DISCRIMINATION
in Elite Public
Schools

DISCRIMINATION
in Elite Public Schools

INVESTIGATING BUFFALO

Edited by
Gary Orfield
Jennifer B. Ayscue

Published by Teachers College Press, 1234 Amsterdam Avenue, New York, NY 10027

Copyright © 2018 by Teachers College, Columbia University

All rights reserved. No part of this publication may be reproduced or transmitted in any form or by any means, electronic or mechanical, including photocopy, or any information storage and retrieval system, without permission from the publisher. For reprint permission and other subsidiary rights requests, please contact Teachers College Press, Rights Dept.: tcpressrights@tc.columbia.edu

Library of Congress Cataloging-in-Publication Data

Names: Orfield, Gary, editor.
Title: Discrimination in elite public schools : investigating Buffalo / edited by Gary Orfield, Jennifer B. Ayscue
Description: New York, NY : Teachers College Press, [2018] | Includes index.
Identifiers: LCCN 2018000328| ISBN 9780807759356 (pbk. : alk. paper) | ISBN 9780807759363 (cloth : alk. paper) | ISBN 9780807777121 (ebook)
Subjects: LCSH: Public schools—New York (State)—Buffalo. | Educational equalization—New York (State)—Buffalo
Classification: LCC LA339.B9 D57 2018 | DDC 371.0109747/97—dc23
LC record available at https://lccn.loc.gov/2018000328

ISBN 978-0-8077-5935-6 (paper)
ISBN 978-0-8077-5936-3 (hardcover)
ISBN 978-0-8077-7712-1 (ebook)

Printed on acid-free paper
Manufactured in the United States of America

25 24 23 22 21 20 19 18   8 7 6 5 4 3 2 1

Contents

Acknowledgments		vii
1.	Great Schools Perpetuating Inequality *Gary Orfield*	1
2.	Buffalo's Choice Schools and the Civil Rights Issues *Jennifer B. Ayscue*	27
3.	Buffalo History and the Roots of School Segregation: The Rise of Buffalo's Two-Tiered School System *Jenna Tomasello*	42
4.	Segregation and Unequal Academic Outcomes in Buffalo's Criteria-Based Schools *Jongyeon Ee*	55
5.	Clearing the Pathway: Recognizing Roadblocks to Entry into Buffalo's Top-Tier Schools *Brian Woodward and Natasha Amlani*	74
6.	How to Make Competitive Schools of Choice More Accessible and Equitable *Jennifer B. Ayscue and Genevieve Siegel-Hawley*	92
7.	Research, Politics, and Civil Rights: What Happened to Our Recommendations *Gary Orfield and Jennifer B. Ayscue*	116
Postscript: What We Learned *Gary Orfield*		133
About the Contributors		142
Index		147

Acknowledgments

We would like to acknowledge the many people who contributed to this important study. The collaboration of the Buffalo Public Schools staff was paramount, particularly Will Keresztes for making things happen; Eileen Bohen for her coordination; Mark Frazier and staff, who responded to our many requests for data; Maria Giardino, for assisting Mr. Keresztes; and others who helped behind the scenes in Buffalo. We are grateful to the many parents, students, teachers, and administrators who responded to surveys and participated in interviews, as well as all of the Buffalo residents who met with us, wrote or called us, and shared their concerns about and wishes for a school system that could expand choice and opportunity for more of the youth of Buffalo. Rev. George Nicholas of the Lincoln Memorial United Methodist Church provided space and recruited parents for one of our field tests.

After our study concluded, several people remained in contact with us, and we are grateful for their ongoing commitment to improving the opportunities for Buffalo students. We pledged to be available to answer questions after our work was done, and we have done that, answering questions from Samuel Radford and members of the District Parent Coordinating Committee. We want to thank Dr. Barbara Seals Nevergold, current president of the Buffalo Board of Education, for informing us about the recent developments in Buffalo. None of this work would have been possible, of course, without the initial investigation by the U.S. Department of Education's Office for Civil Rights and their negotiation with Buffalo Public Schools leaders that produced the agreement leading to our work there.

On our research team, in addition to the contributing authors of this book, we would like to acknowledge Dr. Erica Frankenberg for her dedicated work throughout this study. We are also grateful to our on-the-ground volunteers in Buffalo, Sara Asrat and Jenna Tomasello, who worked tirelessly during the site visits, shepherded our researchers to many a meeting, organized and led survey field tests, and provided overall indispensable support and consultation. Other key collaborators in Buffalo were Rhonda Ried and the staff at Cornerstone Research & Marketing, who carried out the survey work, and Caroline Taggart, who shared her suggestions on survey data collection. Thanks go to Dr. Mindy Kornhaber of Pennsylvania State University for sharing her expertise on testing. Laurie Russman worked miracles of coordination and communication.

Finally, we are extremely grateful for the support and love of our families—Patricia, Brandon, Linda, and Don.

CHAPTER 1

Great Schools Perpetuating Inequality

Gary Orfield

This book is about a high-stakes system of school choice. Choice is something that has the sound of freedom and opportunity, but the most important choices in this study are made by the schools, not the parents, and the students who are chosen for the best opportunities tend to be from the groups that have had the best opportunities all their lives. School choice often offers the only chance for poor students of color in big cities to receive the kind of education that is regularly provided for middle-class White and Asian families—but do they get that chance? What kinds of real choices do they have? Who else is deciding on their choices and making rules that limit those choices?

Choice has many meanings, and people often read into the term what they wish it to be (and often is not). From the perspective of the individuals and groups who do not actually have a choice, it can be seen as a mockery—something that only deepens social and economic gaps that already hold back their children. The choice at the center of this book is about excellent opportunities that turn out to be virtually unavailable to those who need them most. This book is about dissecting the system that led to such a result and suggesting a path toward expanding real choice for all—about building into the system policies and practices that expand the most valuable opportunities. Our research explores the maze of an urban choice system, describes and documents its twists and turns, and outlines a path to a better system. The authors are not writing about a theory or a data set but about a real, high-stakes civil rights battle on the ground. We were charged to investigate a major urban choice system through a study that took place in a city deeply divided by race and politics. Although it is about one city, what we learned is directly relevant to many communities, and we hope that educators, activists, parents, and policymakers will come with us through the maze and gather ideas about designing methods for building better, clearer, stronger systems of equitable choice in order to allocate the best educational opportunities in their communities.

If you were living in a poor central city that had one great, nationally ranked high school and one elementary school that prepared students very well for that school, and most of the remaining schools were failing badly to reach state standards, how important would it be for your children to attend the schools that had a clear path to excellent colleges? To ask the question is to answer it. That is the situation in Buffalo, an old urban school system in an impoverished city. It is not surprising that the nationally ranked high school, City Honors, was the focus of a major civil rights battle, because in a city with a very large majority of non-White students, few were admitted to this powerful school. Ironically, the school was created as a result of a civil rights case that rested on extensive proof of a history of racial discrimination by both the school district and the city government. After the court order was dropped, the school abandoned its desegregation goal and became a school of privilege. When desegregation had been ordered decades ago, the court found that the city had policies that fostered residential segregation in what was one of the nation's most segregated housing markets, therefore bearing part of the responsibility for segregated schools. This and other problems had not been solved when the court ordered the desegregation plan ended.

This book addresses only one significant aspect of the many inequities of urban education: how to allocate access to the best schools in cities with few good options. We (scholars with the Civil Rights Project) have written often about other broad issues, including the intense double and triple segregation in our cities and metropolitan areas and all the ways it is related to unequal opportunities and unfair outcomes, dropouts, school suspension, federal aid policy for impoverished schools, special education discrimination, and other issues; many studies are available at civilrightsproject.ucla.edu. In this book, we address the issue of access to elite public schools because there often is a small supply of very good schooling opportunities in highly distressed older cities, and getting admissions right from the standpoint of civil rights and racial justice is intrinsically important. Studying access also raises questions about other opportunities and, of course, about the possibility of growing the supply of great schools. It would be ideal if all our schools were excellent paths to college and opportunities, but after generations of promises and hundreds of reform plans and many billions of dollars, that has not been achieved across any big segregated city. The Supreme Court, in the 1954 *Brown v. Board of Education* decision, concluded that "segregated schools are inherently unequal." The decision addressed schools segregated by state law, but it appears that the Court's assertion holds true much more broadly, as is evident in the unequal opportunities in family, neighborhood, and schooling that are endemic to non-White schools with a large majority of children living in poverty.

Buffalo, when under its desegregation order, was a national leader in using magnet schools with strong integration policies to successfully produce excellent schools that were intended to be integrated through parent choice, drawing both White and non-White children to schools with well-integrated faculties. The theory behind those magnet schools was that choice was not an end in itself but a way to use unique educational incentives to produce voluntarily integrated schools. It was choice in the service of a more basic value: creation of diverse schools with strong mechanisms for assuring access for students of color that everyone would want to attend. After the courts ended the desegregation plan, however, and the enrollment strategy was left up to local officials, the desegregation goals and processes were dropped, and the best magnet schools became highly selective exam schools. The virtual absence of Black and Latino students triggered opposition that led to a federal civil rights complaint and, eventually, an agreement between the school district and the federal Office for Civil Rights (OCR) for an independent examination of the forces that had produced the problem as well as suggestions for changing the district's choice system to remedy discrimination and to produce wider access and more integration. This book is the result of that research, through which we learned a great deal.

The Buffalo situation is not, of course, unique. There are test-driven exam schools of great prestige in a number of cities across the country. Several of those schools are nationally famous, and they tend to face similar problems as the ones in Buffalo. Many former civil rights–era magnet schools as well as charter schools now operate increasingly like exam schools, with selective admission policies. In addition to their widespread applicability, the lessons we learned in Buffalo are also especially timely. Now that choice is the central theme of the Trump administration's education policy, the unique access to data provided by the Buffalo investigation creates an unprecedented opportunity to understand the dynamics of an urban choice system that federal investigators found to be discriminatory. Our research team gathered and analyzed evidence on the various ways in which choice constrained opportunities for students of color. We learned about the choices parents, teachers, and students wanted as well as the politics and social divisions that made it hard to change the existing choice system. Thus, this book should be of interest to a wide array of educators, parents, civil rights leaders, and community groups across the nation who are struggling to turn the power of choice toward equity.

EXAM SCHOOLS AND CRITERIA-BASED SCHOOLS

Exam schools and criteria-based schools are schools of choice in a radically different sense than magnet schools, where students traditionally enrolled because of their interests and special efforts were made to assure racial diversity. The choice in schools with highly selective admissions processes is not being made by students and families but by the schools, which use methods very strongly linked to the advantages in preparation enjoyed by students from more educated and more affluent families and neighborhoods. Exam schools are able to select extraordinarily well-prepared students through competitive academic admissions criteria. When left to their own control, exam schools as well as other schools often do whatever they can to attract and hold the best-prepared students, those who are likely to be the easiest and most interesting to teach and whose high achievement levels will produce recognition and credit for the success of the school in the various rating systems such as that of the *U.S. News & World Report*. Exam schools also tend to attract and hold excellent teachers and have a very strong record with colleges, which want excellent students from big cities.

While there had been few highly selective exam schools in the United States before the magnet school movement, there were some highly visible and prestigious examples in a few cities, including San Francisco, Boston, and New York. Some of these strong schools were created as desegregation strategies in the heyday of magnet school development in the 1970s. They existed only because of desegregation plans and federal desegregation aid but they positioned themselves to be more like the super-elite exam schools in New York City such as Bronx Science and Stuyvesant, where only the very top test-takers were admitted and graduates seemed to receive a kind of golden pass to the Ivy League. Since there never had been a citywide desegregation plan in New York City, there was no tradition of making diversity one of the schools' fundamental values even though New York State was the most segregated state in the nation for Black students and among the most segregated for Latinos.

In Boston and San Francisco, there were successful lawsuits by disgruntled parents to end the special outreach that the districts had been conducting for students of color, including the set-aside of some seats for students of color at Boston Latin. The San Francisco desegregation plan was lost in large part because of a challenge from one group in the city's Chinese American community over the integration ceiling on the share of students of Chinese descent in Lowell High School, which had been a strict exam school before desegregation. The integration effort did not harm the stellar reputation of the school across the country, and it did significantly increase access for the city's Black and Latino students, though a number of very talented students of color declined to enroll when they were offered a chance because of what was seen as an unwelcoming and isolated atmosphere. Boston Latin School, the nation's oldest public school, also suffered no loss of prestige when one-third of its seats were set aside for decades for African Americans and Latinos, who made up the vast majority of the district's students. But after a White parent won a lawsuit against the plan, underrepresented minority students became a far smaller group.

Although comprehensive research on exam schools is very limited, one recent study identified approximately 165 exam schools across the United States in 2012 (Finn & Hockett, 2012). In the last several years, at least 11 of those 165 exam schools have had federal civil rights investigations pending against them because of disproportionately low admissions and enrollment of students of color. In New York City, all eight specialized exam high schools faced civil rights investigations. In Buffalo, the subject of this book, all eight of the district's criteria-based schools, which include two exam schools, faced civil rights investigations.

The choice system that we were asked to investigate in Buffalo—composed of criteria-based schools—has special terms and dimensions. Criteria-based schools are slightly different from exam schools in that criteria-based schools do not necessarily require students to take an entrance examination, as is the case in exam schools. Criteria-based schools, also referred to as competitive-admissions schools or selective-admissions schools, have entrance criteria that students must meet in order to be admitted. The criteria might include grades, attendance records, teacher or parent recommendations, interviews or auditions, or other factors. Using these definitions, in Buffalo, all eight schools under investigation were criteria-based schools, and two of those eight, City Honors and Olmsted, could also be considered exam schools because they require students to take a cognitive abilities assessment in order to be admitted. Prior to our investigation, a specific level on this exam was an absolute requirement for admission to City Honors.

Just because a school is called a magnet or an exam school does not make it a great school. For example, a study of Chicago exam schools found no net average benefit to students attending selective-admissions schools in comparison to those attending nonselective schools (Allensworth, Moore, Sartain, & de la Torre, 2016). This does not mean, of course, that nationally famous schools like San Francisco's Lowell High or Bronx Science or the North Carolina School of the Arts or Boston Latin School do not have life-transforming impacts on many students over many years. Based on national ratings, City Honors appears to be in that category. Statistics such as graduation rate, college-going rate, and success in college are doubtless affected by selection bias, since the school admits virtually no student who is unlikely to succeed as best the school can measure it. Much of the impact of a school like City Honors comes from the ability of the school to attract and hold very strong faculty, and the fact that there is a critical mass of students ready for very accelerated courses where such students may learn as much from one another as from the teachers. One of the most important advantages of attending such a school is that its students and faculty benefit from a very strong positive stereotype that creates a powerful network of connections, leading straight into good colleges and other opportunities. College admissions officers eagerly seek out students from such schools. The large number of non–public school students taking the exam required for admission to City Honors, for whom enrollment would mean a transfer back into Buffalo Public Schools (BPS) from private and charter schools, is a marker of its powerful reputation.

Admissions policies based substantially on examination scores are a classic example of what is often called "color-blind" policy, a policy that allocates critical opportunities on the basis of what are seen as race-neutral measures of merit. We live in a world of important examinations, of course, where tremendous weight and significance are attached to the SAT, the ACT, the Graduate Record Examination (GRE), the Medical College Admission Test (MCAT), high school exit tests, and a host of other exams. The performance data collected from important exams create the impression that we have a scientific way of measuring potential for benefiting from an educational opportunity. Advocates argue that high-stakes tests provide a fair measure of a student's ability to perform in school or college and that these tests, therefore, are nondiscriminatory ways of allocating opportunities. From a civil rights perspective, however, the fact that the test scores are systematically lower for the groups most discriminated against in society, and that those gaps extend from generation to generation, raises serious questions.

The testing industry and scholars of assessment agree that, while tests may predict performance, they should never be used as the single criterion for allocating important life opportunities (American Educational Research Association [AERA], American Psychological Association [APA], & National Council on Measurement in Education [NCME], 2014; Heubert & Hauser, 1999). Among many reasons for this belief is the finding that there are very strong associations between income and parent education levels and test scores. This association suggests that the achievement measured on tests is often not innate but reflects very different opportunities that groups of students have received during their development. If that is true, then allocating opportunities on the basis of tests will systematically reward those who have already had the best opportunities and exclude those who have had the worst, regardless of what potential they may have that has not yet been developed. If the excluded group has experienced a history of discrimination that denied them strong preparation, reliance exclusively on tests can perpetuate the effects of that discrimination. We know from longitudinal research on affirmative action that when students of color are admitted to the nation's most highly rated colleges even though their test scores are significantly lower, they graduate at high rates and achieve high levels of success in their careers (Bowen & Bok, 2000). Many other dimensions of the limitations of testing have been explored in the research literature. For our purposes, however, it is enough to say that the way tests are commonly viewed greatly oversimplifies the issues. Many educators assume that tests measure what they actually cannot measure and that they are precise enough to justify making very important decisions about life chances. Using tests in these ways is seen by their very creators as illegitimate. Excessive reliance on test results is very likely to perpetuate the status quo, giving it legitimacy and telling the winners that the system is based on meritocracy and that they deserve the best opportunities because they are the best.

RACISM, DISCRIMINATION, AND THE MARKET

Some scholars treat situations such as apparently color-blind choice and testing processes as "color-blind racism," a seemingly contradictory but evocative term used in sociologist Eduardo Bonilla-Silva's (2017) powerful work on systemic racism. He defines color-blind racism as an ideology of denial of the significance of race in a society that has abandoned many of the policies of the civil rights era. It is, he argues, a widely held view among White people in the United States—a belief that the historic discrimination in American society was addressed by the civil rights movement and that there are no longer strong institutional barriers preventing non-White people from succeeding. This worldview further holds that we have entered an era in which race has little impact, and therefore claims of discrimination based on race cannot be justified.

This view is widely held in spite of very large and persistent gaps in education, income, jobs, housing, and family wealth. Advocates of color-blind policy face the need to explain these strikingly unequal results. The typical response is to view these problems as a sign that something is wrong with the group that does not take advantage of the *opportunities* that are fairly offered. In our society, where many believe that explicit claims of racial superiority are no longer acceptable, the claim will be that something is wrong with the institutions and the people whose job it is to educate African Americans and Latinos and that something is wrong with their culture that leads them not to succeed in a fair, nonracial setting.

Speaking of what he saw as the particularly pernicious impact of segregation, Martin Luther King Jr. said, "It gives the segregator a false sense of superiority and the segregated a false sense of inferiority because those on the White side of the line concluded that they must deserve the superior status and goods they received and the segregated non-Whites too often internalized the idea that they could not compete because of the many ways they had never been prepared to compete or given a fair chance" (King, 1963). That distortion is central to what Bonilla-Silva called color-blind racism—it refuses to see the continuing segregation as caused by discrimination and simply accepts the status quo. Because those who embrace the view see no continuing discrimination, they conclude that it does not exist. And the truth is, it does not exist in the old Southern ways of overt racial exclusion. However, even though the current sorting mechanisms are far less direct than the old overt practices, they are almost equally as effective at excluding students of color.

In the contemporary civil rights period, the key question is: Did the institution adopt a set of policies that had the clearly predictable consequence of perpetuating or deepening racial inequalities, and did the institution reject alternatives that would have produced more equitable results? The way to allocate spaces in highly desirable schools is greatly complicated by a profound division between Whites and non-Whites over whether or not minorities face discrimination now. Public opinion polls, with few exceptions, tend to show a sharp difference in understanding of racial inequality between Whites and Blacks, with Whites seeing little persistent discrimination and Blacks seeing systemic discrimination and believing that the government should act (Gallup Editors, 2014). It is true, of course, that it is easy to see segregation, particularly in housing and schools, in virtually any metro area and to see major gaps in patterns of employment and income. Since nearly everyone agrees that there was discrimination in the past and outcomes have never been equal, the advocates of color-blindness need an explanation. A majority of Whites tend to believe that government has done enough. A majority of Blacks and Latinos tend to think much more needs to be done. This difference arose clearly in the public debate over the Buffalo choice plan. One side kept asserting that selection based on test scores was a fair, race-neutral method that had been accepted in the community. The opposing position, held by many in Buffalo's Black community, was exemplified in the complaint to OCR, which stated that the system was perpetuating inequality and harshly restricting good opportunities for Black students.

The idea of school choice relying on standardized tests fits into the color-blind theory. After all, proponents of this theory claim that tests are scientific, involve no personal judgment, and have a scientific basis. What could be more fair? If the results are unequal, it is too bad, but some groups prepare their children better and those children work harder and deserve the most challenging schools.

Those arguments imply an underlying faith in the efficiency of Adam Smith's (1776) "invisible hand" concept, by which the market rewards the effective seller and weak or bad businesses fail; the competition between many sellers and informed buyers creates efficiency without explicit restrictions or regulations. This theory is strongly embraced by many of America's richest businesspeople and their foundations, including the Gates Foundation, the Broad Foundation, and the Walton Family Foundation (Tompkins-Stange, 2016). Their faith in this theory seems extreme, since private businesses are actually substantially regulated in modern nations, in good measure because of a history of violations of the law and undermining of markets by private businesses over time. (Even Adam Smith believed that markets need regulation at certain points in time.) Consistent with violations by businesses, there also have been numerous instances of schools exploiting weak regulations to transfer money earmarked for education expenditures to private coffers (Hiaasen & Mcgrory, 2011).

Although non-public schools must meet the curriculum required by state law, there is virtually no supervision of the ways in which the education is delivered and increasingly less oversight of the qualifications of the educators. Many states have no certification for private school teachers and few if any specific requirements (U.S. Dept. of Education, 2009). Since both charter schools and private schools can vary in a myriad of ways, these decisions do not rest on these schools demonstrating superior educational quality—only on a faith that they must be better by definition. Evaluating the non-public schools in Buffalo was not part of our assignment, but we did not realize when accepting the task that we would be operating at a time of a major attack on the public schools by charter advocates, who had gained control of the public school board and were determined to use their majority to pursue this goal even in the midst of a civil rights investigation.

The conservatives in Buffalo took the position that the correct solution for expanding and equalizing education was shutting down schools with low scores and selling them to charter operators. The metaphor of choice in markets has become a central element in the discussion of education policy. If one blames the schools that serve students of color for students' weak performance on tests, the blame also extends to teachers and teacher organizations—central targets of both Republican and Democratic presidents since 1980. The idea driving this line of reasoning is that the teachers unions are too powerful in the politics of school board and state government elections, since the teachers unions are often the biggest pressure group affecting educational decisions. Conservatives since 1980 have made a continuous attack on government, casting it as an inefficient and parasitic provider of education. Although the United States is the most economically unequal of the major world democracies, with massive gaps in educational success that statistics show are strongly related to the race and poverty levels in schools, the basic argument of choice advocates is that the problems of "failing" schools have nothing to do with economic and social stratification. Instead, they claim that the problems are caused by the public school system monopoly, which fights very strongly to protect the status quo in order to retain job perks and block reforms. This argument is totally unlike the theory of the social reform era of the 1960s, when the basic problems were seen as poverty and discrimination.

The choice advocates believe that market forces can get rid of bad schools and teachers and will give better choices to those failing in the existing system, especially if the schools can be run by leadership or corporations outside the public school system. Markets will foster equity, they argue, because Black and Latino families will have the kinds of choices that White and Asian families currently receive as a result of buying their homes in areas with good schools. Everyone will have a chance to choose, the choices will be fair, and the best schools will admit on the basis of merit, shown through things like test scores and grades and the determination of the family to find out about the choices and figure out what would be best for their children.

At the time when we conducted our study, the central assumption about the problems of racial inequality held by a majority of the Buffalo school board members was that the issues of racial inequality could be successfully resolved in a market setting without any policies directly aimed at changing outcomes for historically disadvantaged racial groups. They believed that the market would achieve those outcomes through the choices of families of color. The contrast could not have been sharper when those views were compared with the views of the community group that saw the outcome of the Buffalo choice system as a discriminatory mechanism for excluding non-White students.

If the conservative assumption is wrong and markets not only fail to equalize opportunities and outcomes but actually tend to deliver the best choices to the families that are already ahead and the worst options to the families with the least education and connections, then the authorities have created a system that looks fair and color-blind only to those who operate well in the markets and testing systems. Naturally, those who succeed want to preserve a system that works well for them and that they view as just. If there is inequality, they believe that it must be because something is wrong with the groups that do not have the initiative and determination to find and take advantage of the good opportunities.

In fact, choice systems do often result in the children of the most privileged families getting the best choices, which actually increases the racial inequality in outcomes (Orfield & Frankenberg, 2013). The reality is that racial inequality is not a relatively minor set of issues that can be resolved by a market system. Instead, there is a deeply entrenched and self-perpetuating system of double segregation in schools, by both race and poverty. The system is perpetuated by very limited family and community resources, inferior local schools, less knowledge of the complex choice system among families with fewer resources, and no network that connects those families with the best options and informs them about how to prepare for and take advantage of those options. For markets to be fair, market theory assumes that all participants have good information. In fact, as our study would show, there can be a market information system assumed to work for all that is actually invisible to the great majority of families. Because all of these inequalities are so deeply rooted—very visible to families of color and invisible to many White families—a choice system is only likely to achieve different results when the goal of expanding access is explicit and is supported by processes that overcome the inequalities and open up the transformative and positive choices to those normally excluded from them.

Critics of race-conscious civil rights policies, which often include, for example, the majority on the Supreme Court, assume that there was serious discrimination in the past, especially in the Jim Crow South, but that it was basically cured in the civil rights era. As noted above, those people believe that the inequalities we see today are largely the consequences of choices that minorities make about where to live, what kind of education they want, their own focus and discipline, their culture, and the fact that they are simply not adequately prepared for better jobs and higher education. Aside from personal and community problems, they argue, the basic obstacles are public schools, teachers unions, and excessive welfare state support preventing Blacks and Latinos from pulling themselves up in the ways that European ancestors did in the United States. Race-conscious remedies, they believe, are totally inappropriate in a society that is post-racial and, in key respects, color-blind. Segregation is not a problem, they argue, if it is the product of a choice process that is a fair way to allocate access to valuable institutions. They maintain that imposing race-conscious solutions when race is no longer a serious cause of inequality is manifestly unfair to Whites. That is the basic conservative argument, and it is accepted by a large share of the White population and a small share of the Black and Latino populations as well.

On the other side, most researchers, civil rights leaders, non-White community leaders, and liberals see racial prejudice and discrimination still acting powerfully in many institutions. They see the "color-blind" philosophy as being a smoke screen to permit denial of racial animus and discrimination, which are manifest in many situations, such as the police murders of young men of color that inspired the Black Lives Matter movement and many protests across the United States. They do not believe that African Americans and Latinos choose to live in the most dangerous communities with the fewest resources or send their children to clearly inferior schools with less experienced teachers and more limited curriculum or be rejected for jobs and mortgage loans. They do not believe that election laws restricting the power of their communities are post-racial, to say nothing of demagogic statements falsely claiming that disproportionate shares of the immigrant population are rapists or murderers.

Similar themes and issues can also be seen in the political arena. Racial themes have played a part in many U.S. elections over time. However, these issues had been muted in most recent national campaigns until 2016, when the campaign of Republican candidate Donald Trump allied itself with the most conservative elements in the White community, made no real reach for non-White votes, and generated meetings teeming with racial anger (Dickerson & Saul, 2016; Peters, Thee-Brenan, & Sussman, 2016). The campaign was a reminder that racial animosity is alive and operating on a large scale in our society.

The Buffalo criteria-based system is an example of color-blind racism (and, for some, more overt racism), stratification, and, ultimately, social reproduction. It is not surprising that the Buffalo school board member who was most hostile to our civil rights research (and the idea of federal civil rights enforcement) was Carl Paladino, the co-chairman of Donald Trump's New York primary campaign. The importance of focusing on the racial substructure of school choice is all the more urgent in a society where the 2016 national election showed a dramatic reemergence of openly race-based issues and appeals in national politics.

SEGREGATION AS A CENTRAL REALITY

Severe racial separation has been and continues to be a central reality in Buffalo. The city, school district, and metro region of Buffalo are plagued by segregation and inequality. The civil rights battle is a product of the isolation of students of color in inferior segregated schools and the reality of resegregation in the city's best schools after court-ordered desegregation was abandoned. Residentially, the city has been among the nation's most segregated for generations. So has the school district, except for the period in which the federal court ordered the implementation of a citywide desegregation plan and required the city to pay for it. This segregated landscape separates the Black community from the best educational options.

Segregation, like choice, is a seemingly simple term that can have complex and confusing meanings, and experts disagree about the best ways to measure it. This book contains much data on and discussion of segregation, and since the term is used differently in various contexts, it is important for readers to understand how we use it here and why we believe this use is appropriate for our purposes. *Segregation* is sometimes used in a legal context, as in "segregation laws" or "*de jure* segregation." These terms refer to unconstitutional public policies requiring racial separation, such as the laws of 17 U.S. states before the *Brown v. Board of Education* decision in 1954. Segregation caused by intentional action by public officials is unconstitutional, violates the Fourteenth Amendment to the Constitution and the 1964 Civil Rights Act, and can trigger broad legal remedies. This study arises from a complaint under the Civil Rights Act, and occasionally this study refers to unlawful segregation when discussing the legal dimensions of segregation.

In social science research, segregation has a very different meaning, referring to statistical measures of racial separation, whatever the cause may be. This book includes such measures for Buffalo. When we discuss the level of segregation, we are talking about a statistical measurement of the severity of the separation. The statistics show the level of racial isolation, not what caused it. Of course, there are various ways to measure this segregation. The three basic ways in research are measures of isolation of students of a certain race or ethnicity, measures of divergence from random distribution by race or ethnicity, and measures of the level of exposure of students of one race or ethnicity to students of other groups, which we call the exposure index. Each of these measures tells us something, and they can be measured at various levels of geography and over time—separation among students, among schools, among census tracts or neighborhoods, in a city, in a metro area, in a state, or in other units.

A number of scholars, particularly those with backgrounds in housing segregation work and demography, tend to measure the extent to which the schools in a district or metro area or the neighborhoods in a city reflect the overall population distribution of that area. In doing so, they are measuring the randomness of distribution among the racial and ethnic groups studied. This measure is called the dissimilarity index or segregation index or, in its multiracial form, H. This index varies from zero, when each unit has the racial proportions of the city or the school district being studied, to 100, when there is absolute segregation and each school or neighborhood is exclusively populated by one group or the other. This measure can be quite informative when measuring two groups, both significantly represented in the overall population of the area studied. However, we did not use it in our work in Buffalo because in a typical central city school district population, for instance, with 85% Black students, the index would define a 95% Black school as quite integrated and a 50-50 school as quite segregated. Such results would make no sense in terms of the history or the sociology of school desegregation. We focus instead on measures that show the proportion of students attending schools with various levels of isolation from or contact with other groups, the social facts that relate to students' actual lived school experiences that are likely to have impacts on them (rather than statistical randomness, which is unlikely to affect them).[1]

Theories of the educational consequences of desegregation rely on actual significant interracial contact at the school and classroom levels. Accordingly, we examine the share of Black or Latino students, for example, who attend schools with varying percentages of White enrollment—schools ranging from those that are virtually entirely non-White to those in which students of color attend school with a substantial share of White students. The exposure index gives the average level of contact between Black or Latino students and Whites in a district or a metro area. If average Black exposure to Whites was 40% under a desegregation plan and has fallen to 10% after the plan ended, for example, that finding would show considerable resegregation.

The statistics show that Buffalo has a very high level of racial separation in schools, with very few Whites in the school district, double segregation by both race and poverty, extremely limited contact between Black students and White students, and no recent progress. Since access to the few strong schools can be a life-changing experience in an extremely stratified city, and such opportunities are far too limited, it is very important that such chances be made available to non-White and poor students from families with little education and few resources and that the number of such schools be expanded. However, as already noted, these opportunities in Buffalo go largely to students from communities that already have far greater resources and serve mostly White, Asian, and middle-class students.

UNEQUAL EDUCATION

Schooling is extremely unequal in America, as the society has reached a point of profound economic inequality and school integration policies have been largely abandoned in public schools following reversals by the Supreme Court (Carter & Welner, 2013; Duncan & Murnane, 2011). Our schools are so clearly unfair in many respects and the inequality is so deeply related to race and poverty that education not only fails to achieve equal opportunity for the groups that start behind but often broadens and deepens the inequality by giving the most stimulating and powerful education to the most privileged social groups and the most affluent communities.

It has become the norm for the weakest and most poorly regarded schools in communities of deep, persistent poverty to have the least experienced teachers for their students, who start furthest behind (Clotfelter, Ladd, & Vigdor, 2005; Jackson, 2009). Racial segregation in schools is at its highest level in a half-century, and the schools serving students of color are usually doubly segregated by poverty as well as race (Orfield, Kucsera, & Siegel-Hawley, 2012). Most schools attended by students of color cannot offer any significant race or class diversity for a multitude of reasons, including the racial and economic segregation in the housing market (Denton, 2001; Frankenberg, 2013; Massey & Denton, 1993); the fragmentation of most of our metropolitan areas into many separate school systems (Ayscue & Orfield, 2014; Bischoff, 2008); the dismantling of desegregation plans, which often made major differences for decades following the civil rights revolution of the 1960s (Orfield & Eaton, 1996; Reardon, Grewal, Kalogrides, & Greenberg, 2012); and the massive demographic shifts in the last half-century (Frey, 2014).

Nor can those schools offer a real chance for mobility for the non-White communities that are now producing a huge share of the nation's school-age children. In a period when social and urban policies are weak and poorly financed, the reality is that welfare programs for the poor have greatly diminished, a substantial share of young men of color have been incarcerated (Alexander, 2010), social mobility has declined markedly, and people without higher education have been experiencing declines in real income for a generation. Deeply unequal education can cut off the only real opportunity for mobility.

None of these conditions is absolute, of course. There are students and determined families who find a way to success in spite of the severe odds against them. There are students selected by affirmative action programs at strong universities who are given a powerful opportunity as they reach college age and succeed, but the way is narrow and the numbers few. These conditions make access to truly excellent public schools urgent.

CHOICE AS A PROCESS

Choice sounds like an event, a decision made at some point. But seriously understanding why choice works the way it often does requires examining the stages of educational choice. Choice, particularly individual choice without equity policies to promote diversity, is a kind of unregulated market. In such markets, especially when the choices are complex, those with the best information, the most resources, and the clearest understanding of the system have substantial advantages. Research shows that those resources are very unequally distributed and that the best-educated and best-connected groups have great advantages, particularly when the choices and the processes to make the choice are complicated (Fuller & Elmore, 1996; Orfield & Frankenberg, 2013; Scott, 2005).

The choice process usually involves several steps. First, parents have to know that a choice exists. Second, they need to understand what the choices are and which might be best for their children. Third, they need to know the deadlines, get the forms, discuss alternatives and seek information, and act in time, which is often more than 6 months before the next school year begins. Fourth, the child often must be tested and/or submit information or perhaps get recommendations or have an interview. Fifth, some large groups of children may be rejected or advised not to apply because they have disabilities or are English learners (ELs). Sixth, there must be a way for the child to get to the school, if transportation is not provided. Seventh, there is no real or lasting choice unless the child is welcomed, treated fairly, and helped to catch up with students who have been given far better preparation, even though they may have no more talent or determination than those who have received weaker preparation. A fair and lasting choice does not happen by accident. Left unattended and unregulated, choice systems are likely to replicate or even intensify the stratification in the community.

As we have thought about this process, it has become clear to us that school choice actually has many meanings, many possible ways of operating, and potentially many different outcomes. Various permutations would have decisively different consequences. During the civil rights era, choices expanded, but choice was subordinated to a higher goal of desegregation when necessary. Now choice is largely about individual families seeking advantages. Choice processes vary, based on which schools are included or excluded from the choice process, what kind of information is provided (especially to disadvantaged and non-English-speaking families), what kind of recruitment and outreach takes place, whether or not all students have a right to enroll, whether there are a variety of prerequisites and sorting mechanisms, and what kinds of curriculum, counseling, and support are available at the school.

When choice systems are regulated and include diversity goals and civil rights protections, they can facilitate desegregation (Cobb & Glass, 2009). For example, magnet schools have an attractive theme around which curriculum and instruction are developed, and because magnet schools are not tied to attendance boundaries, diverse families from across traditional attendance zones often choose magnet schools that are a better fit for their children than their traditional neighborhood schools (Goldring & Smrekar, 2000). Magnet schools that include diversity goals, conduct outreach to diverse communities, and provide free transportation are associated with higher levels of racial integration (Siegel-Hawley & Frankenberg, 2013). However, unregulated forms of choice without diversity goals or civil rights standards tend to stratify and segregate students (Orfield & Frankenberg, 2013).

Using a choice system as a way to achieve integration and opportunity for students of color is a limited strategy, since in most districts only a modest segment of the schools are authentic schools of choice, and many do not provide the incentives and support needed to make the choices real. Moreover, a great number of parents do not understand the often complex processes and take action far enough in advance in a country where a child can simply materialize on the first day of school in his or her neighborhood and be enrolled. Nevertheless, it is an important and powerful option for those who do gain access to the best choices. And sadly, and most importantly, it is the only option available to most children of color in cities to escape a dismal progression of weak public schools and similar charter schools in communities of deeply entrenched and self-perpetuating inequality. So it is worth doing right and worth pursuing the civil rights challenges when the students most in need are rarely admitted, as is the case in Buffalo as well as many other places in America.

CHOICE DURING THE CIVIL RIGHTS ERA AND TODAY

The civil rights era was the only time in our history when school districts made sustained efforts to give access to much more successful schools to African American students and sometimes also to Latino and American Indian students. The basic ways of providing this access were through two mechanisms: (1) mandatory programs (often resulting from court orders), which forced districts to reassign students and teachers with the goal of integrating the schools, including the best schools, and (2) choice programs, including magnet schools, voluntary transfers, and controlled choice plans combined with several key civil rights policies, which created educational incentives through recruitment and selection policies that pursued diversity as a central goal.

Mandatory Programs

Particularly in situations in which a school desegregation plan covered much or all of the metropolitan housing market, mandatory programs produced the highest level of lasting integration, but there have been almost no new plans of this kind in the last third of a century (Orfield, 2001). In 1991, the Supreme Court authorized the dissolution of desegregation plans even if equality had never been achieved, and the clearly predictable consequence was a return to double segregation by race and poverty (*Board of Education v. Dowell*, 1991; Orfield & Eaton, 1996). Since that decision, most urban plans have been terminated, and segregation of both Blacks and Latinos has consistently increased (Reardon et al., 2012).

In several further decisions, the Court allowed lower courts to dismantle parts of desegregation plans even when the plan had never been fully implemented at any time (*Freeman v. Pitts*, 1992). The Supreme Court blocked city–suburban desegregation plans although they presented the only feasible remedy in many areas given how few Whites or middle-class residents with public school children were left in the central city (*Milliken v. Bradley*, 1974). The Court left a little hope alive in a decision that found that when there were no viable remedies in the city, a court could order a state government to pay for some remedial educational programs (*Milliken v. Bradley II*, 1977). But in 1995, the Supreme Court ruled that such efforts constituted a temporary remedy and did not have to be pursued until there was evidence of educational success (*Missouri v. Jenkins*, 1995). The trial court had approved efforts to open magnets in the city to attract students from the suburbs in an effort to remedy the segregation in the city, but the Supreme Court struck that down. The decisions left segregated students of color with no chance for the courts providing either integrated or well-funded schools.

Choice Programs:
Magnet Schools, Voluntary Transfers, and Controlled Choice

The most popular voluntary integration policies were magnet schools and voluntary transfer policies with integration goals and race-conscious recruitment and admissions policies to assure diversity and stability. Another policy used in a number of districts is called controlled choice, which requires all families to rank their top several choices in order of preference and then assigns students to their highest-ranking school that is compatible with the diversity plan. When this approach is used to produce diverse schools, although most students might get their first choice, some have to take lower choices in order to prevent resegregation of the school. Another common plan, M-to-M transfer (majority-to-minority), specifies that students have the right to transfer to a school where their presence would increase diversity but not to a school that they would make more segregated. These plans existed for many years.

When magnet schools were created to provide a new form of regulated choice-based desegregation strategy in the 1970s, civil rights requirements and goals were built into magnet school recruitment and admissions policies and other forms of choice after the enactment of the 1964 Civil Rights Act and the Magnet School Assistance Program. Schools could use incentives and parent choice, but only within limits that would actually produce substantial desegregation. Requirements included a simple choice process; a system in which families, not schools, made the choices; a distinctive curriculum to motivate choices; a school-level plan for diversity with targeted recruitment strategies to be used when the school's diversity fell short; and preference given to students whose presence increased diversity. The development of magnet schools and the creation of the federal Magnet

Schools Assistance Program, as well as the fact that magnets decreased the necessity of mandatory student reassignments, created expansion of schools of choice, many of which became popular and integrated schools in their districts.

A radical policy change during the Reagan administration and subsequent legal changes by the Supreme Court in 1991 and 1992 began to rapidly undermine this effort. In 1981, the federal government repealed the federal desegregation assistance program and greatly reduced funding for voluntary desegregation and went into the courts advocating the termination of desegregation court orders. By the time of the George H. W. Bush administration, conservative appointments to the Supreme Court had moved the Court to a position holding that desegregation orders were temporary and giving the lower courts a directive to dissolve them when the court thought a reasonable local effort had been made to comply with the order (*Board of Education v. Dowell*, 1991). After *Dowell* was decided, there was a steady process of terminating the orders and eliminating the role of the federal courts, which left magnet schools in the hands of local school boards without any federal guidelines, except for those schools seeking federal funds from a small remaining federal magnet school program.

At that point, desegregation of Black students, which had reached its high point in the late 1980s, began a steady reversal. In many cities, the magnet schools dropped or gradually abandoned the civil rights policies. As a result, the magnet schools resegregated, with some becoming heavily non-White, low-income schools. Others became very disproportionately White schools, sometimes adopting various screening procedures that cut the representation of minority students. During this same period, charter schools were launched as schools of choice largely outside the control of the elected officials and public school authorities, receiving increasing federal subsidies while not being subject to the magnet school equity provisions.

A final blow came in the 2007 Supreme Court decision in the *Parents Involved* case and the related guidance issued by the George W. Bush administration. In one of its most criticized civil rights decisions, the Court overturned precedents and outlawed the major choice programs that had been used voluntarily by school districts for years to keep choice programs integrated (*Parents Involved in Community Schools v. Seattle School District No. 1*, 2007). Assigning students by race for integration purposes was legal when the district was implementing a court-ordered remedy but not after the courts had released the district, as the court in Buffalo had done. The Supreme Court was divided 5-4 on the central issue in a majority ruling written by Justice Anthony Kennedy, which found that there were compelling reasons for integration, but that in a voluntary plan, no student could be assigned or denied an assignment on the basis of his or her race. At the same time, he said that race-conscious efforts that did not include such assignments of individuals were valid, giving some examples such as redistricting school attendance boundaries. This decision meant, in effect, that many of the policies that had been required when the federal magnet school program was established were now illegal. The case created a fierce debate within the Court.

In the aftermath of the case, two major school districts, both studied by the Civil Rights Project, have created programs designed to bring together students by considering the race of their immediate neighborhoods, and that action has been upheld by two courts in California (Chavez & Frankenberg, 2009). If a school holds seats or gives preference, for example, to students in a segregated Black or Latino neighborhood, it is likely to produce access for students who would otherwise not have had a chance to be admitted. It is legal for schools to consider any nonracial variable in admitting students, such as a family's home language, the poverty level of the neighborhood, low test scores, or many other possible variables. Unfortunately, however, these strategies are more complicated and less efficient than directly considering a student's race and can often identify students who are already highly represented in the schools, such as Asian immigrants with highly educated parents who temporarily have low incomes shortly after immigration—students with high human capital who have experienced no discrimination and are unlikely to live in an area of concentrated, persistent poverty (Reardon, Yun, & Kurlaender, 2006). But civil rights enforcement combined with funding and technical assistance could make these practices more common and could open up more opportunities for excluded students. The Civil Rights Project surveyed students and parents in Jefferson County (Louisville, KY) and helped the district develop a new desegregation plan that has now been in effect for several years, continuing more than 4 decades of countywide school integration supported by large majorities of parents and students (Orfield & Frankenberg, 2011).

The *Parents Involved* (2007) decision led the George W. Bush administration to advise school districts to do nothing that would explicitly pursue integration, overinterpreting the decision, which said that integration was a compelling interest in education and that some kinds of race-conscious policies were permissible as long as they did not involve decisions about individual students. For example, in some school districts, preference was extended to students from Black or Latino neighborhoods to increase diversity. But the decision sped the abandonment of conscious integration efforts. There was pressure both from families of potential students and from within some schools for the schools to drop all consideration of race and to adopt admissions policies and requirements that favored students with the highest test scores and grades, who were usually students from more affluent families with highly educated parents. It was in this context that the schools of choice in Buffalo resegregated.

CHARTER SCHOOLS

As the mandatory and choice programs that had been designed to create access for students of color to stronger schools began to dissolve, a major new system of choice, charter schools, emerged in the early 1990s. However, it had none of the civil rights policies that produced diversity in the earlier choice programs that were explicitly designed to secure such access. Over a period of 3 decades, the administrations of Bill Clinton, George W. Bush, Barack Obama, and Donald Trump have strongly fostered and favored charter schools, while magnet school development has been starved in federal budgets and desegregation requirements have been undermined. Conservatives favored charter schools for their independence from school districts and, usually, teachers unions. Liberals saw charters as better than private school vouchers since they were at least in the public sector, but many have tried to limit their growth.

The basic idea of charter schools is that segregated neighborhood-based schools are fine and that the only reason their schools had been so unsuccessful during generations of segregation was because they were controlled by public school boards and limited by teachers union contracts. Individual entrepreneurs and the market, advocates claimed, could solve the problems of inequality (Chubb & Moe, 1990). During the period beginning with the Reagan administration's *A Nation at Risk* report in 1983 until the enactment of the Every Student Succeeds Act in 2015, the basic underlying assumption was that the social conditions surrounding schools did not matter and that if there were sufficiently harsh sanctions or if the control of school boards and teachers' organizations could be ended, schooling would flourish. The assumption that the federal government should set standards and require harsh sanctions, using federal dollars for leverage, was central to the No Child Left Behind Act, which was enacted in 2002. The 2015 law, however, was an implicit acknowledgment of the failure of 14 years of federal sanctions under the No Child Left Behind Act and a decision to punt most policy issues to the states.

A huge cautionary note for the expectations for this new semiprivate choice system of charter schools came from the results of a large and deeply unsuccessful experiment with choice in the 1960s. "Freedom of choice" was implemented in many Southern school districts. The theory behind freedom-of-choice plans was that if students were given a chance to voluntarily transfer to a school where their transfer would increase integration, that would be enough to satisfy the requirements of the *Brown v. Board of Education* decision of 1954. By 1965, the federal government was requiring that all students be given an easy process to ask for a transfer and that the school district must provide transportation to those who requested a transfer. However, the plan left White schools with only a handful of Black students, many of whom felt isolated and unwelcome, and their families came under pressure for making the choice. At the same time, the system left the Black schools of the South totally segregated. The failure to create any substantial desegregation is the reason why this approach was rejected as a remedy for unconstitutional segregation by a unanimous Supreme Court decision in the 1968 case *Green v. Board of Education of New Kent County*, which required that districts have plans that actually integrated the students and teachers at all schools.

Only after requirements for actual change were articulated by both the Court and the Lyndon Johnson administration was there a dramatic increase in the level of integration and real access to strong White schools for students of color. The goal for the jurisdictions with a history of illegal actions producing segregation was now to try to make all the schools substantially integrated. The federal government provided funds to help the schools with their efforts and to improve race relations within the desegregated schools. For a time, choice was simply shut down as an alternative in these cases. The rise of intentionally integrated magnet schools was the development that revived the hope that choice could be combined with equity. Once magnets dropped desegregation strategies, the old questions came back, creating conditions that led to our involvement in Buffalo.

INVESTIGATING SEGREGATION AND DISCRIMINATION IN THE CHOICE STRUGGLE

The civil rights dimension of the choice struggle has produced demands for changing procedures for selecting students for the best schools so that the student body better reflects the community. When a school system is under a court order to repair the damages caused by official action that segregated the schools, students and teachers can be assigned or denied assignment to increase integration. In other circumstances, after a court order ends or before the district has been found to be illegally discriminating, civil rights lawyers normally have to prove that the segregation was *intentionally* caused. This burden is enormous, since local officials will almost always give another reason for the segregation, such as admitting the students with the highest test scores. The U.S. Department of Education, however, has special powers under Title VI of the 1964 Civil Rights Act, which forbids discrimination in any school district or other institution receiving federal aid. OCR can examine the result of patterns of local actions, and if it finds them discriminatory, it has to prove discriminatory impact but does not have to prove that there was an intent to discriminate. If OCR finds discrimination, it has the authority to cut off federal funds to the district, a very powerful sanction, which usually generates a negotiation and a settlement. OCR very rarely took any enforcement actions under the George W. Bush administration or other previous conservative administrations, but it was revived during the Obama presidency. This action led to appeals to OCR in the form of complaints from citizens' groups in several cities about the segregation of elite, highly selective schools, some of which had previously been diverse, excellent schools operating under civil rights policies.

A legal investigation or finding of discrimination does not mean that, to remedy the violation, a selective school cannot continue to operate as a very demanding and excellent school, as virtually all of the nation's most selective colleges do. It does mean that, to correct the violation, diversity must become a basic goal and be institutionalized in goals and processes that actually produce more diversity. Of course, those processes cannot violate Supreme Court rulings and are likely to require more investment in outreach and recruitment, more integration of faculty and staff, and adoption of more sophisticated, multidimensional measures of excellence and promise of students, as the nation's colleges do. It need not be a rationing of precious scarcity. There is nothing to prevent school officials from expanding capacity or creating another school with the same or similar excellent features. This could, in fact, be one of the best outcomes of these conflicts. The bottom line is that these selective schools offer valuable opportunities, and if our city schools are to be more effective in creating mobility for historically excluded groups, we have to find a way to open them up to more diverse student bodies as we did in the civil rights era. This work will require effort and resources, but it is an excellent, life-changing investment that will enrich the education of all students. The Buffalo story, spelled out in the pages of this book, shows that solving this challenge will require serious and persistent enforcement of the law as well as effective leadership by local educators and school authorities.

THE BUFFALO STORY

This book is about a serious civil rights conflict and focuses on extensive research that we implemented on competitive-admissions choice schools, or criteria-based schools, in BPS. In 2014, a group of Buffalo parents saw that access to the city's best schools was stratified along racial lines and filed a civil rights complaint with OCR about discrimination in BPS's criteria-based choice system. OCR opened an investigation of the district's eight criteria-based schools, and initial findings appeared to substantiate the claim. That created a threat that the district might lose essential federal funds, the ultimate sanction for violations provided by the 1964 Civil Rights Act. Consequently, the district negotiated an agreement with OCR to commission an independent assessment of the issues and eventually negotiated a settlement. The Civil Rights Project was selected from among bidders to carry out this study. The book's authors were deeply involved in the research to identify barriers to equitable access in the recruitment, application, and enrollment processes in BPS's criteria-based schools and to propose changes that the school board would be required to consider under the OCR agreement.

Struggles over access to the small number of seats in very-high-quality schools are most intense in older central cities with a small minority of White residents and extreme racial and economic polarization. In many such cities, although there are mayors and school board members of color, the local constituencies have been divided ideologically by the charter school movement, and the parents in the highly selective public schools tend to be strongly committed to the traditional way of operation. Those parents are very concerned about the loss of exclusivity for their schools, and they believe that the quality of the school will decline substantially if "less qualified" students are admitted. In those districts, the scarcity of strong college preparatory education is extreme and the demands from parents and communities who see it as a life-or-death issue for their children can become very intense. Buffalo is such a city, and BPS is such a school district.

This book takes the reader into complex and strongly contested terrain. There was no developed pathway for conducting this kind of investigation. The study team recognized inherent difficulties in creating equity within a complex choice process but understood our assignment as making it more equitable, not restructuring the school district or abandoning the system. The authors do not oppose the creation of demanding special schools of choice in urban communities and have not proposed shutting down existing schools. Our fundamental concern is with operating them fairly across the lines of race, ethnicity, poverty, and immigrant status. We believe that in schools of choice, as in our most selective colleges, diversity is an asset and that many students from homes and neighborhoods with limited resources are capable of succeeding in demanding schools without any lowering of standards if the process is managed appropriately. Research also shows that for White students, diversity helps prepare them to live and work successfully in a very diverse society.

Efforts to increase access to excellent schools in our big cities are efforts to activate the last vestige of such opportunities in a post–civil rights urban society where we have retreated both in terms of creating access to better middle-class schools and financially equalizing schools in rich and poor communities. Or, of course, these efforts could begin something very different. They could be the first step in turning around decades of shrinkage of rights for students of color. They could help clarify that only by facing the results of race-blind policies that produce resegregation can we begin to make more and more people and leaders understand that we have fallen into a pit of self-perpetuating segregation and inequality and that it will take conscious action to turn that around. Not only would some students of color and children living in deep poverty receive life-transforming opportunities, but we could realize that it is not necessary to limit these opportunities so rigidly. We could decide to create more great and diverse schools that would offer these chances to many more of our students. And seeing both the depths of inequality and the transformative possibilities could awaken the need for a much more serious focus on reversing the resegregation of many cities and big sectors of suburbia and creating schooling and housing opportunities that could be the base for a truly integrated society. This issue is very important at this juncture in our history, and it could have even greater importance in helping us find the way out of a social dead end.

We are very conscious of the fact that the federal government's pursuit of BPS was a product of the far more active enforcement of civil rights law under the Obama administration after a virtual shutdown of OCR during the George W. Bush administration. Subsequently, the Trump administration quickly signaled sharp changes in both OCR and the Department of Justice, supporting local autonomy and federal deregulation and reversing the government's position in civil rights litigation. We know that the country is deeply polarized on civil rights policy and that future federal administrations may take very different positions. Researchers must be aware of the political reality, but our assignment was to tell the truth as best as we could document it and propose policy changes that our research told us were feasible in Buffalo and could be successfully implemented. We understood that researchers have the power only to recommend, but we had the unusual agreement the parties had negotiated that forced the district to at least respond to our recommendations, and OCR had powerful sanctions it could use. Once research is done, others make the decisions, but good research can have a long shelf life as issues evolve and communities and the law change. The issues can be taken up by state officials, by educational officials and administrators, through litigation by civil rights groups, and by forces within communities as local politics evolve. This book raises issues that will continue to be contested in federal and state courts and in local educational policymaking over the coming years, both in Buffalo and, we expect, in other communities facing similar problems. It was a privilege to be given this responsibility, and we hope that others will take on similar challenges in other communities.

ORGANIZATION OF THE BOOK

This book explores longstanding racial inequalities in the highly segregated city of Buffalo, examines BPS's competitive-admissions choice system, and identifies policies that could address barriers to access and opportunity in BPS as well as in the many other choice systems across the nation. In Chapter 2, Ayscue introduces the Buffalo investigation. She describes the nature of school choices in Buffalo and the allegations in the Buffalo parents' complaint to OCR. This chapter offers a glimpse into the authors' role as researchers on the firing line as they faced the challenge of conducting excellent research in a troubled district with intense political and racial divisions. In Chapter 3, Tomasello describes the history and context of the city of Buffalo and the BPS school district through the eras of school segregation, desegregation, and resegregation, leading up to the recent civil rights investigation. In Chapter 4, Ee examines overall enrollment trends in the district compared to criteria-based schools, with a focus on disparities in enrollment by race and poverty. She also investigates the extent to which the proportion of students of color and socioeconomically disadvantaged students is associated with academic outcomes in criteria-based schools and in comparison to the rest of the district. Ee underscores the grave academic consequences of segregation in Buffalo's choice system. In Chapter 5, Woodward and Amlani describe five major categories of barriers that posed challenges for BPS students of color, low-income students, and ELs when both applying to and accessing criteria-based schools: information, preparation, admissions criteria (particularly the cognitive skills testing requirement at two of the criteria-based schools—City Honors and Olmsted), support services, and availability of choices. In Chapter 6, Ayscue and Siegel-Hawley detail the changes the research team recommended for BPS's criteria-based schools, grounded in research literature about how to make choice fair as well as policy guidance from the federal government. In Chapter 7, Orfield and Ayscue describe the responses from BPS and OCR to our recommendations. In the Postscript, Orfield shares the lessons we learned, some of them relevant to a broad range of issues and studies, as well as the many significant questions that remain.

This book's authors demonstrate that without intentional effort, competitive-admissions choice systems are likely to exacerbate inequality and segregation. However, they strongly contend that comprehensive efforts to reduce barriers could be used to create competitive-admissions choice systems that are not only more desegregated but also more equitable and accessible to all students.

NOTE

1. For further analysis of these issues, see Orfield, G., Siegel-Hawley, G., & Kucsera, J. (2014). *Sorting out deepening confusion on segregation trends.* Los Angeles, CA: The Civil Rights Project/Proyecto Derechos Civiles.

REFERENCES

Alexander, M. (2010). *The new Jim Crow: Mass incarceration in the age of colorblindness.* New York, NY: The New Press.

Allensworth, E. M., Moore, P. T., Sartain, L., & de la Torre, M. (2016). The educational benefits of attending higher performing schools: Evidence from Chicago high schools. *Educational Evaluation and Policy Analysis, 39*(2), 175–197.

American Educational Research Association (AERA), American Psychological Association (APA), & National Council on Measurement in Education (NCME). (2014). *Standards for educational and psychological testing.* Washington, DC: AERA.

Ayscue, J. B., & Orfield, G. (2015). School district lines stratify educational opportunity by race and poverty. *Race and Social Problems, 7*(1), 5–20.

Bischoff, K. (2008). School district fragmentation and racial residential segregation: How do boundaries matter? *Urban Affairs Review, 44*(2), 182–217.

Board of Education v. Dowell, 498 U.S. 237 (1991).

Bonilla-Silva, E. (2017). *Racism without racists: Color-blind racism and the persistence of racial inequality in America* (5th ed.). Lanham, MD: Rowan & Littlefield.

Bowen, W. G., & Bok, D. (2000). *The shape of the river: Long-term consequences of considering race in college and university admissions.* Princeton, NJ: Princeton University Press.

Brown v. Board of Education of Topeka, 347 U.S. 483 (1954).

Carter, P. L., & Welner, K. G. (Eds.). (2013). *Closing the opportunity gap: What America must do to give every child an even chance.* New York, NY: Oxford University Press.

Chavez, L., & Frankenberg, E. (2009). *Integration defended: Berkeley Unified's strategy to maintain school diversity.* Los Angeles, CA: The Civil Rights Project/Proyecto Derechos Civiles.

Chubb, J. E., & Moe, T. M. (1990). *Politics, markets and America's schools.* Washington, DC: Brookings Institution Press.

Clotfelter, C. T., Ladd, H. F., & Vigdor, J. L. (2005). Who teaches whom? Race and the distribution of novice teachers. *Economics of Education Review, 24*(4), 377–392.

Cobb, C. D., & Glass, G. V. (2009). School choice in a post-desegregation world. *Peabody Journal of Education, 84*(2), 262–278.

Denton, N. A. (2001). The persistence of segregation: Links between residential segregation and school segregation. In j. a. powell, G. Kearney, & V. Kay (Eds.), *In pursuit of a dream deferred: Linking housing and education policy* (pp. 89–119). New York: Peter Lang.

Dickerson, C., & Saul, S. (2016, November 10). Campuses confront hostile acts against minorities after Trump's election. *New York Times*. Retrieved from www.nytimes.com/2016/11/11/us/police-investigate-attacks-on-muslim-students-at-universitieshtml

Duncan, G., & Murnane, R. (Eds.). (2011). *Whither opportunity? Rising inequality, schools, and children's life chances*. New York: Russell Sage Foundation.

Finn, C. E., & Hockett, J. A. (2012). *Exam schools: Inside America's most selective public high schools*. Princeton, NJ: Princeton University Press.

Frankenberg, E. (2013). The role of residential segregation in contemporary school segregation. *Education and Urban Society, 45*(5), 548–570.

Freeman v. Pitts, 112 S. Ct. 1430 (1992).

Frey, W. H. (2014). *Diversity explosion: How new racial demographics are remaking America*. Washington, DC: The Brookings Institution.

Fuller, B., & Elmore, R. F. (Eds.). (1996). *Who chooses? Who loses? Culture, institutions, and the unequal effects of school choice*. New York, NY: Teachers College Press.

Gallup Editors. (2014, December 12). Gallup review: Black and White differences in views on race. Retrieved from news.gallup.com/poll/180107/gallup-review-black-white-differences-views-race.aspx

Goldring, E., & Smrekar, C. (2000). Magnet schools and the pursuit of racial balance. *Education and Urban Society, 33*(1), 17–35.

Green v. Board of Education of New Kent County, 391 U.S. 430 (1968).

Hiaasen, S. & Mcgrory, K. (2011, September 19). Florida charter schools: Big money, little oversight. *Miami Herald*. Retrieved from www.miamiherald.com/news/special-reports/cashing-in-on-kids/article1939199.html

Heubert, P., & Hauser, R. M. (Eds.). (1999). *High stakes: Testing for tracking, promotion, and graduation*. Washington, DC: National Academy of Sciences.

Jackson, K. (2009). Student demographics, teacher sorting, and teacher quality: Evidence from the end of school desegregation. *Journal of Labor Economics, 27*(2), 213–256.

King, Jr., M. L. (1963). Letter from Birmingham Jail. Retrieved from www.thekingcenter.org/archive/document/letter-birmingham-city-jail-0

Massey, D. S., & Denton, N. A. (1993). *American apartheid: Segregation and the making of the underclass*. Cambridge, MA: Harvard University Press.

Milliken v. Bradley, 418 U.S. 717 (1974).

Milliken v. Bradley II, 443 U.S. 267 (1977).

Missouri v. Jenkins, 115 S. Ct. 2938 (1995).

Orfield, G. (2001). Metropolitan school desegregation: Impacts on metropolitan society. In j. a. powell, G. Kearney, & V. Kay (Eds.), *In pursuit of a dream deferred: Linking housing and education policy* (pp. 121–157). New York: Peter Lang.

Orfield, G., & Eaton, S. E. (Eds.). (1996). *Dismantling desegregation: The quiet reversal of Brown v. Board of Education*. New York, NY: The New Press.

Orfield, G., & Frankenberg, E. (2011). *Diversity and educational gains: A plan for a changing county and its schools*. Los Angeles, CA: The Civil Rights Project/Proyecto Derechos Civiles.

Orfield, G., & Frankenberg, E. (Eds.). (2013). *Educational delusions? How choice can deepen inequality and how to make schools fair*. Berkeley, CA: University of California Press.

Orfield, G., Kucsera, J., & Siegel-Hawley, G. (2012). *E pluribus . . . separation: Deepening double segregation for more students*. Los Angeles, CA: The Civil Rights Project/Proyecto Derechos Civiles.

Parents Involved in Community Schools v. Seattle School District No. 1, 551 U.S. 701 (2007).

Peters, J. W., Thee-Brenan, M., & Sussman, D. (2016, November 9). Exit polls confirm stark divisions along racial, gender and economic lines. *New York Times*. Retrieved from www.nytimes.com/2016/11/09/us/politics/election-exit-polls.html

Reardon, S. F., Grewal, E. T., Kalogrides, D., & Greenberg, E. (2012). *Brown* fades: The end of court-ordered school desegregation and the resegregation of American public schools. *Journal of Policy Analysis and Management, 31*(4), 876–904.

Reardon, S. F., Yun, J. T., & Kurlaender, M. (2006). Implications of income-based school assignment policies for racial school segregation. *Educational Evaluation and Policy Analysis, 28*(1), 49–75.

Scott, J. (Ed.). (2005). *School choice and diversity: What the evidence says*. New York, NY: Teachers College Press.

Siegel-Hawley, G., & Frankenberg, E. (2013). Designing choice: Magnet school structures and racial diversity. In G. Orfield & E. Frankenberg (Eds.), *Educational delusions? Why choice can deepen inequality and how to make schools fair* (pp. 107–128). Berkeley, CA: University of California Press.

Smith, A. (1776). *The wealth of nations*. London, England: Methuen & Co.

Tompkins-Stange, M. E. (2016). *Policy patrons: Philanthropy, education reform, and the politics of influence*. Cambridge, MA: Harvard Education Press.

U.S. Department of Education, Office of Innovation and Improvement. (2009). *State regulation of private schools* Washington, DC: Author.

CHAPTER 2

Buffalo's Choice Schools and the Civil Rights Issues

Jennifer B. Ayscue

The Buffalo Public Schools (BPS) system, located in Upstate New York on the eastern shore of Lake Erie, serves one of the state's largest school districts. A once-great industrial center, the city of Buffalo has experienced a long-term decline since the mid-20th century. Buffalo is currently one of the nation's most segregated cities and metropolitan areas (Kucsera & Orfield, 2014). In 2013–2014—the year when the civil rights complaint was filed—the district's enrollment was predominantly Black (54% in 2013), with smaller shares of White (21%), Latino (16%), and Asian students (6%). The overwhelming majority of students (81%) were low-income. In 2013–2014, BPS operated 69 schools that enrolled almost 37,000 students. Eight of the district's 69 schools were criteria-based schools that offered students access to unique educational programs and exceptional academic opportunities.[1] In other districts, criteria-based schools might also be referred to as "competitive-admissions schools" or "selective-admissions schools." These schools have entrance criteria, such as grades, tests, attendance records, teacher or parent recommendations, and interviews or auditions, that students must fulfill in order to be accepted for admission to the school.

THE OCR COMPLAINT AND RESOLUTION AGREEMENT

Buffalo's magnet schools were originally designed in 1976 with desegregation requirements. They were created under a federal court desegregation order, which was issued after the court held that both the school system and the city government had a long history of discrimination (*Arthur v. Nyquist*, 1976). The plan was dropped after a 1991 Supreme Court decision (*Board of Education of Oklahoma City v. Dowell*, 1991) ruling that desegregation orders were temporary, and the choice process was turned over to local officials who, in 1997, eliminated the mechanisms that had fostered school diversity. In 2014, a group of parents filed a complaint with the U.S. Office for Civil Rights (OCR) of the U.S. Department of Education alleging that BPS "discriminated on the basis of race and national origin by using admissions criteria that disproportionately excluded non-White students from enrollment in the district's 'criteria-based' schools" (Blanchard, 2014). OCR began an investigation of the claim and found evidence of significant statistical disparities. For each of the district's eight criteria-based schools, OCR identified the admissions criteria, the number of applicants, and the admissions rates by race/national origin. OCR found that there were statistically significant differences in the admissions rates between White and non-White students, particularly between White and Black students, in six of the eight criteria-based schools. OCR found the most severe violations in two schools—City Honors and Olmsted. These initial findings were sufficiently serious that the district agreed to resolve the matter before OCR concluded the investigation. This important OCR case has broad national implications.

In June 2014, BPS voluntarily agreed to implement a resolution agreement to resolve the complaint allegation. The resolution agreement required BPS to hire a consultant "to study and make recommendations" designed to "provide all students with equal access and an equal opportunity to participate in these programs." The consultant, who had to be approved by OCR, was to "examine and make recommendation to address the root cause(s) of any disparity in enrollment and admissions rates of minority students in these schools" (U.S. Department of Education, New York Office for Civil Rights, 2014, p. 1). The agreement provided that the consultant would produce a report that the district was required to consider. The district would determine the action it would take based upon the consultant's recommendations, subject to OCR acceptance. OCR identified several specific areas that the district must consider as part of this process: parent/guardian and student outreach, academic counseling services, training for district staff/administrators, remedies for individual complainants' children, data maintenance, and monitoring of changes.

In July 2014, BPS issued a Request for Proposal for a consultant to review and assess the criteria-based schools. Our team of researchers from the Civil Rights Project at the University of California, Los Angeles, submitted a proposal in August 2014. We were selected by BPS and approved by OCR, and charged with analyzing application, admission, and enrollment rates at the criteria-based schools. Given OCR's initial findings regarding disproportionality in admissions, we were not required by OCR to examine all eight of the criteria-based schools; however, we chose to do so in an effort to create more comprehensive and systematic change that would impact students across the district and be sustainable over time. We were responsible for conducting surveys and focus groups with parents, students, and district and school faculty and staff to identify the barriers to equitable access in the recruitment, application, and enrollment processes in the criteria-based schools. We were also tasked with proposing changes that the school board would be required to consider.

As is often the case when doing civil rights work that has lasting consequences for children's life opportunities, this work was challenging. In the politically and racially divided City of Buffalo, there was strong support as well as resolute opposition to changing anything about the criteria-based school system. However, before we describe our approach to engaging in conversations to explore various perspectives, it is essential to understand the terminology of school choice systems as well as the process that governs the choices available in Buffalo's criteria-based schools.

SCHOOL CHOICE TERMINOLOGY

Magnet schools are public schools that typically have a focused theme along with innovative curriculum or instructional methods that are aligned with the theme. They often do not have entrance criteria but instead draw students from across an entire school district or set of multiple school districts through their "magnetizing" theme, curriculum, or pedagogy. In this book, we are focusing on a very specific type of magnet school. We are examining magnet schools that do have entrance criteria, often termed *selective magnet schools*, and more specifically those that have academic entrance criteria. Such schools are often referred to as *competitive-admissions magnet schools/competitive-admissions schools of choice* or *academically selective magnet schools/academically selective schools of choice*. In the most recent comprehensive study of such schools, Finn and Hockett (2012) use the term *exam schools* and identify the following six characteristics to describe exam schools: (1) public schools, (2) high schools, (3) whole-school models, not a program or school within another school, (4) schools that offer academic curriculum intended to prepare students for college, (5) schools that have an academically selective admissions process, and (6) schools that have an admissions process that is academically competitive in that the number of applicants exceeds the number of available seats, or applicants could be denied admission based on academic merit in comparison to other applicants or the school's standards for admissions. Finally, BPS uses the term *criteria-based school*, a broader concept referring to a school that requires that students meet a certain set of criteria, which includes academic criteria in some cases but not in other cases. City Honors and Olmsted, which require students to take an entrance exam, would meet the definition of exam schools, while the district's six other criteria-based schools are not exam schools. We use the terms *competitive-admissions school of choice*, *selective-admissions magnet school*, and *criteria-based school* interchangeably throughout this book. When referring specifically to City Honors and/or Olmsted, we also use the term *exam school*.

THE BPS CRITERIA-BASED SCHOOL SYSTEM

Each of BPS's eight criteria-based schools has a different theme and set of accompanying admissions criteria (Table 2.1). While the criteria-based schools are perceived to be of better quality and in higher demand than the rest of BPS's schools,

Table 2.1. BPS Criteria-Based Schools

School Name	Grade Level	Theme	Admissions Criteria
Olmsted Elementary 64	K–4	Gifted and talented	• Preliminary screening (K) • IQ test (K–1) • Cognitive abilities test (2–4) • Teacher inventory (1–4) • Parent inventory (K–4)
Olmsted Middle and High 156	5–12	Gifted and talented	• Cognitive abilities test • New York State English language arts and mathematics assessments • Grades (9–12) • Parent inventory • Teacher recommendation
Buffalo Academy of Visual and Performing Arts 192	5–12	Visual and performing arts	• Audition • Grades • Teacher recommendations
City Honors 195	5–12	International baccalaureate (IB)	• Cognitive abilities test • New York State English language arts and mathematics assessments • Grades • Teacher recommendation • Attendance
Leonardo da Vinci 212	9–12	College prep	• New York State English language arts and mathematics assessments • Grades • Teacher recommendations • Attendance
Emerson School of Hospitality 302*	9–12	Hospitality	• New York State English language arts and mathematics assessments • Grades • Teacher recommendation • Attendance
Hutchinson Central Technical High School 304	9–12	College prep, pre-engineering	• Entrance aptitude test • Grades • Teacher recommendation
Middle Early College 415	9–12	Dual enrollment in high school and community college	• Grades • Attendance • Behavior • Teacher recommendations • Interview

* As of 2014–2015, Emerson School of Hospitality 302 was no longer a criteria-based school. However, we include it as a criteria-based school because it was a criteria-based school at the time when the OCR complaint was filed and was part of OCR's investigation of the district's criteria-based schools.

there are also two tiers of criteria-based schools. Among the criteria-based schools, each school has a different reputation, and there is a clear division in perceived quality and desirability between Olmsted Elementary 64, Olmsted Middle and High 156, and City Honors 195 versus all other criteria-based schools. Olmsted 64 and 156 have gifted and talented programs, and City Honors, the most desired of all the district's schools, operates the international baccalaureate (IB) program.

As is the case in districts across the nation, BPS's criteria-based schools are highly sought after and consistently receive more applications than there are slots available. In many cases, middle-class White parents view these schools as the only acceptable option for their children, refusing to send them to any other schools in BPS and instead opting to enroll them in nearby charter or private schools or to move to another school district if they are not admitted to a criteria-based school. The competition over these seats is intense.

Olmsted Elementary 64 and Olmsted Middle and High 156

Olmsted was the site of a pilot program for gifted and talented elementary students in 1979. The success of the pilot led the school to expand to a citywide magnet in 1981 as part of BPS's desegregation plan. In 2008, Olmsted expanded to include a high school, which is a citywide school focusing on gifted education. The high school is not attached to a particular neighborhood.

Olmsted Elementary 64's gifted and talented program is the only criteria-based option for elementary students in BPS. This criteria-based program is part of the larger school, which also enrolls students from the surrounding neighborhood (an affluent, predominantly White area of the city) and houses a Spanish dual-language immersion program. Students who wish to enroll in the gifted and talented program at Olmsted Elementary must meet certain criteria. Kindergarten applicants are invited by appointment to participate in a locally developed screening by school staff. All applicants participate in some form of testing, an IQ test (Stanford-Binet Intelligence Test) for kindergarten and 1st-grade applicants and a cognitive abilities test (InView) for 2nd-, 3rd-, and 4th-grade applicants. Parent inventories are required for all applicants, and teacher inventories are required for 1st- through 4th-grade applicants. A school-based folder review committee then meets to select qualified applicants.

Students who have attended the gifted and talented program at Olmsted Elementary 64 are automatically admitted to attend Olmsted 156 for 5th grade. All other students applying for grades 5 through 8 at Olmsted 156 must take a cognitive abilities test (InView) during one of two testing times in the fall. After students receive notification of whether or not they met the minimum cutoff score on the cognitive abilities test, they must submit additional application materials, which include results from the New York State English language arts and mathematics assessments, a parent inventory, and a teacher recommendation. For students applying to attend Olmsted 156 for high school, in addition to the criteria already described, students must also submit their grades in English language arts, mathematics, social studies, and science. The school review committee then selects qualified applicants.

City Honors 195

In 1975, the City Honors program was established as a site of progressive education. In his 1976 decision in *Arthur v. Nyquist*, Federal Judge John T. Curtin ordered BPS to desegregate, at which point City Honors became one of the first two magnet schools created in Phase I of BPS's desegregation plan. In 1989, the IB program was established at City Honors. Currently, City Honors is an IB World School that offers both the IB Middle Years Program for students in 5th through 10th grades and the IB Diploma Program for 11th- and 12th-grade students.

The school is consistently ranked among the top high schools in the nation. In 2013, *Newsweek* ranked City Honors as the number-one school in the state of New York, the number-one school in the Northeast, and number 22 in the United States. This ranking was based on six factors: graduation rate, college acceptance rate, average number of AP/IB/AICE tests taken per student, average AP/IB/AICE score, average SAT/ACT score, and percentage of students enrolled in at least one AP/IB/AICE course. City Honors had a graduation rate of 100%, and 98% of students were college-bound. Students took an average of 2.4 AP/IB/AICE tests and scored an average of 2.6 on AP tests. The average SAT score was 1792, and the average ACT score was 26.3. With such high levels of academic achievement, City Honors is often referred to as "the gem of the city," and Buffalo residents express pride in the school regardless of whether or not their children attend it.

Because City Honors has such an exceptional academic reputation, parents are persistent in trying to gain access for their children to attend. As one middle-class White BPS parent explained, "People say, 'If I don't get into City Honors, I'm moving out of the city.'" In fact, some families whose children have been denied enrollment at City Honors have subsequently enrolled them in charter schools, private schools, or schools in other districts. They continue to retest and reapply to City Honors until they are granted admission, at which point they move back into the BPS district.

Admission to City Honors is based on five criteria. Similar to Olmsted, City Honors applicants must take a cognitive abilities test (InView) during one of two testing administrations in the fall. After receiving notification of whether or not they met the minimum threshold at or above the seventh stanine on the cognitive abilities test, students must submit additional application materials. To be considered for admission, students must also perform at or above the seventh stanine on the New York State English language arts and mathematics assessments. A grade point average of 85% or higher is required in English language arts, mathematics, social studies, and science. Applicants must also submit attendance records that demonstrate at least an 85% attendance rate as well as a teacher recommendation. The school review committee then determines who is admitted.

City Honors School, Buffalo, NY

Photo by Lindsay DeDario

OUR ROLE AS RESEARCHERS

To learn more about the admissions, application, and enrollment processes at the eight criteria-based schools, our research team gathered extensive data from a diverse group of participants. In addition to analyzing enrollment and achievement data (as described in Chapter 4), we conducted interviews, focus groups, and surveys. In order to identify the primary barriers to accessing the district's criteria-based schools, we used an exploratory sequential mixed-methods approach. That is, we began with a qualitative research phase of interviews and focus groups to explore participants' views. After analyzing the data from this phase, we used the information to create a second, quantitative phase with a survey instrument that was well suited to our sample of participants (Creswell, 2014).

Ultimately, we collected data from 1,741 people through the following methods: individual or small-group site-based interviews with 6 district officials; phone interviews with 8 principals; focus group interviews with 117 parents, 62 students, 9 administrators (8 of whom had previously participated in phone interviews), and 19 teachers and counselors; online surveys from 295 school staff and 290 8th- and 9th-grade students; phone surveys conducted in Spanish and English with 860 parents; 73 emails; and 10 phone calls. Throughout this process of data collection, we remained committed to seeking participation from low-income parents and students as well as from parents and students of color—the very parents and students who had been marginalized and denied enrollment in the criteria-based schools. During the data-collection process, it was important to listen carefully, document responses, and explore ideas from multiple perspectives.

Finding Participants

In recruiting participants, our goal was to obtain maximum variation by hearing from as many parents, students, and school and district staff members as possible. Because this study was the result of a resolution agreement between BPS and OCR, we benefited from the assistance of BPS in gaining access to participants. However, we also wanted to ensure that we engaged with a diverse range of participants and were not limited to those who might be inclined to respond to outreach from BPS. Therefore, we used multiple approaches to recruiting participants, including outreach from BPS, outreach from key members of the religious community, direct recruitment from the research team, and open opportunities publicized to the entire community. Ensuring that the research team was effective in outreach to multiple stakeholders was critical because the district was often disorganized and unsuccessful in its efforts to communicate with the community. For families who did not speak English, the lack of communication and information was an even greater barrier, as the district did not provide any written materials or outreach in any languages other than English. Moreover, the district had difficulty gathering a sufficient number of parents to complete the field tests of our interview protocols and surveys; hence, it was extremely important to devise multiple ways to give voice to the community.

To recruit parent participants for our interviews and focus groups, we contacted school district leaders and a pastor of an African American church, all of whom facilitated direct connections with parents in the Buffalo community. These parents allowed us to pilot-test our interview protocol, an important step in ensuring that our interview questions were valid and would lead to responses that advanced our study's aims. These parents also helped to spread the word about the study, increasing our visibility in the community. We generated a phone message and an email message to publicize our focus group meetings, and these messages were delivered to all parents of BPS students. Our focus group meetings were also publicized on the BPS website. In addition, we attended a District Parent Coordinating Council meeting, which was aired on the local public news station, and announced our focus group meetings on the air. Finally, we conducted focus groups with formally organized parent groups, some of which had specific interests, such as multilingual education and special education. We conducted our parent interviews and focus groups both during the day and in the evening. All meetings were held at a centralized location accessible by public transportation. A total of 117 parents participated in focus groups or interviews, ranging from 15 minutes to 1 1/2 hours. Despite our multiple efforts to recruit diverse groups of parents, a disproportionately large share of parent participants represented the two exam-based criteria schools—City Honors and Olmsted—which limited our access to marginalized communities. For this reason, the parent survey, described below, was particularly important in giving voice to low-income parents of color and Spanish-speaking parents.

To recruit student participants, we relied more heavily on BPS staff. Focus groups were conducted during the school day either at schools or at a centralized location to which transportation for students was provided. BPS district staff arranged for student leaders to meet with us in small groups at a centralized location. While we were appreciative of this vocal group of participants, we also wanted to meet with other students and therefore arranged site visits at two schools: one criteria-based and one non-criteria-based school. These visits were important for allowing us to interview a more diverse set of students; however, it is also important to note that the selection of the students for our focus groups was facilitated by school principals. As a result, we are not certain that we obtained a truly representative sample of students. A total of 62 students participated in focus groups, ranging from 30 to 60 minutes in length. Student participants represented 11 BPS high schools, including five criteria-based schools and six non-criteria-based schools.

It was also essential to hear from district and school personnel. A total of six district staff members participated in individual or small-group discussions, lasting approximately 1 hour each. District staff who participated included the director of student placement and registration, director of multilingual education, director of special education, supervisor of clerical staff, supervisor of student placement, and supervisor of the front office at Central Registration. We conducted individual 1-hour phone interviews with principals from all eight criteria-based schools as well as a 2-hour, in-person focus group with the eight principals and the vice principal from one criteria-based school. In addition, we interviewed two administrators from a non-criteria-based school. A total of eight counselors participated in a 2-hour focus group conversation. These counselors represented four pre-K–8 schools, one 5–8 school, and four 9–12 schools, including both criteria-based and non-criteria-based schools. School staff, including teachers, counselors, and instructional coaches from four schools, participated in 1-hour small-group discussions at their respective schools, which included two criteria-based schools and two non-criteria-based schools. These focus groups included a total of 10 teachers, eight counselors, and one instructional coach. In addition, Orfield met individually with school board members. Although all board members were invited to participate, one who was strongly opposed to the OCR investigation and our study of BPS, as will be described below, declined to participate in a meeting.

In addition to recruiting participants for our focus groups, we also wanted to encourage participation from parents and students who were unable to attend the focus group meetings. Therefore, we provided a telephone number and email address at which parents, students, staff, and community members could contact us if they wanted to participate but were unable to attend our meetings. Providing a phone number was important and, in fact, was created at the request of a participant who expressed difficulty—on behalf of some members of the community, particularly low-income families—in accessing the Internet and emailing us. We announced our contact information on the local public news stations, and when we conducted interviews and focus groups, we also distributed our contact information to all participants, encouraging them to share it with others. When we were contacted via telephone or email, we responded within 24 hours and requested information from everyone who contacted us. We received 10 phone calls and 73 emails.

Even with these multiple and varied attempts to solicit participants from diverse groups of participants, we acknowledge that our general appeals to students, parents, and staff might have resulted in a sample that is not fully representative of the population. Instead, a random sample of participants might have been preferable. However, this approach was not feasible due to organizational and logistical constraints at BPS.

Developing Trust and Asking Valid Questions

In all our interactions, we made it clear that our role as researchers was to listen and learn from our participants, the people who possessed the expertise and had been living the experience. By conveying this message as well as clearly articulating the goals of our study, we believe that we were able to establish trust and a shared sense of responsibility for contributing to meaningful changes in BPS's criteria-based school system. It was important to listen and gain perspective from everyone, both those who were normally included as well as those who had been excluded from previous conversations discussing the BPS criteria-based school system. Again, emphasizing that the research team wanted to expand opportunity rather than decrease rigor and close down schools helped to minimize criticisms.

In our interviews and focus groups, we asked questions that explored the following topics: the number, location, and theme of criteria-based schools; communication and outreach; advertisement; school reputations and peer pressure; early awareness of the relationship between academic performance and enrollment in criteria-based schools; course offerings to prepare students for enrollment in criteria-based schools; admissions requirements; application process; enrollment and registration policies and procedures; guidance counselors; support services available at criteria-based schools; and transportation. In the interviews and focus groups, we used a semistructured protocol. We established a general set of questions that ensured that we covered similar topics with all participants but also gave us the flexibility to ask open-ended questions, probe more deeply, and allow the conversation to take turns into unanticipated topics, an important part of learning from our participants who possessed more knowledge and experience than we did about the situation and the barriers that students of color faced in BPS. Although it was tempting to begin formulating suggestions for change, we did our best to remain cognizant of our listening role and continuously attempted to listen to participants' responses without prematurely jumping into brainstorming policy recommendations. We wanted to remain open to hearing the statements of all the participants and recording all of their insights.

Listening and Documenting Responses

To facilitate the listening process during interviews and focus groups, we paired each interviewer with a second member of the research team who was responsible for taking notes. The second team member could also provide another set of ears to suggest probing questions if the primary interviewer did not pick up on an important topic or response from a participant. To ensure accurate documentation of data, we also audio-recorded all interviews and focus groups with parents, school staff, and district staff. Due to district restrictions, we were not able to audio-record student focus groups, so we relied solely on notes for student data. Four research team members were involved in conducting interviews and focus groups.

Using Multiple Sources of Information

To triangulate our data, we used multiple sources of data, including participants with different roles as well as different data collection techniques, and multiple investigators, as previously noted. In addition to the interviews and focus groups described above, we conducted phone surveys with parents and online surveys with students and school personnel. The surveys were important because they allowed us to reach more people and provided a more representative sample of participants.

The survey questions were informed by our interview and focus group findings. Survey questions explored issues related to the location and themes of criteria-based schools, school reputations, access to information, preparation in earlier grades, the application process, guidance counselors, support services, transportation, and beliefs about barriers.

We worked with a local professional survey research firm to conduct a phone survey of parents of 9th-grade students, including parents of children who had applied to criteria-based schools (both those who had been accepted into the schools and those who had been denied acceptance) as well as parents of children who had not applied to criteria-based schools. An independent firm administered the survey to the two groups of parents. We took several steps to gain access to a diverse set of parents, particularly those from marginalized groups. To ensure that we were not further marginalizing parents due to language barriers, the survey was conducted in both English and Spanish. BPS's communication is always conducted in English; therefore, providing an opportunity for Spanish-speaking families to have their voices heard was essential because their voices had been silenced prior to this study. We also knew that it was important to obtain the most recent contact information for parents, particularly because we wanted to reach low-income parents, who are often more highly mobile and whose phone numbers might change more frequently than others. Therefore, 9th-grade homeroom teachers gathered parents' phone numbers from their students just days before our survey was conducted. Parents were randomly selected for survey participation. The firm made up to 15 attempts to reach each parent. A total of 860 parents participated in the phone survey, including 459 parents whose children attended criteria-based schools and 401 parents whose children did not.

Alongside the parent survey, we conducted an online student survey of 8th- and 9th-grade students. All 8th- and 9th-grade students received a flier inviting them to participate in the survey; a link to the survey was also prominently displayed on the homepage of the BPS website. We had hoped to administer the survey to students during class time in order to maximize participation, but because we were administering our survey in the spring, the need to preserve class time for students' exam preparation precluded us from conducting the survey then. Students had one week to complete the survey. The 1-week time frame for completion of the survey was shorter than desired, but again, in order to prevent interference with students' exam schedules, this short time frame was necessary. A total of 290 8th- and 9th-graders completed the survey. The student survey explored the same types of topics as the parent survey.

We administered an online survey to teachers, counselors, and administrators across BPS. An email containing the survey link was sent to BPS staff (approximately 4,000 people) from the Superintendent's Office and was available for 2 weeks. A total of 295 BPS staff completed the survey. As an indication of the level of interest of the respondents, more than 100 of the 295 participants included notes explaining their attitudes, raising questions, and offering suggestions. This level of engagement is unusually high for such surveys, and we deeply appreciate the contributions of those staff and teachers. Teachers, counselors, and administrators are central to the educational process, so it is desirable, when possible, to have their support for needed changes.

Analyzing the Data

After collecting these multiple forms of data, we analyzed the data and used the analysis to develop recommendations that would make a direct impact on BPS policy. For this study, we first conducted interviews and focus groups that allowed us to develop a broad understanding of the situation in BPS and the potential barriers that existed for students of color and low-income students in attempting to enroll in criteria-based schools. We analyzed this data using open coding and then developed categories to identify common themes and barriers (Merriam, 2009). We wrote analytic memos to describe categories of barriers.

Next, we used what we had learned from the interviews and focus groups to inform the development of survey questions, allowing us to pose more specific and focused questions related to the barriers we had identified through the interviews and focus groups. We analyzed survey responses separately for each group of participants, identifying common sentiments as well as areas of disagreement. We then explored the results across the groups.

POLITICAL AND RACIAL DIVISION

As might be expected when doing civil rights work, this research process was not easy. It was necessary, but difficult, to conduct high-quality research in a troubled district with the intense political and racial division that exists in the community and on the school board. However, it is likely that the weight of OCR and the threat of possible termination of federal funding provided incentives to the district to facilitate a smooth process. BPS district and school representatives were extremely cooperative with our requests.

We found that participants were very open in discussing the current recruitment, application, and admissions processes for criteria-based schools. Numerous parents, students, and community members were eager to share their insights and experiences in an effort to bring about change that would benefit students' educational opportunities and outcomes. Yet in this politically and racially divided city (as is described in Chapter 3), there was also strong opposition to changing anything about the process, mostly coming from White middle-class parents whose children were benefiting from the current processes. Resistance also was expressed by some members of the school board, again most strongly from one politically prominent White member of the racially divided school board. Regardless of their stance, participants provided many comments and shared insights that allowed us to better understand the current processes and the barriers that students had been facing during various phases of the process.

It is clear from our experience in Buffalo that all parents want a high-quality education for their children, and many emphasized the need to improve all of the district's schools, not just the criteria-based schools. We understood, however, that our role was strictly limited to the issues related to the criteria-based schools. There was strong disagreement about the role of criteria-based schools in providing opportunities to the city's students. Some, often middle-class White families, held steadfast to the ideas of meritocracy, argued that the testing and assessment procedures showed that their children were the most prepared, and believed that their children deserved the opportunities they had received to attend criteria-based schools. They did not believe that the criteria-based schools had a stratifying or segregating effect; as one parent contended, "I believe the whole complaint is sort of ridiculous." Also critical of the OCR investigation and our work in BPS was the White majority faction of the racially divided school board, one of whom declined to meet with Orfield. Carl Paladino, a former conservative candidate for governor, expressed the most virulent resistance to expanding opportunity and access to the criteria-based schools and tried to block our efforts, writing in an email to Orfield, "Get out of the way" (Staff, 2015). (He subsequently was removed from the school board in August 2017, due to disclosing confidential school board information.) In contrast, others put forth views that "choice is important, but I don't think it's actually available to everybody who lives in the city." They asserted that the effect of the choice process was segregative: "The school system is back where we were. I think it's a segregated system and I think that privileged kids end up at the choice schools." These dichotomous views about the criteria-based system are grounded in strongly held and opposing broader beliefs regarding the extent to which racism pervades the city and school district, as well as how the criteria-based school system creates social stratification and results in social reproduction as White, middle-class students are able to gain access to the best educational opportunities in the district while low-income students of color attend segregated and often less strong schools.

The stakes in the study were high, and opinions varied widely about how the choice process should work and who should receive access to the district's criteria-based schools. However, no one, including our research team, wanted to shut down or lower the academic quality of the criteria-based schools. As a Black BPS father explained, "Please understand, we do not want anything to happen to our City Honors. . . . I don't have a kid in City Honors, but I'm prouder of City Honors than I am of being a citizen of Buffalo." The puzzle of how to both preserve good options in a troubled city and make them more accessible to the large majority of non-White students who have previously had very limited access was the central challenge. It is because of the life-changing effect of attendance at one of the district's criteria-based schools that the struggle over access and equity in criteria-based schools was, and continues to be, so strong in Buffalo. This book explores the ways we learned about the roots and mechanisms of the inequality and formulated remedies, how the local battle evolved, and what the implications are, both for Buffalo and more broadly for elite public schools of choice across the nation.

NOTE

1. As of the 2014–2015 school year, Emerson School of Hospitality 302 was no longer a criteria-based school; however, we include it as a criteria-based school because it was a criteria-based school at the time when the OCR complaint was filed and was part of OCR's investigation of the district's criteria-based schools.

REFERENCES

Arthur v. Nyquist, 415 F. Supp. 904 (1976).
Blanchard, T. C. J. (2014). U.S. Department of Education, New York Office for Civil Rights letter of determination. Retrieved from www2.ed.gov/about/offices/list/ocr/docs/investigations/more/02141077-a.pdf
Board of Education of Oklahoma City v. Dowell, 498 U.S. 237 (1991)
Creswell, J. W. (2014). *Research design: Qualitative, quantitative, and mixed methods approaches* (4th ed.). Los Angeles, CA: SAGE Publications.

Finn, C. E., & Hockett, J. A. (2012). *Exam schools: Inside America's most selective public high schools.* Princeton, NJ: Princeton University Press.

Kucsera, J., & Orfield, G. (2014). *New York state's extreme school segregation.* Los Angeles, CA: The Civil Rights Project/Proyecto Derechos Civiles.

Merriam, S. B. (2009). *Qualitative research: A guide to design and implementation.* San Francisco, CA: Jossey-Bass.

Newsweek. (2013, May 6). *2013 America's best high schools. Newsweek.* Retrieved from www.newsweek.com/2013/05/06/america-s-best-high-schools.html

Staff. (2015, February 12). Civil rights consultant calls out Paladino for attempts to '"intimidate."' *The Buffalo News.* Retrieved from buffalonews.com/2015/02/12/civil-rights-consultant-calls-paladino-attempts-intimidate/

U.S. Department of Education, New York Office for Civil Rights. (2014). Resolution agreement: Buffalo Public Schools OCR Case No. 02-14-1077. Retrieved from www2.ed.gov/about/offices/list/ocr/docs/investigations/more/02141077-b.pdf

CHAPTER 3

Buffalo History and the Roots of School Segregation
The Rise of Buffalo's Two-Tiered School System

Jenna Tomasello

The current civil rights conflicts in Buffalo reflect deep features of Buffalo's history. This chapter describes the history and context of the City of Buffalo, the greater metropolitan area, and Buffalo Public Schools (BPS) through the era of school segregation, desegregation under court order, and the process of resegregation leading up to the recent civil rights investigation. Buffalo is characteristic of many old former industrial centers but has maintained exceptionally high levels of poverty and residential segregation to the present time. These trends are important in understanding Buffalo's story and the various factors that led to the disparities identified in the federal Office for Civil Rights (OCR) complaint and confirmed during the investigation. Multiple sources, including scholarly articles, legal documents, newspapers, and maps, were synthesized to describe the history and context of poverty and segregation in Buffalo, the metropolitan area, and BPS.

HISTORICAL BACKGROUND AND CONTEXT OF THE CITY OF BUFFALO AND THE METROPOLITAN AREA

Industry and Population Change

Buffalo had notable accomplishments generations ago as an important and prosperous city. In 1825, the Erie Canal was completed, linking New York City with the Great Lakes and the American interior and making Buffalo a major port (National Park Service, n.d.). By connecting Lake Erie to the Hudson River and therefore the Great Lakes to the Atlantic, the canal allowed for mass importing and exporting of goods, particularly wheat (Glaeser, 2007; National Park Service, n.d.). With the invention of the steam-powered grain elevator in 1841, Buffalo became "the world's leading grain port," attracting immigrants from throughout Europe (Glaeser, 2007, para. 4). Shipping goods by water to the surging cities of the Midwest and great national markets created economic power. Given the economic opportunities associated with being "one of the largest grain storage and processing centers in the world," Buffalo grew in population from 10,000 in 1831 to 352,000 in 1900 (City-Data, n.d., para. 5). In fact, it was the eighth-largest city in America when the 20th century began (U.S. Bureau of the Census, 1998). In the early 1900s, Buffalo began milling wheat and exporting flour throughout the country and the world, using hydroelectric power harnessed from Niagara Falls (National Park Service, n.d.). The combination of water-based transportation and abundant energy not only benefited the mills but also attracted businesses, including the Lackawanna Steel and Iron Company, Union Carbide, and Aluminum Company of America (Glaeser, 2007). Buffalo's population peaked in 1950 at 580,132, making it then the 15th-largest city in the nation ("Buffalo, New York," n.d.; see Figure 3.1).

Following World War II, like most industrialized cities, Buffalo began to experience a rapid decline due to several factors. First, the St. Lawrence Seaway opened in 1957, connecting the Great Lakes to the Atlantic, providing an option for direct transport on large ships and marking the beginning of Buffalo's decline as a port and rail center (Glaeser, 2007; National Park Service, n.d.). In Buffalo, as in other major Rust Belt cities such as Pittsburgh, Cleveland, St. Louis, Cincinnati, Detroit, Milwaukee, and Chicago, businesses began to pull out of the area, jobs vanished, and people moved out of the city to the suburbs (City-Data, n.d.; Crandall, 1993). The Erie Canal became virtually irrelevant with the advent of modern highways, and the interstate system and improvements to electricity transmission made proximity to Niagara Falls less important (Glaeser, 2007).

Shifting housing patterns also contributed to Buffalo's decline. Older industrial cities had boomed during World War II when jobs increased and there was a dearth of new housing due to rationing. But after the war, suburbanization quickly took hold, spurred by mass production of suburban tract housing and G.I. Bill–subsidized mortgages for returning soldiers, as well as affordable new suburban housing for the baby boomers. Most of the new suburban housing was for Whites only, since it was a generation later when the federal Fair Housing Act was passed (Abrams, 1955, 1965; U.S. Commission on Civil Rights, 1961). Following World War II, Buffalo was a textbook example of housing policy that drew Whites out of the city into highly segregated White suburbs.

Beginning in the 1950s, Buffalo experienced population loss, including much of its middle class (Glaeser, 2007; Figure 3.1). Concurrent with Buffalo's declining industry and overall shrinking population, thousands of Southern Blacks migrated into the city (Taylor, 1996). Amid the wartime worker shortage, Black workers were drawn to Buffalo's good unionized jobs, and as a result, its Black population grew by 433% from 1940 to 1970 (Yin, 2009). At the peak of Buffalo's influx of Southern Blacks during the 1970s, Buffalo experienced most of its population loss (Glaeser, 2007). In other words, Blacks moved into Buffalo and Whites left at the same time that deindustrialization hit the city. As Buffalo's White, middle-class residents moved to the suburbs, property values in the city began to decline, allowing for low-income families to take their place and diminishing the local tax

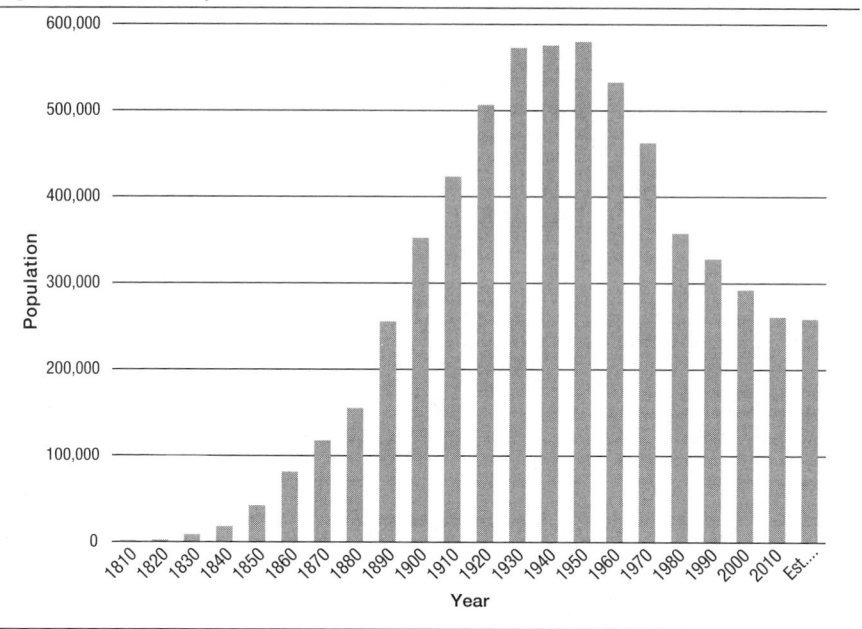

Figure 3.1. Buffalo Population Growth and Decline

Source: Buffalo, New York (n.d.).

base (Glaeser, 2007; Taylor, 1996; Yin, 2009). While efforts have been under way in Buffalo since the 1970s to curb population loss and attract new businesses, progress has been slow (Glaeser, 2007).

With an overall poverty rate above 30%, Buffalo is currently the third-poorest city in the country, behind only Detroit and Cleveland (Thomas, 2014). Even more extreme is the fact that 54% of Buffalo's children are growing up in families below the poverty line (Rey, 2016). The "White flight" that took place in the 1970s continues; both the inner-ring and outer-ring suburbs of Buffalo are, with few exceptions, overwhelmingly White, and the city and Niagara Falls are "predominantly non-White" or "diverse" (University of Minnesota Law School: Institute on Metropolitan Opportunity, 2010). The City of Buffalo and Niagara Falls continue to experience population loss, and so do the surrounding inner-ring suburbs, including North Tonawanda, Tonawanda, Cheektowaga, Depew, West Seneca, and Lackawanna (University of Minnesota Law School: Institute on Metropolitan Opportunity, 2000–2008). In contrast, the population of the outer-ring suburbs—Grand Island, Amherst, Clarence, Lancaster, Elma, Aurora, Orchard Park, and Hamburg—is relatively stable or growing.

Segregation Trends

Examining recent segregation patterns within the City of Buffalo and across the greater metropolitan area helps explain the poverty and segregation trends in BPS, and illuminates important roots of the current disparities found by OCR. Buffalo is one of the most segregated metropolitan areas in the country and one of the older industrial "hypersegregated" cities largely untouched by a half-century of fair housing laws. Thus, in addition to having a high poverty rate, Buffalo consistently ranks among the most racially segregated cities in the country (Jacobs, Kiersz, & Lubin, 2013). The racial composition of Buffalo's overall population is 46% White, 39% Black, 11% Latino, 3% Asian, 3% two or more races, and less than 1% Native American (U.S. Census Bureau, 2013a; Figure 3.2). Buffalo's racial demographics do not reflect larger New York State (NYS) or national trends. Buffalo's proportion of Black residents is more than twice as large as NYS and the country, while its proportions of Asian, Latino, and White residents are significantly smaller (U.S. Census Bureau, 2013b).

Buffalo has maintained persistent patterns of residential segregation, particularly in terms of White–Black residential dissimilarity (Kucsera & Orfield, 2014; Yin, 2009). Moreover, according to Yin (2009):

Figure 3.2. 2013 Population by Race: USA, Buffalo, and New York State

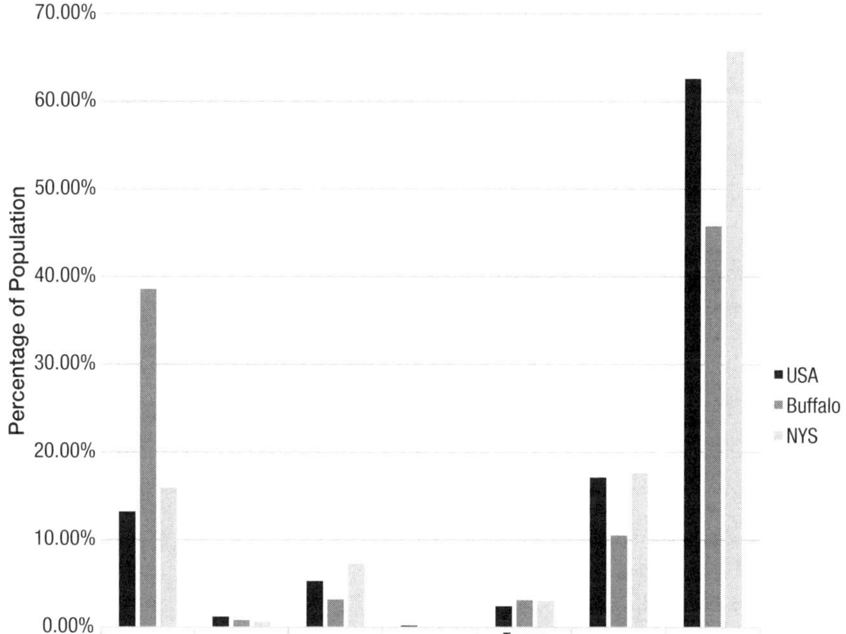

	Black	American Indian	Asian	Native Hawaiian	Two or More Races	Hispanic or Latino	White
USA	13.20%	1.20%	5.30%	0.20%	2.40%	17.10%	62.60%
Buffalo	38.60%	0.80%	3.20%	0.00%	3.10%	0.50%	45.80%
NYS	15.90%	0.60%	7.30%	0.00%	3.00%	17.60%	65.70%

Source: U.S. Census Bureau, 2013a, 2013b.

[W]hile the 1990 and 2000 censuses show that residential segregation declined to some extent from its extremely high levels nationwide, data for Buffalo reveal the persistent and striking high level of Black–White residential segregation in both the city and the metropolitan area. (p. 2753)

Thus, while national trends in Black–White residential segregation have decreased, Buffalo has maintained high levels of segregation.

An examination of segregation in the entire Buffalo metropolitan area indicates that between 2000 and 2010, Buffalo's suburbs have remained "predominantly White" (with the exception of Lackawanna, which shifted from "predominantly White" to "diverse") to a very unusual extent (University of Minnesota Law School: Institute on Metropolitan Opportunity, 2000–2008, 2010). According to Orfield et al. (2015), "The major suburbanization of families of color that has taken place in recent decades in most large metro [areas] simply has not occurred in Buffalo" (p. 3).

This situation is problematic for Buffalo, as Orfield et al. (2015) explain:

The process of continually building new white middle-class suburban developments in a metro with declining population produces lower density. A new suburban infrastructure in a declining metro cannot afford to continuously draw out the more successful families with resources further and further away from the city center and declining suburbs, which is left with a poor, poorly educated and heavily non-white population and a weak core to handle the central functions of a major metro. Without an ability to work together and to successfully train the young people who make up the future workforce, the area will continue its long decline. (pp. 3–4)

In addition to Buffalo's segregation across urban-suburban boundary lines, the City of Buffalo is also known to be segregated by neighborhood. While the city appears quite diverse in overall population figures, it is deeply segregated at the neighborhood level. In the early 1900s, prior to Buffalo's influx of Southern migrant workers, the Black community was small and the neighborhood in which most Black residents lived was somewhat integrated, with Blacks sharing residential space with German, Italian, and Irish neighbors (Taylor, 1996; Yin, 2009). In the mid-1900s, as noted earlier, Buffalo's Black population increased dramatically while Whites took advantage of federal subsidies and moved to the suburbs (Yin, 2009). At the same time, discriminatory housing, lending, and real estate practices kept Blacks in specific neighborhoods within the city (Kucsera & Orfield, 2014). According to Yin (2009), "[By 2000,] over 85 percent of the city's Black population lived on the east side of Main Street" (p. 2735). By that time, "whites had decreased to 51.8 percent of the city's total population and Blacks had increased to 37.2 percent" (Yin, 2009). Thus, while the City of Buffalo has retained a significant overall White population—46% according to the most recent census data (Figure 3.2)—the majority of Whites live on the northern, west side of Main Street (i.e., NY Route 5) and south of Interstate 190, while the majority of Blacks live on the east side of Main Street (Yin, 2009). In addition, outside of the city, there is also a substantial Black population in Niagara Falls (Desktop Explorer, 2013). These data suggest that Buffalo's title as one of the most segregated cities in the nation applies to both the central city (i.e., within city boundaries) and the entire metropolitan area (i.e., across urban-suburban boundary lines).

In sum, once an economically thriving city, Buffalo began a steady decline during the mid-1900s with the collapse of the manufacturing industries in the Northeast. After that, population shifts occurred, with Whites moving out to the suburbs and Blacks being segregated into certain neighborhoods within the city. With White flight came poverty, decreased property values, and therefore a shrinking tax base to support the city's infrastructure. These factors have also made Buffalo unsuccessful at attracting new business, thereby perpetuating its economic troubles. With a predominantly poor, non-White urban core and more affluent White suburbs, Buffalo has maintained consistently high levels of segregation and poverty in recent decades.

BPS AND THE ERAS OF SCHOOL SEGREGATION, DESEGREGATION, AND RESEGREGATION

Era of Segregation

In 1867, the first Buffalo desegregation case was filed. Henry Moxley, a prosperous Black barber, sued the school district superintendent for "assault and battery, for forcibly removing black children from the school, in violation of the 1866 Civil Rights Act" (Mosey, 1998, p. 1). The plaintiff lost the case, and it was not until 1872, with pressure from the community, that Black children were allowed to attend the public schools of Buffalo (Mosey, 1998).

Once Black children were allowed in the public schools, psychological and intelligence testing was used to track and isolate them. According to Mosey (1998), "[As early as 1915,] black students, labeled as retarded or overaged, would find their way to special schools with a compensatory curriculum based on what had been determined as their low abilities and special needs" (p. 65). Not only were Black students overrepresented in these "special schools," but in 1918 the Board of Education characterized these schools as being in "intolerable condition" (Mosey, 1998, p. 66). Thus, starting in the early 1900s, Black students in Buffalo experienced both separate and inferior curricula and facilities.

As discussed previously, Buffalo's Black population grew rapidly between 1940 and 1970 with the migration of Southern Blacks (Taylor, 1996; Yin, 2009). During this period, the isolation of Blacks became more pronounced, especially Black students in the schools. At this time, reading achievement tests were used to "segregate and isolate students with language difficulties—students such as southern Blacks and eastern and southern Europeans" (Mosey, 1998, p. 104). As a result, such students were placed in separate, lower-track programs starting at early ages (Mosey, 1998). Again, BPS deliberately segregated students through the mid-1900s.

Era of Desegregation

Nearly 100 years after the first school desegregation case in Buffalo was filed, a group of parents appealed to the New York State Commissioner in 1964 "regarding the racial imbalance [in BPS] . . . and the failure of the Board of Education to alleviate such issues" (Kucsera & Orfield, 2014, p. 15). The commissioner "mandated a plan for mitigating racial imbalance," and in response, the board "created a voluntary desegregation program, consisting mainly of one-way busing of black students into majority white schools" (Kucsera & Orfield, 2014, p. 15). However, the plan "allowed 2,000 to 4,000 white students to transfer from desegregated schools to predominantly white schools, effectively undermining the desegregated neighborhoods and schools" (Orfield et al., 2015, p. 5). Over the course of 7 years, the board ignored or rejected other revised plans or programs, and by 1972, BPS was more segregated than it had been previously (Kucsera & Orfield, 2014).

During the early 1970s, federal courts began ordering Northern city school districts to desegregate if they were found to be *de jure* (i.e., by law, intentionally) segregated. In 1972, a coalition of Black and White parents, the NAACP, and the Citizens Council on Human Relations filed a lawsuit claiming that BPS was both *de facto* (i.e., by fact, but not required by law) and *de jure* segregated, and alleging that city officials were intentionally operating a segregated school system (Orfield et al., 2015). The Supreme Court's 1973 decision in *Keyes v. School Dist. No. 1, Denver* set the standards for proving illegal segregation outside the South. In *Arthur v. Nyquist* (1976), the federal district court ruled that "the public schools in Buffalo had been purposely segregated," and thus required the district to desegregate. The court found

> both the school district and the Buffalo city government guilty of intentional unconstitutional actions producing segregation of schools and housing in Buffalo. The school district was found guilty of intentionally segregating teachers and staff and manipulating boundaries and transfer policies to preserve access to white schools for white students who might otherwise have had to attend schools with African Americans. (Orfield et al., 2015, p. 6)

The BPS desegregation plan, established following the *Arthur v. Nyquist* case, included multiple phases—the first three of which were completed—and involved school closings, magnet schools and programs, voluntary school transfer programs, and mandated busing (Kucsera & Orfield, 2014; Mosey, 1998). In Phase One, which began in 1976, attendance zones were redrawn, 10 schools were closed (5 majority Black and 5 majority White), and two magnet schools—that is, specialized or themed schools designed to promote voluntary desegregation by attracting

Buffalo History and the Roots of School Segregation 49

diverse groups of students—were opened (Orfield et al., 2015, p. 6). During Phase Two, which began in 1977, eight more magnet schools were established, and a few years later, the majority of the magnet schools achieved racial balance. In 1979, the court mandated that the two remaining predominantly Black high schools be converted into a citywide magnet school called Buffalo Vocational Technical Center. Phase Three began in 1980 and involved the establishment of six early childhood centers from preschool through 2nd grade, two with mandated assignments and four with no fixed assignments (Orfield et al., 2015).

According to Orfield et al. (2015), "The system of magnet schools was so appealing that of the 30,000 students who were bused, 85% of families chose their own desegregated schools and only one in seven [students] faced mandatory desegregation" (p. 7). The Buffalo desegregation plan was so successful that the *New York Times* hailed it as a "national model of integration" (Winerip, 1985). School Superintendent Eugene Reville became nationally known for his integrated magnet program. The success of the Buffalo program, which was strongly supported by New York Senator Daniel Patrick Moynihan, helped to stimulate and strengthen the federal Magnet Schools Assistance Program.

Era of Resegregation

Changes in federal law and policy helped facilitate resegregation in Buffalo's schools. The changes included severe cuts to magnet school funding under the Reagan administration and weakened desegregation standards by the U.S. Supreme Court in the 1991 decision *Board of Education of Oklahoma City v. Dowell*, which authorized federal courts to terminate desegregation plans. In turn, before Phase Four of the BPS desegregation plan could be initiated, the court declared in 1995 that the district was unitary (i.e., no longer operating a dual system of segregated schools), thus lifting its desegregation order and cutting off the requirement that the city government pay for the magnet schools (Mosey, 1998). Had Phase Four been implemented, it would have addressed faculty affirmative action, more integration of elementary schools, and other issues. Some of these issues paralleled those we addressed 2 decades later in our report. According to Kucsera and Orfield (2014), "[Following unitary status,] the district experienced dramatic fiscal problems and severe white flight" (p. 16). Without court oversight, the city budget, which had been the major source of funding to maintain the successful magnet schools, ended its investment (Orfield et al., 2015). While some of the magnet schools were retained, numerous special features of the schools were cut, thereby losing their attraction to many families (Kucsera & Orfield, 2014).

On top of these factors, in 1997, White parents filed a lawsuit against BPS claiming that their daughter was the victim of reverse discrimination after being denied admittance into a magnet school, City Honors. Despite having a high qualifying score, their daughter was not admitted, while three students of color with lower qualifying scores were admitted. The parents claimed that the admissions criteria—specifically the racial quota—discriminated against White students. With pressure, their daughter was eventually admitted to City Honors. This lawsuit sparked debate in Buffalo about the use of racial set-asides, common in desegregation plans, to assure that both White and non-White students enrolled in the schools. On the one hand, some city leaders asserted that ending racial set-asides would lead to the resegregation of magnet schools, while other city leaders maintained that continuing to use race as a factor would lead to additional lawsuits. By 2000, all use of racial quotas for admittance into criteria-based schools in Buffalo was abandoned (Orfield et al., 2015).

Today, the progress made during the 20 years of the *Arthur v. Nyquist* (1976) desegregation order has been largely undone (Byrnes, 2014). With New York State recently branded as having "the most segregated schools in the country," schools within BPS are prime examples (Kucsera & Orfield, 2014, p. vi); hence, an OCR complaint was recently filed against BPS. With the exception of the district's period of court-ordered desegregation, which was successful even though the city remained heavily residentially segregated, BPS has persistently operated a dual system of separate and unequal schools. From explicitly excluding Black students from the district schools before 1872, to using intelligence testing to track Black students and other special populations of students into separate and inferior schools and programs, to manipulating boundaries and transfer policies to undermine desegregation efforts, to dissolving magnet programs and abandoning diversity goals in criteria-based school admissions, it is no accident that schools in Buffalo are among the most segregated in the nation at the present time.

BPS DEMOGRAPHIC AND SEGREGATION TRENDS

As the largest city school district in Upstate New York, BPS serves approximately 31,815 students across 57 schools (New York State Education Department, 2013–14). In the 2013–2014 school year, the enrollment was 50% Black, 21% White, 17% Latino, 7% Asian, and 3% multiracial (New York State Education Department, 2013–2014). The growing segments of the population in the district, as across the Northeast, were Latino and Asian.

Significant demographic differences in BPS in the 2013–2014 academic year compared to statewide public schools in New York (NYS) include the enrollment of Black, White, and Latino students, as well as economically disadvantaged students, students with disabilities, and limited English proficient (LEP) students. Compared to NYS, BPS serves nearly three times as large a share of Black students (50% versus 18%), but less than half as large a share of White students (21% versus 46%; Figure 3.3). BPS also has a significantly smaller Latino population compared to NYS (17% versus 25%; Figure 3.3.). Over the past decade, BPS has consistently enrolled more than twice as many Black students as White students. However, both groups are steadily declining, while the district's enrollment of Asian and

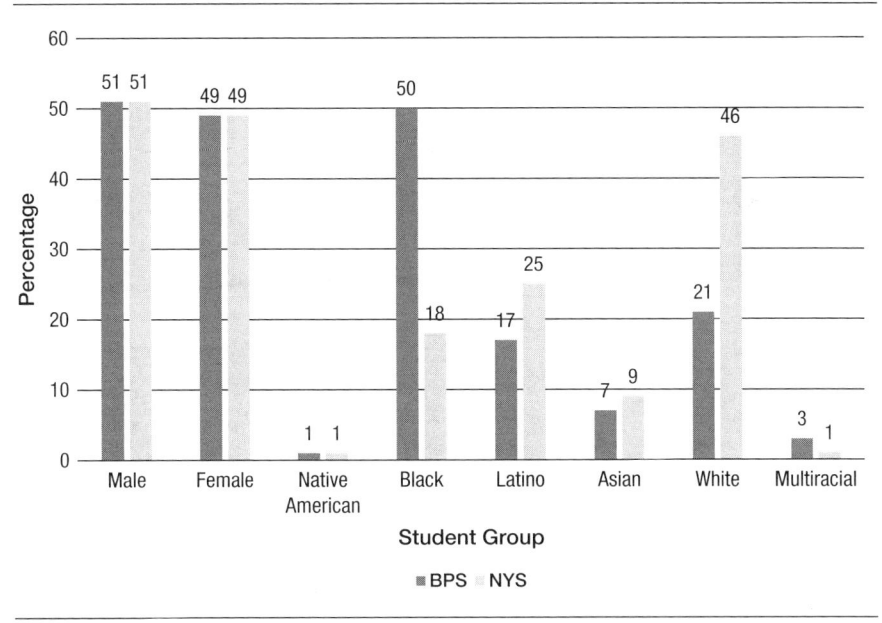

Buffalo History and the Roots of School Segregation　　51

Figure 3.3. 2013–2014 Enrollment of Students by Gender and Race/Ethnicity

Student Group	BPS	NYS
Male	51	51
Female	49	49
Native American	1	1
Black	50	18
Latino	17	25
Asian	7	9
White	21	46
Multiracial	3	1

Source: New York State Education Department, 2013–2014.

Latino students is growing (New York State Education Department, 2013–2014). These data suggest significant between-district, Black–White segregation across the Buffalo metropolitan area. These enrollment trends echo the area's persistent residential segregation, as discussed earlier.

Enrollment data of other groups of students reveal that BPS also serves more economically disadvantaged (free and reduced-price lunch eligible [FRL]) students, students with disabilities, and LEP students than does NYS as a whole (Figure 3.4). In BPS, 76% of students are classified as economically disadvantaged, compared to 53% in NYS; 21% of BPS students have disabilities compared to 16% in NYS; and 13% of BPS students are classified as LEP compared to 8% in NYS (Figure 3.4). These data demonstrate that BPS serves a larger share of students with special needs compared to schools in NYS more generally.

Compared to the other school districts in the Buffalo-Niagara Falls metropolitan area, BPS also serves significantly more FRL students (University of Minnesota Law School: Institute on Metropolitan Opportunity, 2015). According to 2015 data, not a single elementary school within the City of Buffalo had fewer than 47% of students who qualified for FRL, whereas nearly the opposite was true for the surrounding suburban elementary schools. Echoing the poverty and segregation trends in the City of Buffalo, BPS schools are more heavily segregated by both race and class when compared to other school districts in the greater metropolitan area.

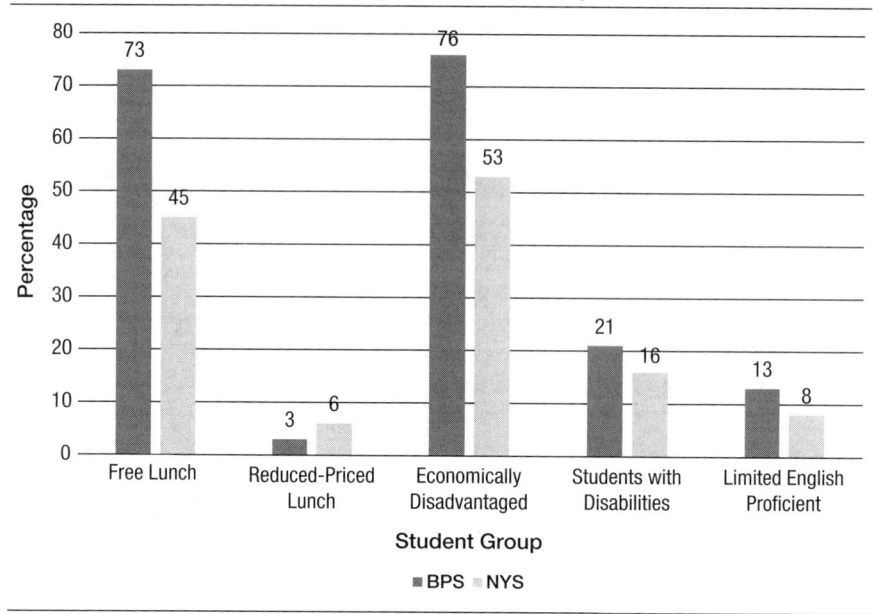

Figure 3.4. 2013–2014 Enrollment of Other Student Groups

Student Group	BPS	NYS
Free Lunch	73	45
Reduced-Priced Lunch	3	6
Economically Disadvantaged	76	53
Students with Disabilities	21	16
Limited English Proficient	13	8

Source: New York State Education Department, 2013–2014.

CONCLUSION

The City of Buffalo and BPS have struggled since the beginning of Buffalo's economic decline in the mid-1900s. Both the city and the greater metropolitan area have maintained extremely high levels of residential segregation by race and class for decades, directly impacting BPS. Despite this persistent residential segregation, BPS created a successful system of magnet schools during a period of court-ordered desegregation to achieve integration. However, since BPS achieved unitary status in the 1990s, magnet schools have abandoned integration goals and urban-suburban population shifts have increased between-district segregation, therefore facilitating resegregation in BPS. Today, many disparities remain, leading to the perpetuation of a two-tiered system of inequitable educational opportunity. The city's history of race relations and persistent patterns of separation and inequality set a very important context for the federal OCR investigation of the city's system of school choice.

REFERENCES

Abrams, C. (1955). *Forbidden neighbors*. New York: Harper.
Abrams, C. (1965). *The city is the frontier*. New York: Harper.

Arthur v. Nyquist, 415 F. Supp. 904 (1976).

Board of Education of Oklahoma City v. Dowell, 498 U.S. 237 (1991).

Buffalo, New York. (n.d.). Retrieved September 19, 2017, from en.wikipedia.org/wiki/Buffalo,_New_York

Byrnes, M. (2014, April 11). Buffalo was once a model for integration. Now the vast majority of its public schools are segregated. *The Atlantic: City Lab*. Retrieved from www.citylab.com/equity/2014/04/how-buffalos-once-diverse-schools-became-some-most-segregated/8823/

City-Data. (n.d.). Buffalo: History. Retrieved from www.city-data.com/us-cities/The-Northeast/Buffalo-History.html

Crandall, R. W. (1993). *The continuing decline of manufacturing in the Rust Belt*. Washington, DC: Brookings Institution.

Desktop Explorer. (2013, February 12). The 10 most segregated U.S. cities visualized with GIS. [Web blog post]. Retrieved from desktopexplorer.wordpress.com/2013/02/12/the-10-most-segregated-cities-visualized-with-gis/

Glaeser, E. L. (2007, October 19). Can Buffalo ever come back? *The New York Sun*. Retrieved from www.nysun.com/opinion/can-buffalo-ever-come-back/64879/

Jacobs, H., Kiersz, A., & Lubin, G. (2013, November 22). The 25 most segregated cities in America: 5. Buffalo-Niagara Falls, NY. *Business Insider*. Retrieved from www.businessinsider.com/most-segregated-cities-in-america-2013-11

Keyes v. School Dist. No. 1, Denver. 413 U.S. 189 (1973).

Kucsera, J., & Orfield, G. (2014, March). *New York State's extreme school segregation: Inaction, inequality, and a damaged future*. Los Angeles, CA: Civil Rights Project/Proyecto Derechos Civiles.

Mosey, G. J. (1998). *Testing, tracking, and curriculum: The isolation of black students in the Buffalo Public Schools from 1917 to 1956* (Doctoral dissertation). Retrieved from UMI Dissertations Publishing. (UMI No. 9816387)

National Park Service. (n.d.). A brief chronology of the development of the City of Buffalo. Retrieved from www.nps.gov/thri/buffalotimeline.htm

New York State Education Department. (2013–2014). *Enrollment data: Buffalo city school district*. Albany, NY: Author.

Orfield, G., Ayscue, J., Ee, J., Frankenberg, E., Siegel-Hawley, G., Woodward, B., & Amlani, N. (2015, May). *Better choices for Buffalo's students: Expanding and reforming the criteria schools system*. [A Report to Buffalo Public Schools]. Los Angeles, CA: The Civil Rights Project/Proyecto Derechos Civiles.

Rey, J. (2016, October 1). More than half of Buffalo children live in poverty, new census figures show. *The Buffalo News*. Retrieved from buffalonews.com/2016/10/01/half-buffalo-children-live-poverty-new-census-figures-show/

Taylor, H. L. Jr. (1996). Black in Buffalo: A late century report. *Buffalo: Magazine of the Buffalo News*. Retrieved from ubwp.buffalo.edu/aps-cus/wp-content/uploads/sites/16/2015/04/Black-in-Buffalo.pdf

Thomas, G. S. (2014, January 2). Buffalo's poverty rate tops 30 percent, making it America's third-poorest city. *Buffalo Business First*. Retrieved from www.bizjournals.com/buffalo/news/2014/01/02/buffalos-poverty-rate-tops-30.html

University of Minnesota Law School: Institute on Metropolitan Opportunity. (2000–2008). Buffalo region: Percentage change in population by municipality, 2000–2008 [map]. Retrieved from www.law.umn.edu/sites/law.umn.edu/files/metro files//bu_popch.pdf

University of Minnesota Law School: Institute on Metropolitan Opportunity. (2010). Buffalo region: Community type by municipality, 2010 [map]. Retrieved from www.law.umn.edu/sites/law.umn.edu/files/metro-files//bu_rtype00.pdf

University of Minnesota Law School: Institute on Metropolitan Opportunity. (2015). Buffalo region: Percentage of students eligible for free or reduced-price lunch by elementary school, 2015 [map]. Retrieved from www.law.umn.edu/sites/law.umn.edu/files/metro-files/bu_fred15.pdf

U.S. Bureau of the Census. (1998). Table 13. Population of the 100 largest urban places: 1900. Retrieved from www.census.gov/population/www/documentation/twps0027/tab13.txt

U.S. Census Bureau. (2013a). Buffalo city, New York quickfacts. Retrieved from quickfacts.census.gov/qfd/states/36/3611000.html

U.S. Census Bureau. (2013b). New York, United States quickfacts. Retrieved from quickfacts.census.gov/qfd/states/00000.html

U.S. Commission on Civil Rights. (1961). *Housing*. Washington, DC: U.S. Government Printing Office.

Winerip, M. (1985, May 13). School integration in Buffalo hailed as a model for U.S. *The New York Times*. Retrieved from www.nytimes.com/1985/05/13/nyregion/school-integration-in-buffalo-is-hailed-as-a-model-for-us.html?pagewanted=all

Yin, L. (2009). The dynamics of residential segregation in Buffalo: An agent-based simulation, *Urban Studies, 46*(13), 2749–2770.

CHAPTER 4

Segregation and Unequal Academic Outcomes in Buffalo's Criteria-Based Schools

Jongyeon Ee

Disparities in academic achievement among students of color have become wider over the past decades, particularly in schools located in areas of concentrated poverty. Under some school choice systems that ignore issues of race and poverty, some students may have access to strong schools with challenging peers and educational programs while other students find their access very limited. In order to attend the most competitive schools in the Buffalo Public Schools (BPS), students in the district must apply and are selected using several criteria. A civil rights complaint was filed in 2014, claiming that this process resulted in racial disparities among students who attended these schools; accordingly, the Civil Rights Project was engaged to conduct research to identify barriers to equitable access in BPS's criteria-based schools. This chapter examines overall enrollment trends in the district and its criteria-based schools, and focuses on relationships between race and poverty. It also explores different types of segregation—by race, socioeconomic status, and language—and overall intergroup contacts of students. It further investigates to what extent schools' academic outcomes are associated with the share of students of color as well as the proportion of socioeconomically disadvantaged students. This chapter shows that Buffalo's schools are highly segregated by race, class, and language, and that this segregation is strongly related to school outcomes.

DEMOGRAPHICS OF BPS

Racial diversity in American public schools has grown rapidly and transformed the classroom landscape over recent decades. Between 1970 and 2013, the percentage of White students dropped from 79% to 50% at the national level (Orfield, Ee, Frankenberg, & Siegel-Hawley, 2016). During this time, the proportion of Latino students climbed from 5% to 25%, and that of Asian students increased from 0.5% to 5%. The Black share of enrollment remained relatively stable, at about 15% (Orfield et al., 2016).

BPS, which is one of New York's largest school districts, has also experienced a rapid change in student demographics. Mirroring national trends, there has been a noticeable increase in the Hispanic and Asian proportions in the district in recent years. Concurrently, the White and Black shares dropped significantly, although BPS still has a large Black majority. Amid these shifts, the overall size of BPS's total enrollment increased by 3.5% between 2011 and 2015 (Table 4.1). In 2014–2015, the district's total enrollment was more than 38,000, and over half of the district's students were Black (52%). The next-largest racial groups were Whites and Latinos, accounting for 20% and 17% of the district's enrollment, respectively. In addition to the demographic changes in racial groups, the proportion of English learners (ELs) grew from 9% to 12% during the same period, reflecting an influx of Latino and Asian students. The share of low-income students whose families were poor enough to be eligible for free or reduced-price lunch (FRL) has been consistently high during this time period, reaching its peak in 2013 (81%) and declining slightly to 78% in 2015.

RACE AND POVERTY:
CRITERIA-BASED SCHOOLS VERSUS NON-CRITERIA-BASED SCHOOLS

In 2014–2015, BPS had eight criteria-based schools that enrolled close to a seventh of the district's students. Comparing enrollments shows that the two types of schools—criteria-based and non-criteria-based—are quite dissimilar, especially in terms of the growth rate of enrollment and the percentages of White and Black students (Tables 4.2 and 4.3). First, the growing enrollment in criteria-based schools stood out in comparison to non-criteria-based schools. From 2011 to 2015, total enrollment in criteria-based schools grew by 15.3%. In contrast, the number of students attending non-criteria-based schools increased by only 1.9%, which was even lower than the district-wide growth rate (3.5%). These comparisons indicate that the demand for criteria-based schools has been increasing over recent years. In addition, in 2015, the proportion of White students in criteria-based schools was twice as large as the White share in non-criteria-based schools (36% versus 18%). Conversely, in 2015, the proportion of Black students in criteria-based schools was 10 percentage points lower than in non-criteria-based schools (43% versus 53%).

In addition to the disproportionate racial shares, criteria-based schools also have significantly smaller shares of low-income students and ELs than non-criteria-based schools. More than 80% of the students who attended BPS's non-criteria-based schools in 2015 were from low-income families, compared to 57% in criteria-based schools. Nearly one in seven students attending BPS's non-criteria-based schools in 2015 were ELs, but there were almost no ELs in criteria-based schools (1.3%). Some of the differences in outcomes relate to different shares of students with serious learning challenges. ELs, often from immigrant families, have been a growing share of the city's population, but they have had little access to these special schools.

Table 4.1. Student Demographics in Buffalo Public Schools, 2011-2015

Year	No. of Schools	Total Enrollment	White	Black	Latino	Asian	AI	Multiracial	Low-Income	EL
						PERCENT (%)				
2011	70	36,967	22.0	57.1	13.8	4.0	1.3	1.8	79.1	9.1
2012	70	36,683	21.5	55.6	15.1	4.9	1.2	1.8	78.1	9.6
2013	69	36,994	21.1	54.1	15.7	5.7	1.1	2.3	81.0	10.3
2014	70	37,936	20.7	52.7	16.3	6.5	1.0	2.7	76.9	11.4
2015	72	38,279	20.1	51.7	17.1	7.1	0.9	3.0	77.8	12.2

Source: Data from New York State Education Department (NYSED; 2017a). Notes: Data include charter schools. AI: American Indian; ELs: English learners.

Table 4.2. Student Demographics in Criteria-Based Schools, 2011-2015

Year	Total Enrollment	White	Black	Latino	Asian	AI	Multiracial	Low-Income	EL
					PERCENT (%)				
2011	4,605	39.9	43.7	10.7	3.5	1.3	0.9	53.9	1.4
2012	4,617	39.6	42.5	12.0	3.5	1.2	1.1	52.8	1.6
2013	4,974	38.1	42.9	13.1	3.3	1.0	1.6	57.3	1.5
2014	5,210	36.4	43.1	13.7	3.9	1.0	1.9	50.6	1.4
2015	5,308	35.8	42.9	13.8	4.5	0.7	2.2	56.5	1.3

Source: Data from NYSED (2017a). Note: AI: American Indian; ELs: English learners.

Table 4.3. Student Demographics in Non-Criteria-Based Schools, 2011-2015

Year	Total Enrollment	White	Black	Latino	Asian	AI	Multiracial	Low-Income	EL
					PERCENT (%)				
2011	32,362	19.5	59.0	14.2	4.1	1.3	1.9	82.7	10.1
2012	32,066	18.9	57.5	15.5	5.1	1.2	1.8	81.7	10.7
2013	32,020	18.5	55.8	16.1	6.1	1.1	2.4	84.7	11.7
2014	32,726	18.2	54.2	16.8	7.0	1.0	2.8	81.1	13.0
2015	32,971	17.6	53.1	17.7	7.5	0.9	3.2	81.2	13.9

Source: Data from NYSED (2017a). Note: AI: American Indian; ELs: English learners.

RELATIONSHIP BETWEEN THE SHARE OF POOR STUDENTS AND THE SHARE OF STUDENTS OF COLOR

Given the large percentage of students of color in the district, nearly 70%, we examined the relationship between the combined shares of Black and Latino students and the proportion of socioeconomically disadvantaged students in schools. We then identified where criteria-based schools were located in terms of the association between race and poverty. To explore the relationship, we conducted a pairwise correlation analysis and found a very strong and positive correlation ($r = 0.440$, $p < 0.001$) between the poverty rate and the proportion of students of color. Figure 4.1 shows that students of color were concentrated in high-poverty schools. Specifically, the major cluster at the top right corner in Figure 4.1 indicates that schools with a larger percentage of non-White students had a higher percentage of low-income students, which we call double segregation: segregation by both race and poverty. Criteria-based schools also followed this pattern, but varied considerably. While Emerson School of Hospitality and Middle Early College High School are near the cluster of non-White and poor schools, some criteria-based schools (e.g., City Honors and Frederick Olmsted 64) are extreme outliers, given the distribution of schools in the district. As the top left corner of the graph shows, the district also has a significant number of largely White schools with a high

Figure 4.1. Relationship Between the Share of Low-Income Students and the Share of Black and Latino Students in BPS, 2014–2015

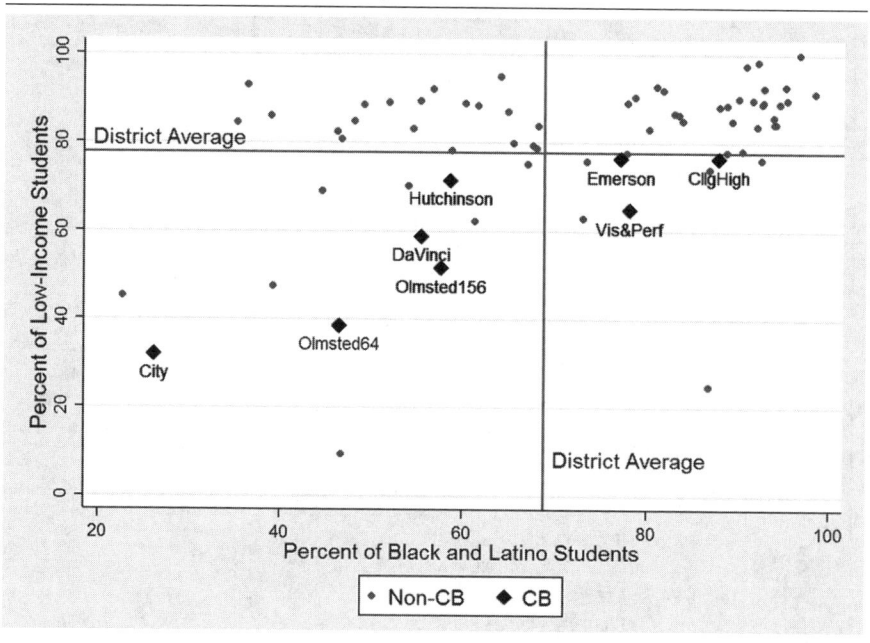

Source: Data from NYSED (2017a).

Segregation and Unequal Academic Outcomes in Buffalo's Criteria-Based Schools   59

percentage of poor students and a small proportion of non-White students. In central cities with very few Whites, we often find that the remaining Whites are far poorer than the Whites in the suburbs.

DEMOGRAPHICS OF INDIVIDUAL CRITERIA-BASED SCHOOLS

From 2011 to 2015, most criteria-based schools experienced gradual increases in overall student enrollment. However, student demographics for individual criteria-based schools, the non-White share in particular, vary tremendously.

With respect to the non-White share of enrollment in criteria-based schools, the schools could be categorized into two groups: schools enrolling a larger percentage of non-White students and those enrolling a smaller percentage of non-White students, compared to the overall district enrollment (see Table 4.4). Specifically, Emerson, Middle Early College High, and Visual Arts & Performing Arts were predominantly non-White schools, enrolling close to 80% or higher Black and Latino students. Hutchinson, da Vinci, and Olmsted 156 enrolled slightly less than 60% of non-White students but still reflected the district's average share of Black and Latino students. In contrast, City Honors and Olmsted 64, the schools that the Federal Office for Civil Rights singled out for discrimination in admissions processes and the two criteria-based schools that require an entrance exam, enrolled less than 50% non-White students. For example, Black and Latino students accounted for merely one-quarter of the total enrollment at City Honors, and its student demographics differed dramatically from the overall district's student populations. In terms of the comparison of the binary groups of Black and White students, Figure 4.2 shows substantial differences across the criteria-based schools. In this figure, we also confirmed that there was disproportionate enrollment of White students in most criteria-based schools. The White share of enrollment of City Honors, in particular, was three times as large as the average White share in BPS.

Figure 4.2. Percentage of Black and White Students in Criteria-Based Schools, 2014–2015

School	% White	% Black
District	20.1	51.7
City Honors	63.2	19.1
College High	11.9	76.9
Da Vinci	37.9	41.2
Emerson	18.7	58.7
Hutchinson	31.0	42.1
Olmsted 156	33.4	45.0
Olmsted 64	45.4	27.5
Visual & Performing	19.6	63.7

Source: Data from NYSED (2017a).

Table 4.4. Student Demographics in Criteria-Based Schools, 2014–2015

School	White	Black	Latino	Asian	AI	Multiracial	Low-Income	EL
District	20.1	51.7	17.1	7.1	0.9	3.0	77.8	12.2
City Honors	63.2	19.1	7.1	6.7	0.6	3.3	32.0	0.0
da Vinci	37.9	41.2	14.1	5.3	0.5	1.0	58.8	1.9
Emerson	18.7	58.7	18.4	0.9	0.7	2.7	76.4	1.8
Hutchinson	31.0	42.1	16.4	8.0	1.4	1.0	71.5	1.0
Middle Early College High	11.9	76.9	10.8	0.3	0.0	0.0	76.6	0.7
Olmsted 156	33.4	45.0	12.6	5.9	1.0	2.2	51.6	2.0
Olmsted 64	45.4	27.5	19.0	1.6	0.2	6.4	38.5	3.5
Visual & Performing	19.6	63.7	14.4	0.7	0.7	0.9	64.8	0.7

Source: Data from NYSED (2017a). *Notes:* AI: American Indian; ELs: English learners. Data include charter schools.

Segregation and Unequal Academic Outcomes in Buffalo's Criteria-Based Schools   61

Next, we explored the proportions of low-income students and ELs attending criteria-based schools. More than three-fourths (78%) of BPS students came from socioeconomically disadvantaged households (Figure 4.3). Some criteria-based schools reflected a similar percentage of low-income students; however, some did not. Of all criteria-based schools, low-income students were the most underrepresented at City Honors (32%) and Frederick Olmsted 64 (39%). As noted above, these two schools also had the smallest percentage of Black students among all criteria-based schools.

In addition, one in eight students in the district were identified as ELs. However, they were literally nonexistent at some criteria-based schools (e.g., City Honors and Hutchinson Central Technical) and did not exceed 4% of the total student enrollment at all criteria-based schools. Given the rising trend of Latino and Asian student populations in the district, the number of ELs will also increase, and civil rights law makes it illegal under the Civil Rights Act for schools to discriminate on the basis of language (as it is considered an element of national origin). However, as Figure 4.4 demonstrates, it was evident that ELs had extremely limited access to criteria-based schools.

Figure 4.3. Share of Low-Income Students in Criteria-Based Schools, 2014–2015

School	Percentage
District	77.8
City Honors	32
College High	76.6
Da Vinci	58.8
Emerson	76.4
Hutchinson	71.5
Olmsted 156	51.6
Olmsted 64	38.5
Visual & Performing	64.8

Source: Data from NYSED (2017a).

Figure 4.4. Share of English Learners in Criteria-Based Schools, 2014–2015

School	Percentage
District	12.2
City Honors	0
College High	0.7
Da Vinci	1.9
Emerson	1.8
Hutchinson	1
Olmsted 156	2
Olmsted 64	3.5
Visual & Performing	0.7

Source: Data from NYSED (2017a).

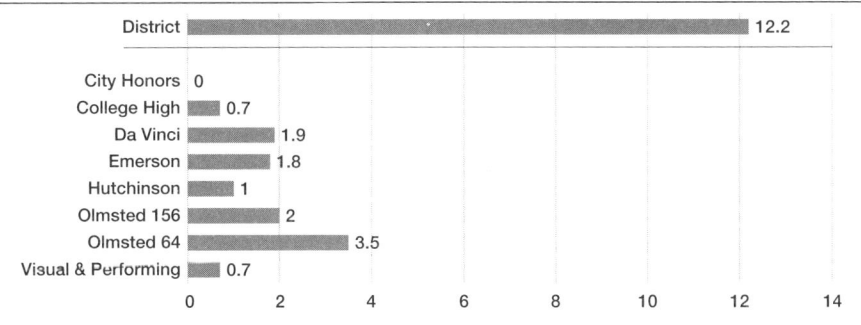

INTERGROUP CONTACT IN CRITERIA-BASED SCHOOLS AND NON-CRITERIA-BASED SCHOOLS

In addition to having access to strong schools, a large body of research demonstrates that all students benefit from the social and educational integration that results from significant contact with students of other races or ethnicities (e.g., Abrams & Killen, 2014; Killen, Crystal, & Ruck, 2007; Mickelson & Nkomo, 2012; Pettigrew & Tropp, 2006; Ready & Silander, 2011). Educational benefits, in particular, are intrinsically related to having access to both tangible and intangible resources, including stimulating peers, a challenging curriculum, high-quality teachers, and ample school funding. In addition to academic success, another vital benefit of attending schools with diverse student bodies is that intergroup contact boosts critical thinking and develops a positive understanding of other groups, critical assets required in a diverse society and work environment.

Unfortunately, these tangible and intangible resources are not equally distributed; rather, they are concentrated in schools serving White (and sometimes Asian) students from middle-class families. In contrast, Black and Hispanic students, as well as immigrant students and ELs, often come from families with fewer economic resources and tend to go to schools lacking these critical resources. Therefore, to increase the benefits of school desegregation, it is essential for all students to have equitable access to necessary resources. One way to provide these benefits is to expand the extent to which students interact with other students from diverse racial and ethnic backgrounds. This chapter uses measures of exposure to investigate the level of interracial contact between various racial groups at BPS's criteria-based and non-criteria-based schools. It also investigates the racial composition of schools that the typical student of each race attends.

Table 4.5 shows the intergroup contact experiences of students attending criteria-based schools and non-criteria-based schools. The results demonstrate that the typical student of each race experiences different levels of intergroup contact, depending on whether he or she goes to a criteria-based or a non-criteria-based school. With regard to the White share, at least 30% of schoolmates were White in criteria-based schools attended by students of all races, whereas the percentage of White schoolmates that the typical non-White student met in non-criteria-based schools was about 17%. In 2014–2015, the typical White student in a criteria-based school had 43% of schoolmates who were also White. But for the typical White student in a non-criteria-based school, only slightly more than one-quarter of schoolmates were White. Furthermore, the share of Black schoolmates that the typical White student in a criteria-based school met was 36%, which was 16 percentage points lower than the district's average share of Black students (52%; Tables 4.1 and 4.5). In comparison, in a non-criteria-based school, the typical White student had 44% Black schoolmates.

Turning to the typical Black student, in a non-criteria-based school, he or she had nearly 60% of schoolmates who were Black and only one in six schoolmates who were White (16%). At a criteria-based school, the typical Black student had 49% of schoolmates who were Black and also had the smallest share of White schoolmates (30%) among the students of all races attending criteria-based schools. However, this figure was still larger than the overall percentage of White schoolmates that the typical White student had in a non-criteria-based school (28%).

Table 4.5. Racial Composition of BPS Schools Attended by the Typical Student of Each Race, 2014-2015

		PERCENT (%)					
Criteria-Based Schools		White	Black	Hispanic	Asian	Low-Income	EL
Racial Composition of School Attended by Typical Student	White Student	42.8	35.8	12.8	5.2	50.0	1.2
	Black Student	29.9	49.4	14.4	3.8	61.7	1.3
	Hispanic Student	33.2	44.6	14.9	4.3	59.1	1.5
	Asian Student	41.1	36.5	13.0	6.5	54.4	1.1
	Low-Income Student	31.7	46.8	14.4	4.4	61.2	1.3
	EL Student	33.7	42.9	16.0	3.8	56.3	2.1
Non-Criteria-Based Schools							
Racial Composition of School Attended by Typical Student	White Student	27.7	43.5	17.3	6.9	76.2	11.7
	Black Student	16.1	58.3	14.8	6.9	81.2	11.3
	Hispanic Student	18.4	42.5	27.4	7.8	80.9	19.5
	Asian Student	17.1	46.0	18.1	14.8	82.6	23.7
	Low-Income Student	18.1	51.9	18.0	7.9	81.9	14.3
	EL Student	16.1	41.9	25.2	13.1	82.9	26.2

Source: Data from NYSED (2017a). *Note:* Analyses did not include multiracial and American Indian students; therefore, the percentages do not add up to 100%.

Hispanic students' intergroup experiences were similar to those of Black students. At a criteria-based school, the typical Hispanic student had 15% of schoolmates who were Hispanic. At a non-criteria-based school, however, more than one-quarter of her or his schoolmates were Hispanic (27%), and this figure was 10 percentage points higher than the overall Hispanic share in BPS (17%).

DOUBLE AND TRIPLE SEGREGATION

This chapter also explores double segregation—segregation by both race and concentrated poverty. These two factors are strongly intertwined across the nation, and BPS is no exception. Double segregation exacerbates educational inequality and adds additional challenges for students, which hinder academic development and success. As demonstrated above, substantial differences in the level of racial segregation emerged between criteria-based schools and non-criteria-based schools. Similar patterns were found with regard to poverty. In 2014–2015, students living in poverty accounted for 78% of the enrollment in the district (Table 4.1). However, in a non-criteria-based school, the typical low-income student had over 80% of schoolmates who were from poor families (Table 4.5). Likewise, in non-criteria-based schools, the typical students of all races except White had more than 80% of schoolmates who were from socioeconomically disadvantaged families. By contrast, in criteria-based schools, the overall low-income percentage that the typical students of all races met ranged from 50% to 62% (Table 4.5). Still, the typical Black student and the typical low-income student in the criteria-based school system had the largest share of poor schoolmates compared to other groups of students.

Turning to ELs, we found that although these students need considerable contact with English-speaking peers to develop English proficiency, they usually attend schools that are linguistically, racially, and economically isolated. The Civil Rights Project uses the term "triple segregation" to indicate this multilayered segregation combining race, class, and language. In BPS schools, where in 2014–2015 one in eight students were ELs (Table 4.1), a notable difference existed between criteria-based schools and non-criteria-based schools in terms of the share of ELs. Triple segregation of ELs stands out more in BPS's non-criteria-based schools than in the district's criteria-based schools. Due to the almost nonexistent percentage of ELs in criteria-based schools, the overall composition of schools attended by an average EL was not substantially different from those of other students. However, in non-criteria-based schools, the typical EL had a larger share of EL schoolmates (26%) than did any other group, and more than double the average EL share that the typical White or Black students met in non-criteria-based schools (12% and 11%, respectively; Table 4.5). Moreover, the low-income proportion in a non-criteria-based school attended by the typical EL was 83%, which was a higher share than typical students of other groups had in their schools (Table 4.5).

Segregation and Unequal Academic Outcomes in Buffalo's Criteria-Based Schools   65

The double and triple segregation, as well as the overall segregation, in BPS shows meaningful distinctions between criteria-based schools and non-criteria-based schools. The results demonstrate that the two school systems create different schooling experiences for students in terms of segregation and that the levels of double and triple segregation in non-criteria-based schools are far higher and more complex than in criteria-based schools. Students from low-income families and non-English-speaking homes who attend non-criteria-based schools experience tremendously limited intergroup experiences related to the quality of their schooling as well.

TEACHER DIVERSITY IN BPS SCHOOLS

Racial diversity among BPS teachers does not reflect the growing diversity in student demographics, and the district shows an extremely limited racial composition of its teachers. In 2014–2015, more than 80% of BPS teachers were White, and as Figure 4.5 portrays, White teachers in criteria-based schools accounted for almost 90% of the teaching staff. By contrast, BPS schools had only a small percentage of Black teachers in 2014–2015: 5% for criteria-based schools and 9% for non-criteria-based schools. The proportions of other racial groups, including Hispanic and Asian teachers, were tiny in both criteria-based and non-criteria-based schools, accounting for about 6% of the total BPS teaching force. These figures show that many students of color in the district do not have the opportunity to interact with diverse teachers. The results also raise questions regarding whether the majority of White teachers have an adequate understanding of different cultures and styles of non-White students and parents.

ACADEMIC PERFORMANCE OF CRITERIA-BASED SCHOOLS

We examined academic performance of criteria-based schools at the high school level and its relationships with poverty and race by analyzing the results of New

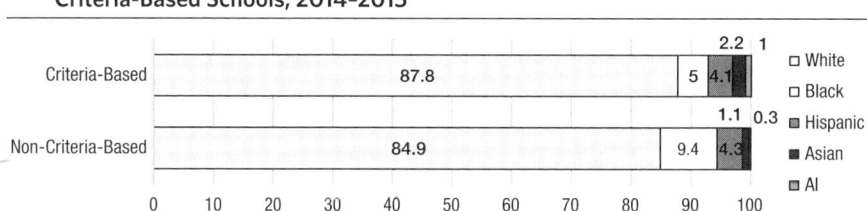

Figure 4.5. Racial Composition of Teachers in Non-Criteria-Based Schools and Criteria-Based Schools, 2014–2015

School Type	White	Black	Hispanic	Asian	AI
Criteria-Based	87.8	5	4.1	2.2	1
Non-Criteria-Based	84.9	9.4	4.3	1.1	0.3

Source: Data from Buffalo City School District (2014). *Note:* Data include elementary, secondary, and other classroom teachers only.

York State's Regents Common Core integrated algebra examination, which is administered to all high school students in the state. Both English language arts and mathematics are necessary and significant courses for college and career readiness. In this chapter, however, we focus on the mathematics results for two reasons. First, mathematics assessment results are more widely distributed than English language arts assessment outcomes in the available data. Mathematics is less skewed by non-school differences in language development as well.

Regarding proficiency levels of the exam, New York State Department of Education sets five performance levels as follows:

Level 1: Does not demonstrate knowledge and skills for Level 2
Level 2: (Safety Net): Partially meets Common Core expectations
Level 3: Partially meets Common Core expectations
Level 4: Meets Common Core expectations
Level 5: Exceeds Common Core expectations

We created combined categories of tested students who scored at Levels 1 and 2 as well as Levels 4 and 5, and we investigated pairwise correlations between academic outcomes and race and poverty. We then identified where individual criteria-based schools were located in the relationships. We found a dramatic association, something that is common in research on educational achievement across the United States (e.g., Orfield & Lee, 2005; Perry & McConney, 2010; Putnam, Frederick, & Snellman, 2012; Reardon, 2011; Rumberger & Palardy, 2005).

RELATIONSHIP BETWEEN THE LOW-INCOME SHARE OF ENROLLMENT AND ACADEMIC PERFORMANCE

First, we explored a relationship between the proportion of socioeconomically disadvantaged students and academic performance in BPS high schools. We analyzed the extent to which schools in BPS varied in terms of the proportion of students who did not meet the Common Core expectations on the integrated algebra test (Figure 4.6).

Based on the data displayed in Figure 4.6, we found a modest but meaningful .21 correlation between the share of students living in poverty and the combined share of students at Levels 1 and 2 on the statewide results of the integrated algebra assessment. This correlation means that schools with a larger share of poor students tended to have more students who were below or well below the standards for their grade. Due to the large spread among individual schools, the correlation was not significant, but the plot clearly shows a major trend in terms of the association. A notable number of Buffalo schools were concentrated in the upper right corner of the graph, indicating that schools with a high share of low-income students also tended to lag far behind in mathematics assessment results. Criteria-based schools followed this district-wide trend, but results for criteria-based

Segregation and Unequal Academic Outcomes in Buffalo's Criteria-Based Schools   67

Figure 4.6. Relationship Between the Share of Low-Income Students and the Proportion of Students Scoring at Levels 1 and 2 on Integrated Algebra, 2014–2015

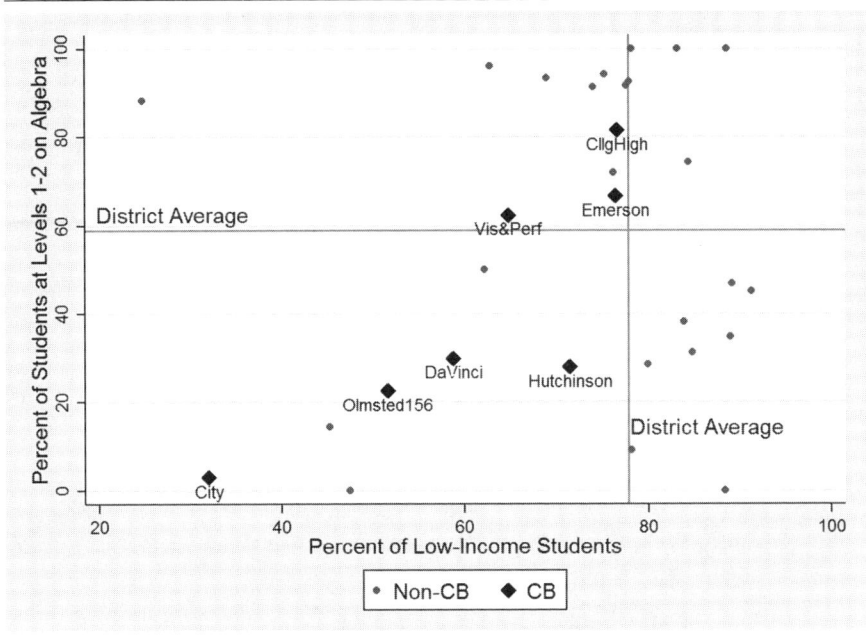

Source: Data from NYSED (2017a) and NYSED (2017b).

schools varied substantially. Most criteria-based schools had less than 30% of students scoring at Levels 1 and 2. City Honors, and to some extent Olmsted 156, in particular, are notable outliers in this distribution, with a very small percentage of students who scored at Levels 1 and 2. However, some criteria-based schools, including Emerson, Middle Early College High, and Buffalo Academy for Visual and Performing Arts, had a larger percentage of students scoring at Levels 1 and 2 on the integrated algebra assessment than the district's average.

Turning to an examination of students scoring at Levels 4 and 5—those who meet or exceed the Common Core standards—we found a strong and negative .55 correlation ($p < 0.01$) between the share of low-income students and the proportion of students scoring at those levels on the integrated algebra assessment. Strikingly, a large majority of BPS schools, including some criteria-based schools, had less than 10% students who met or exceeded the Common Core standards, indicating that a considerable number of high school students in BPS had difficulties with algebra (Figure 4.7). There were a few outliers that had a large percentage of students who outperformed the district, including criteria-based schools such as City Honors and Olmsted 156. In the district, there were few opportunities to attend schools meeting the state standards.

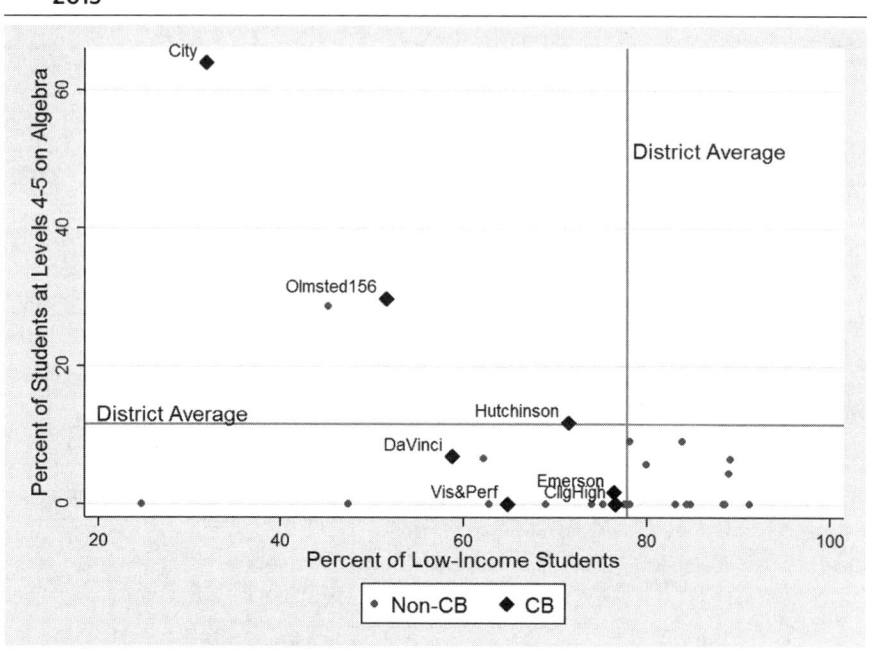

Figure 4.7. Relationship Between the Share of Low-Income Students and the Proportion of Students Scoring at Levels 4 and 5 on Integrated Algebra, 2014–2015

Source: Data from NYSED (2017a) and NYSED (2017b).

RELATIONSHIP BETWEEN COMBINED BLACK AND LATINO SHARES OF ENROLLMENT AND ACADEMIC PERFORMANCE

Employing the same data, we also examined the relationship between the combined shares of Black and Latino students and school-level results on the Common Core integrated algebra exam. Compared to the relationships between the low-income proportion and mathematics results explored above, we found an even stronger association when we focused on the combined share of Black and Latino students. As Figure 4.8 demonstrates, there was a significant and substantial .62 correlation ($p < 0.001$) between the percentage of Black and Latino students enrolled and the proportion of students tested who scored at Levels 1 and 2. The plot also shows the extent to which racial segregation was linked with students' academic outcomes, which in this context are represented by algebra exam results. As the top right corner of the plot in Figure 4.8 reveals, schools with a larger concentration of non-White students had a higher percentage of students who failed to meet the Common Core standards on the integrated algebra exam, and some criteria-based schools—Middle Early College High, Emerson, and Visual & Performing Arts—also belonged to this segregated school group. Recall that these three schools are the same ones with a

Segregation and Unequal Academic Outcomes in Buffalo's Criteria-Based Schools   69

Figure 4.8. Relationship Between the Combined Shares of Black and Latino Students and the Proportion of Students Scoring at Levels 1 and 2 on Integrated Algebra, 2014–2015

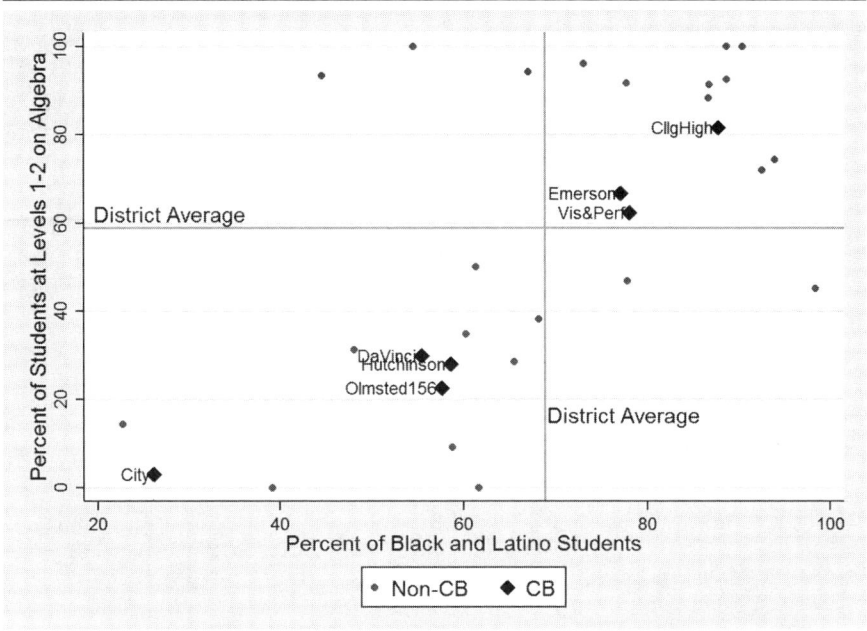

Source: Data from NYSED (2017a) and NYSED (2017b).

larger share of students who scored at Levels 1 and 2, as shown in Figure 4.6, which identified the relationship between low-income students and low performance. By contrast, the rest of the criteria-based schools enrolled a smaller percentage of non-White students than the district's average and had fewer students who did not meet the Common Core expectations on the integrated algebra test. Consistent with the analysis of the relationship between academic performance and the share of low-income students, City Honors in particular was an extreme outlier in this distribution and had a far lower percentage of Black and Latino students than the rest of the schools in the district. It is apparent that segregation has put many students of color in very-low-achieving schools.

We then examined the relationship between the Black and Latino share of students and the percentage of students scoring at Levels 4 and 5 on the Common Core integrated algebra assessment. Similar to the previous plot regarding poverty, the scatterplot shown in Figure 4.9 unveils serious concerns in terms of BPS students' academic performance on mathematics. We found a highly significant and negative .60 correlation ($p < 0.001$) between the percentage of Black and Latino students and the share of students who met or exceeded the Common Core expectations. The majority of BPS schools had less than 10% of students who met these criteria on

Figure 4.9. Relationship Between the Combined Shares of Black and Latino Students and the Proportion of Students Scoring at Levels 4 and 5 on Integrated Algebra, 2014-2015

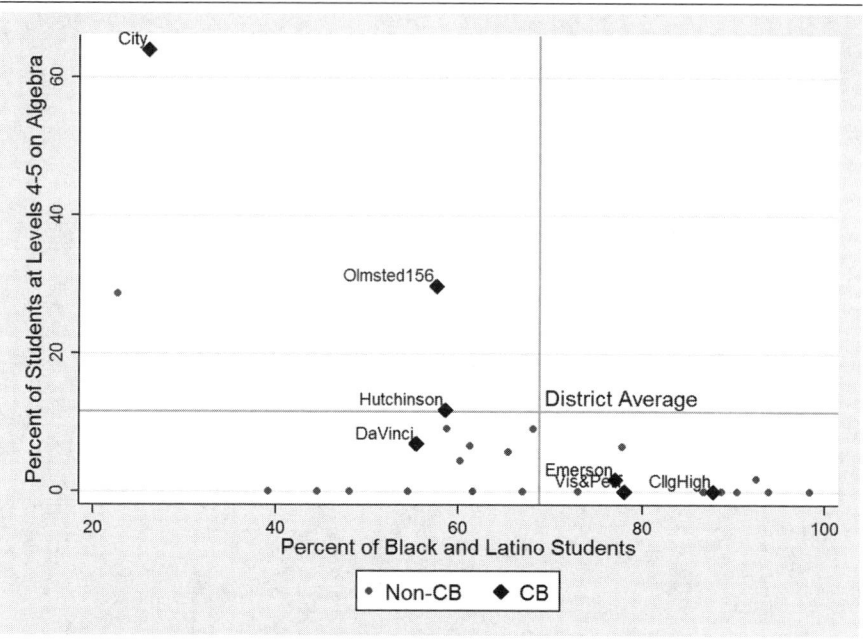

Source: Data from NYSED (2017a) and NYSED (2017b).

the algebra assessment. Some criteria-based schools encountered the same problem as other failing schools. However, two criteria-based schools—City Honors and Olmsted 156—outperformed other schools on this test. Roughly one in three students attending Olmsted 156 performed well on the algebra test. The extreme case was City Honors, where more than 60% of students scored at Levels 4 and 5. The issue here is that this school enrolls a very small percentage of non-White students, significantly lower than the district's overall non-White share. Given that the vast majority of BPS students attended academically failing schools and that only a tiny percentage of students attended schools with competitive programs, the inequality across the district made us ponder a fundamental question regarding the access to fair and equitable opportunities for quality education that every student deserves.

DEEPENING SEGREGATION AND LIMITED ACCESS TO QUALITY EDUCATION

In summary, we found that criteria-based schools differ significantly from non-criteria-based schools in BPS in terms of both racial and poverty concentrations.

The majority of BPS schools are doubly segregated, enrolling a large percentage of students of color from socioeconomically disadvantaged families. Many students of color in the district attend segregated schools where most of their peers are also non-White students living in poverty. Most schools with a substantial share of poor, non-White students are designated under state standards as failing schools, where a predominant number of students do not meet the statewide Common Core standards. Simultaneously, the district is facing a change in student demographics due to the gradual influx of Latino and Asian populations, and the increasing percentage of ELs over the years is evidence of that change. It is apparent that some criteria-based schools, particularly City Honors, Olmsted 64, and Olmsted 156, are highly exclusive and virtually inaccessible to students of color and immigrants who come from low-income families or families with a different home language.

Given this context, the civil rights complaint filed in 2014 regarding unequal enrollment in criteria-based schools posed a timely question on fair access to the quality education that all students deserve. The school segregation by race and poverty in BPS schools that has been confirmed in this chapter is not new. An exclusive school choice system that provides extremely limited opportunities to certain groups of students is not new either. However, the BPS case raises concern about the school choice systems that fail to include diverse student populations in the strongest schools.

A school choice system is a double-edged sword. As the BPS example shows, an exclusive school choice system based mainly on restricted school-specific criteria, such as test scores, can exacerbate the levels of school segregation by race, poverty, and language groups. In contrast, if criteria-based schools create inclusive environments and offer opportunities for quality education to diverse groups of students, they can be strong options for students and their families. We understand that most issues in BPS are closely intertwined with multifaceted problems such as residential segregation, leadership challenges, shortage of high-quality teachers at some schools, and absence of communication with families about school options. However, despite the causes and complexities, the current double and triple segregation of BPS's students, inequitable access to criteria-based schools, and strong relationships among race, income, and academic achievement are unacceptable.

APPENDIX: SEGREGATION STATISTICS (EXPOSURE RATES)

Chapter 4 uses exposure statistics to measure segregation and to capture student experiences of segregation. Exposure of certain racial groups to one another or to majority groups shows the distribution of racial groups among organizational units and describes the average contact between different groups. It is calculated by comparing the percentage of a particular group of students of interest in a small unit (e.g., school) with a certain group of students in a larger geographic or organizational unit (e.g., state or district) to show a weighted average of the composition of a particular racial group. The formula for calculating the exposure rates of a student in racial group A to students in racial group B is:

$$P^* = \sum_{i=1}^{n} \frac{a_i b_i}{A t_i}$$

where

n is the number of small units (e.g., school) in a larger unit (e.g., state or district)
a_i is the number of students in racial group A in the small unit i (school i)
A is the total number of students in racial group A in the larger unit (state or district)
b_i is the number of students in racial group B in the small unit i (school i)
t_i is the total number of students in all racial groups in the small unit i (school i)

REFERENCES

Abrams, D., & Killen, M. (2014). Social exclusion of children: Developmental origins of prejudice. *Journal of Social Issues, 70*(1), 1–11.

Buffalo City School District (2014). Unpublished raw data for internal use.

Killen, M., Crystal, D., & Ruck, M. (2007). The social developmental benefits of intergroup contact for children and adolescents. In E. Frankenberg & G. Orfield (Eds.), *Lessons in integration: Realizing the promise of racial diversity in American schools* (pp. 57–73). Charlottesville, VA: University of Virginia Press

Mickelson, R. A., & Nkomo, M. (2012). Integrated schooling, life course outcomes, and social cohesion in multiethnic democratic societies. *Review of Research in Education, 36*(1), 197–238.

New York State Education Department. (2017a). *2010–2011, 2011–2012, 2012–2013, 2013–2014, and 2014–2015 report card databases*. Retrieved from data.nysed.gov/downloads.php

New York State Education Department. (2017b). *2014–2015 3–8 Assessment database*. Retrieved from data.nysed.gov/downloads.php

Orfield, G., Ee, J., Frankenberg, E., & Siegel-Hawley, G. (2016). *"Brown" at 62: School segregation by race, poverty and state*. Los Angeles, CA: The Civil Rights Project/Proyecto Derechos Civiles at UCLA.

Orfield, G., & Lee, C. (2005). *Why segregation matters: Poverty and educational inequality*. Cambridge, MA: The Civil Rights Project, Harvard University.

Perry, L. B., & McConney, A. (2010). Does the SES of the school matter? An examination of socioeconomic status and student achievement using PISA 2003. *Teachers College Record, 112*(4), 1137–1162.

Pettigrew, T. F., & Tropp, L. R. (2006). A meta-analytic test of intergroup contact theory. *Journal of Personality and Social Psychology, 90*(5), 751.

Putnam, R. D., Frederick, C. B., & Snellman, K. (2012). *Growing class gaps in social connectedness among American youth.* Cambridge, MA: Harvard Kennedy School of Government. Retrieved from www.hks.harvard.edu/saguaro/research/SaguaroReport_DivergingSocialConnectedness 20120808.pdf

Ready, D., & Silander, M. (2011). School racial and ethnic composition and young children's cognitive development. In E. Frankenberg & E. H. Debray (Eds.), *Integrating schools in a changing society: New policies and legal options for a multiracial generation* (pp. 91–113). Chapel Hill, NC: University of North Carolina Press.

Reardon, S. F. (2011). The widening academic achievement gap between rich and poor: New evidence and possible explanations. In G. J. Duncan & R. J. Murnane (Eds.), *Whither opportunity? Rising inequality, schools, and children's life chances* (pp. 91–115). New York: Russell Sage Foundation.

Rumberger, R. W., & Palardy, G. J. (2005). Does segregation still matter? The impact of student composition on academic achievement in high school. *Teachers College Record, 107*(9), 1999.

CHAPTER 5

Clearing the Pathway
Recognizing Roadblocks to Entry into Buffalo's Top-Tier Schools

Brian Woodward and Natasha Amlani

The purpose of this chapter is to highlight barriers that students encountered when seeking to apply to, enroll in, and fully participate in Buffalo Public Schools (BPS) criteria-based schools. In order to examine those barriers, we first review literature about mechanisms of choice systems that can create inequity. Following the literature review, we outline the methodological tools employed; present findings from our surveys, interviews, and focus groups; and then explore multiple stakeholders' perspectives regarding the barriers that currently prevent students of color from having equitable access to criteria-based schools in BPS. The stakeholders include BPS administrators, parents, students, teachers, counselors, district officials, and community leaders. Although it was challenging to connect with some of these people, we believe it was imperative to hear as many voices as possible and learn how school representatives, district personnel, and community members felt about the pathway to top schools. Including the insights of everyone in the community, especially those whose voices were seldom heard, may have provided a sense of empowerment to some who participated while simultaneously bringing a certain level of justice to the investigation.

PRIOR RESEARCH ON BARRIERS IN SCHOOL CHOICE SYSTEMS

A significant appeal for school choice plans in general, and magnet schools in particular, is the ability to attract a diverse student population. Research on criteria-based schools (often referred to as competitive-admissions magnet schools) is limited; therefore, we draw on magnet school literature more broadly to understand how different features of choice systems can lead to diverse schools or heighten stratification. In seeking to attract an integrated student body, magnet schools offer programmatic features that can facilitate the creation of an appealing and racially diverse school. These features include desegregation goals, outreach to diverse groups of students and families, free transportation, accessible locations, and equitable admissions processes (Frankenberg & Siegel-Hawley, 2008). If implemented well, these features can attract many families and facilitate desegregation. However, when not done well, they also can deter students' admittance into the most desirable schools of choice and further entrench segregation.

The ability to conduct outreach effectively has a significant impact on the number and type of students applying to schools throughout a district. Students who are unaware of the admissions requirements and application procedures for magnet schools are disadvantaged if they lack the social capital to find the information (Holme, 2002). However, if outreach is effective and reaches all neighborhoods across a school district, it can increase the likelihood that most students are aware of the opportunities to attend magnet schools. Conducting outreach to a wide range of students requires multiple strategies, such as hosting information centers and having school personnel offer publications directly to students. Outreach should be conducted consistently and evaluated periodically to ensure that all students are reached, which is salient because effective outreach has been associated with a higher level of integration (Frankenberg & Siegel-Hawley, 2008).

Transportation has long been considered one of the most critical factors to ensure that students of all races and income levels have the opportunity to attend their schools of choice (Wells, 1996). For many families, the physical distance between their home and desired school can be a deterrent. Even if transportation is provided by the parents or the district, the time lost each day can be burdensome. Therefore, the location of schools of choice is also important. Locating magnet schools in isolated or remote parts of the district can be an impediment.

It is also important to note that while magnet schools have many features that attract families, often the most important factor for parents when choosing a school for their child is the caliber of its academic offerings (Kleitz, Weiher, Tedin, & Matland, 2000). As a result, despite a number of choice options, the majority of the parents in a district are often vying for the same spots in schools with the highest academic performance records. Since the schools must limit the number of students they accept, this situation creates a dilemma about which students and how many students will be admitted. The next logical question for many is: Are the requirements for admittance into these highly-sought-after schools equitable?

In many of the original desegregation plans, interest, not ability, was the primary basis for assigning students to magnet schools (Frankenberg & Siegel-Hawley, 2008). Although magnet programs often use a variety of factors such as geographic proximity, preferences for siblings, or auditions as benchmarks for entrance into schools, magnet school admissions are sometimes based on competitive admissions criteria such as grade point averages and test scores, despite the concern that using such criteria often leads to inequitable access. Compounding those concerns is the frequent scarcity of available seats. A survey of magnet school staff found that a higher percentage of schools using essays and interviews as part of their admissions criteria reported that they were substantially integrated or had experienced increasing integration during the last decade. Alternatively, magnet schools that employed test scores and/or auditions as admissions criteria reported lower levels of integration. More specifically, the use of grade point average as an admissions factor was correlated with the highest share of schools that reported decreasing integration. These findings support the notion that noncompetitive-admissions schools were more integrated than those using competitive admissions requirements. Thus, admissions criteria can hinder students from accessing schools in a choice system.

Many factors can make some schools more attractive than others to students and parents. A particular theme, a school's academic reputation, or a geographic location are reasons why certain schools are highly desired (Frankenberg & Siegel-Hawley, 2008). A problem arises when families who are better organized or have more information or resources tend to displace those with less information and fewer resources. In order to ensure equitable access to choice options, it is critical to examine barriers that families and students face when seeking access to the most desired schools. The next section explains how our research team gathered and analyzed data from key stakeholders in the BPS district.

METHODS

As described in Chapter 2, the research team employed mixed methods to investigate barriers related to the recruitment, application, and enrollment processes for criteria-based schools in BPS. Through online and telephone surveys as well as semistructured interviews and focus groups, we solicited feedback on recruitment, outreach, communication, information, transportation, preparation in earlier grades, admissions criteria, enrollment and registration policies, and support for English learners (ELs) and students with disabilities. We used multiple approaches to recruit participants, including outreach from BPS, outreach from key members of the religious community, direct recruitment from the research team, and open opportunities publicized to the entire community. Ensuring that the research team was effective when conducting outreach was critical for several reasons, including the low percentage of parents who utilized the district website, the district's practice of providing pertinent information only in English, and the difficulty in getting a sufficient number of parents to participate in the field tests for our interview protocols and surveys. Despite these initial hurdles, our comprehensive approach allowed us to identify numerous barriers to accessing the criteria-based schools.

PARTICIPANTS

We created surveys for three stakeholder groups: parents, teachers and staff, and students. We received responses from 860 parents, including 459 parents of students who applied to criteria-based schools and 401 parents of students who did not apply to criteria-based schools. In each of these samples, approximately half of the participants were African American. The remaining racial composition of the group of parents whose children applied to criteria-based schools was 24% White, 10% Latino, 4% Asian, and 9% other. The remaining racial composition of the group of parents whose children did not apply to criteria-based schools was 16% White, 20% Latino, 5% Asian, and 9% other.

For the teacher and staff survey, we had a total of 295 respondents. We had an unusually high level of engagement and interest from the respondents. More than 100 respondents sent optional notes explaining their attitudes, raising questions, and offering suggestions. We deeply appreciate their contributions. Participants ranged in their role, although most were teachers: 85% teachers, 6% counselors, 5% administrators, and 5% other staff.[1] Participants' length of experience in working with BPS ranged from 1 year to more than 30 years, with most having more than a decade of experience in BPS: 15% with 1–3 years of experience, 25% with 4–10 years of experience, and 60% with 10 or more years of experience. Participants represented all grade levels in BPS: 29% elementary school staff, 27% middle school staff, and 44% high school staff. Some have worked at criteria-based schools and others have not: 64% never worked at a criteria-based school, 23% currently work at a criteria-based school, and 13% worked at a criteria-based school in the past. The racial composition of participants was very similar to the overall composition of BPS full-time staff: 84% White, 10% Black, 6% Latino, 2% Asian, 1% American Indian, and 1% other.

A total of 290 8th- and 9th-grade students participated in our online survey. While there was some variation among student survey participants, the vast majority were students who either had applied and were accepted to criteria-based schools or were currently attending criteria-based schools. Students from 27 different schools participated, although only a handful of schools produced significant numbers of respondents. The largest portions of students were from Leonardo da Vinci (33%), City Honors (21%), Harvey Austin (16%), and Hutch Tech (7%). There were fewer than 10 students representing each of the other 23 schools. White students and students who had applied to and been accepted by criteria-based schools were substantially overrepresented in the sample. Of the total 290 student participants, 48% were 8th-graders and 52% were 9th-graders. The racial composition of the respondents was 44% Black, 32% White, 9% Latino, 7% Asian, and 8% other. Among the student participants, 82% had applied to a criteria-based school, and 65% had been accepted by a criteria-based school. Thus, it is likely that our student survey respondents reflect a group of high-performing students who were actively involved in the criteria-based school admissions process.

A notable portion of students responding to this survey had received their earlier education outside of BPS. Overall, 80% of the total student respondents had attended a BPS elementary school. A closer look reveals that 66% of the White student respondents had attended a BPS elementary school compared to 85% of non-White students. Among those not currently enrolled in a criteria-based school, almost all (98%) of them had attended a BPS elementary school. When asked specifically about private schooling, 6% of criteria-based school students responded that they had attended a private elementary school. In comparison, among the students not currently enrolled in criteria-based schools, none of them had attended a private elementary school. Although this sample is not representative of the total student population, we did offer all students the opportunity to give us their feedback, and the responses of these students deserve our attention.

Beyond the surveys, our interviews and focus groups reached a wide range of key education stakeholders in Buffalo. A total of 62 students from criteria-based and non-criteria-based schools participated in focus groups. In addition, 117 parents, the majority of whom had children attending City Honors and Olmsted, participated in individual, small-group, and town hall–style discussions. Representatives from the following groups also participated: District Parent Coordinating Council, Special Education Parent Advisory Committee, Multilingual Education Advisory Committee, and Buffalo Parent Teacher Organization. Eight counselors from both criteria-based and non-criteria-based schools at all grade levels participated in a focus group. School staff, including 10 teachers, 8 counselors, and 1 instructional coach, participated in focus group discussions. Administrators from all criteria-based schools as well as two administrators from a non-criteria-based school participated in interviews. Six district staff members participated in individual interviews or focus groups. All board members, except for Carl Paladino, who opposed this study, met with Orfield.

In addition to these formal data-gathering opportunities, we set up an email account and publicized it in *The Buffalo News*. We received 10 phone calls and 73 emails from Buffalo residents of various backgrounds.

FINDINGS: BARRIERS TO ACCESS[2]

Based on the surveys, interviews, and focus groups, barriers to accessing criteria-based schools can be grouped into five main categories: information, preparation, admissions criteria, support services, and availability of choices (Table 5.1). Within each category, students encountered multiple barriers while attempting to access criteria-based schools in the BPS district.

Information

Gathering information about the application and enrollment process was challenging for families due to limited and inequitable outreach by BPS as well as

Clearing the Pathway

Table 5.1. Barriers to Accessing Criteria-Based Schools

Information	• Limited outreach and recruitment • Inadequate information at Central Registration • Unclear and complex application process • Lack of materials and support in languages other than English
Preparation	• Disparate preparation in elementary school • Gifted and talented pipeline disproportionately White and middle-class • Higher acceptance rates for students who had attended criteria and charter schools
Admissions Criteria	• Cognitive skills test • New York English language arts and mathematics assessments • Parent and teacher recommendations
Support Services	• Lack of services for ELs • Insufficient support for special education students
Availability of Choices	• Limited number of schools and seats • High interest

difficult interactions at Central Registration. The complexity of the application process and the application forms themselves also create barriers for students of color and ELs.

Disparate outreach efforts. At both the district and school levels, district staff, principals, counselors, and teachers engage in various forms of outreach and advertisement, but these efforts do not seem to be received by parents or students as important sources of information.

More than one-fourth of parents whose children did not apply to criteria-based schools (28%) and 15% of parents whose children did apply expressed that they were not satisfied with their child's school. Almost all parent survey participants reported that they supported the school choice system; however, nearly 60% of the parents of students who did not apply to criteria-based schools said they were not familiar with criteria-based schools in the district. Further, approximately one in five parents whose children did not apply to criteria-based schools reported never having received any information from the district about criteria-based schools. There is a strong preference for school choice among parents in the district but highly unequal knowledge about the criteria-based school system among different groups of parents. The fact that many parents were not satisfied with their child's school and supported the school choice system yet did not apply for their child to attend a criteria-based school suggests that there are likely problems in disseminating information and encouraging applications.

At the district level, district staff expressed conflicting views about outreach. Some district staff described a recent, strong effort to increase outreach, including presentations by district staff in cooperation with community partners about the application process and timeline. The comprehensive outreach included parent meetings, radio announcements, fliers, open houses, and robocalls.

However, other participants noted the many ways in which outreach and advertisement have been limited. For example, the school visits, formerly held as a way of recruiting students, have stopped. Jamborees and road shows, which were common forms of outreach and recruitment in the past, no longer occur. In place of these events, open houses are conducted, but counselors and students contend that transportation can create a barrier for some students and parents to attend these sessions outside of the regular school day. Some district staff expressed concern that while outreach is occurring, they are skeptical that it is occurring at a time and place that make it accessible to all families. In particular, they highlighted the need to improve outreach to "less savvy, less sophisticated parents" as well as to parents who do not speak English.

Currently, there is no targeted outreach to encourage special education students or ELs to apply to criteria-based schools, and all of the outreach in BPS occurs only in English. Thus, perhaps not surprisingly, special education students and ELs are much less likely to apply to criteria-based schools. Among the parents whose children applied to criteria-based schools, one-sixth reported that their child requires special education or EL services. Among the parents of students who did not apply to criteria-based schools, almost twice as large a share of respondents (29%) indicated that their child needs such services. In the group of parents whose children did not apply to criteria-based schools, 11% have a child who was identified as an EL and 18% have a child who has an individualized education plan (IEP) or a 504 plan. Among parents who did not apply to criteria-based schools, majorities of respondents had received no information (52%) or very little information (22%) about services for those groups. Even among parents who applied to criteria-based schools, more than half of respondents (51%) reported that they had received very little or no information from the district regarding services for ELs or special education students.

Further, there is disagreement about whether all schools are promoted and advertised equally by the district. One counselor commented, "I think there has been a concerted effort on the part of the district to push all of the non-criteria-based schools." On the other hand, some counselors and teachers expressed the belief that criteria-based schools as a group are promoted more than non-criteria-based schools. As one teacher explained, "The problem is the promotion of the criteria-based schools that leaves schools like us [non-criteria-based schools] in the shadows." Likewise, a principal from a criteria-based school commented, "The district doesn't do a good job of promoting other schools with good programs."

At the school level, a number of principals noted that they utilize the services the district provides, and while these services are helpful, some principals and teachers feel that the majority of outreach efforts are relegated to individual schools. One principal remarked, "There is piecemeal outreach—the district leaves outreach to us [individual schools] outside of *The Buffalo News* ads and Connect Ed calls." The different approaches to information dissemination are also evident in the survey responses from the BPS teachers and staff—15% of respondents reported that their school provided families with a lot of information about all criteria-based schools, 6% provided a lot about some schools, 19% provided a little about all schools, 16% provided a little about some schools, 8% provided none, 27% did not know, and 10% reported it was not applicable. Different schools implement different outreach strategies, and principals suggested that it would be helpful for advertisement to be more centralized. In part, due to the lack of centralization, schools have different budgets allocated for advertisement; therefore, some schools have higher-quality materials than others.

Even with various school- and district-level efforts to conduct outreach and advertisement, the parents and students who participated in our study cited peer networks as their key source of information. One parent explained, "[I] found out through hearsay about the criteria to get into City Honors." Families generally learn about school options by gathering their own information through peer networks and personal contact with schools. In particular, the most common sources of information for parents are guidance counselors (15%), their children (14%), and other parents (13%). In addition to peer networks, parents also call the schools and speak with principals and guidance counselors to obtain information. Some parents also visit the schools. Parents generally expressed the sentiment that in reality, the responsibility for obtaining information relies on the parents themselves. Many did not see this as a problem. As one parent explained, "If you put in the effort, you create your own opportunities." Another concurred, "As a parent you have to be active to find out all of the information." Similarly, students reported that they get most of their information about schooling options from other people: counselors (51%), teachers (44%), family members (37%), and friends (35%). Facebook and other social media were also important sources of information.

Parents and students generally do not rely on the district's website for learning about schools. They find that the website is often outdated and not user-friendly. Only 5% of parents visited the district website in attempting to gather information about criteria-based schools. District staff expressed a similar concern with the district website. They acknowledged that the website needs improvement, and that addressing this need is currently a priority for district staff. As a related concern, other district staff mentioned the high level of poverty in Buffalo and the limited utility of this approach because computer and Internet access is not readily available to low-income families across the district.

In addition to concerns about the source of information, the timing of when information is acquired varies. For the parents whose children applied to criteria-based schools, 39% reported that they had learned about the criteria-based schools before or during their child's elementary school years, 29% had learned about criteria-based schools during their child's middle school years but before 8th grade, and 21% had learned about the criteria-based schools during their child's 8th-grade year. In contrast, two-thirds of parents whose children did not apply to criteria-based schools reported that they did not know about the academic preparation and courses needed for enrolling their child in a criteria-based school when their child was in elementary or middle school. These disparate findings reveal that one group of parents is aware of and understands the criteria-based system relatively early in their children's educational experience, while many other parents do not know about the system, might never connect with it, and have received little or no information at any stage of their child's educational experience in BPS.

Inadequate information at Central Registration. Both the parents who participated in our study and the staff who work at Central Registration agree that interactions at Central Registration can be challenging. Parents are extremely dissatisfied with multiple aspects of Central Registration, including its location, hours, personnel, and phone communications. Central Registration staff raised additional concerns related to understaffing and the limited ability to communicate in languages other than English.

Parents think the location of Central Registration is not easily accessible, and some expressed concern that it is not accessible by public transportation. They believe that the hours of operation of Central Registration are inadequate and that it closes too early. Parents also believe that the staff at Central Registration are not knowledgeable about the various school options, do not know what programs each school offers, and do not provide consistent responses to the same questions. Parents are often frustrated when they call Central Registration because their calls are frequently unanswered. One parent commented, "The process is very convoluted, and no one seems to have full authority to speak about it downtown."

Central Registration staff are in general agreement with the negative perceptions held by others. They attribute this reputation, in part, to long lines and unpleasant interactions with those who come to their office seeking information. In an effort to address the situation, customer relations training has been provided to the Central Registration staff. An additional concern is that Central Registration is understaffed in multiple areas. First, they need more clerical staff to be able to complete tasks effectively and on time. More specifically, a great deal of time is required to call parents about errors or missing information on applications; more staff are needed to support these labor-intensive efforts. Second, in addition to English, Spanish is the only other language spoken by anyone at Central Registration. They expressed a desire to have multilingual staff who can communicate in at least the top five languages spoken in the district. Despite these concerns, some parents acknowledged that Central Registration has been improving recently.

Unclear and complex application process. There was a consensus among the parents, counselors, teachers, principals, and district staff who engaged in our review that the overall application process is too complex. Parents made many comments on this topic, such as the following: "The process isn't clear. No one knows the process";

Clearing the Pathway

"Parents are in the dark. Parents don't know the facts"; "It was very confusing, and I have a PhD." Almost half of parents whose children applied to criteria-based schools found the application process somewhat difficult (29%) or very confusing and difficult (17%). Parents stated that they were unclear on the application process itself, as well as on the admissions criteria. A parent explained, "The process isn't easy. You really have to know what's going on, and just because you don't know, doesn't mean you don't care about your kid." A veteran BPS teacher concurred:

> Knowledge of these schools' existence, what it takes to be accepted, entrance in schools before high school, process to apply, support throughout the process . . . as a BPS teacher, I do not know all of this! Not only are criteria schools a mystery to students and parents, the whole district and the programs available are extremely confusing, constantly changing, difficult to navigate, and [it's] extremely difficult to obtain information. As a Buffalo teacher for almost 30 years, I still do not know how this district works.

Unlike the parents and teachers, district staff members felt that efforts over the past few years have made the process more accessible. One recent improvement is the publication of a written document describing the application process, thus eliminating the need for parents to track down a staff member in order to understand the steps that need to be taken. However, for non-English-speaking parents, this written material is not very helpful because it is available only in English.

Other areas of the application process still lack clarity, including specifying the selection criteria and describing the process for how individual schools keep a waiting list. Parents who have sought this information on the district's website have frequently been disappointed to find outdated and incomplete information. Parents also expressed anxiety over having their child placed on a waiting list and not knowing how or when they would be notified of next steps.

Beyond the overall process, the application forms and the parent inventories pose significant barriers. Parents expressed confusion about the implications of listing school ranking preferences on the application as well as understanding how to use the correlating codes for each school. In addition, there are conflicting opinions about the paper-and-pencil nature of the application. Some parents expressed frustration about having to go to the physical location of Central Registration to complete the process, while others said that shifting to an online application process would create its own set of challenges. Teachers, counselors, and district staff emphasized that using an online application process would pose an additional obstacle to many low-income parents and students who lack easy access to a computer or the Internet. If the district does adopt an optional online application, several participants noted that it will need to make adjustments from its previous attempt to do so, because the system that was used previously did not meet the district's needs.

The timeline for submitting an application is another concern for many participants because the applications are due in the fall, which some believe is too early in the school year. Staff at Central Registration reported that minority parents, in particular, tend to submit applications after the deadline. Late applications are problematic because students whose applications are submitted on time are placed first. In addition, students who move into the district later in the year are at a disadvantage because seats have already been taken for the next year. District staff are concerned that not all students fit neatly into this timeline and believe that adjustments are needed.

Preparation

In order to be prepared to compete for admissions to criteria-based schools, students must have had access to high-quality preparation in earlier grades. However, given the high levels of segregation in BPS schools, it is likely that students of color and low-income students have had access only to inferior educational opportunities, as tends to be the case with segregated schools. Many students who participated in our study were aware of these inequities. As one student who did not attend a criteria-based school commented, "I always heard that I didn't come from the best school ... When you come from a school with a not-so-great background, you think, 'Oh, I might not be able to get in.'" Another student expressed a similar concern: "If I had better circumstances in my middle school years, I could have gone to a school like City Honors or Hutch." Of the students who currently attend criteria-based schools, 32% believe that their elementary or middle school prepared them for criteria-based schools, and another 35% believe their elementary school prepared them somewhat for criteria-based schools. Only 14% believe that their school did not prepare them. More than three-fourths of all White students believe that their elementary or middle school prepared them for criteria-based schools. However, among non-White students, just over half felt prepared and one-sixth did not feel prepared.

Parents' perspectives on their children's preparation for criteria-based schools are enlightening as well. When parents were asked whether their child's school had provided strong preparation for criteria-based schools, the responses of those whose children applied for admission to a criteria-based school were markedly different from those whose children did not apply. Among the group that applied for such schools, 59% of parents responded "yes" or "somewhat," indicating that most of them believed their children had received strong or somewhat strong preparation. However, among those who did not apply for criteria-based schools, 58% responded no or don't know, indicating that either they believed their children were not well prepared for criteria-based schools or that they were uninformed and disconnected from such pathways for their children. Of the parents whose children did not apply to criteria-based schools, 36% explained they had not received information about the courses needed to prepare for criteria-based schools, 18% indicated that required courses had not been available at the school, 7% reported that a teacher or counselor had discouraged their child from taking courses, and 5% reported that the school had offered courses but there had not been enough space for their child to enroll. Of this same set of parents whose children did not apply to criteria-based schools, when asked about their reasons for not applying, 30% reported that their child had not been qualified or prepared or that their child's academic standing had not been adequate. It is clear from these responses that inequitable preparation in earlier grades contributes to barriers in accessing criteria-based schools.

BPS teachers and staff gave mixed responses about the degree to which their schools prepared students for criteria-based schools. Teachers generally believed that their schools prepared students somewhat but not very well for criteria-based schools. Elementary teachers were most likely to think that their schools did a better job of preparation. Meanwhile, non-White staff (41%) were more likely than White staff (18%) to say that their schools' course offerings do not prepare students well at all for admissions to criteria-based schools. This was the most common response for non-White teachers and staff. For White teachers and staff, the most common response (40%) was that their school prepared students somewhat well.

There seems to be an unofficial pipeline between some elementary schools—such as Olmsted Elementary, a school with a gifted and talented program—and the secondary criteria-based schools. Moreover, students who had attended charter schools for the primary grades were more likely to be admitted to criteria-based schools than students who had attended BPS's primary schools. Of all the students who applied to criteria-based schools, 47% were admitted. However, much larger shares of applicants who had earlier attended criteria-based schools (95%) or charter schools (70%) were admitted to criteria-based schools. These disparate admissions rates reveal the inequitable access to education in BPS and the lack of opportunities that would have sufficiently prepared many students to compete for admission to criteria-based schools.

Admissions Criteria

Numerous aspects of the admissions criteria also raise concerns. Among the problematic requirements are the cognitive skills testing and the parent and teacher recommendations.

Cognitive skills testing. There is a range of views regarding the testing required for admission to City Honors and Olmsted. Some students and most parents who participated in our study are satisfied with the testing requirements and are committed to the tests as part of the process for gaining admission to City Honors and Olmsted. Some participants feel that the testing is necessary to ensure a fair, objective process for applying to City Honors and Olmsted. However, other participants expressed concern regarding the test and did not think it should be part of the admissions criteria. Of the BPS teacher and staff respondents, 65% expressed that the tests should be given some weight, but not a great deal.

When parents were asked to name the biggest challenge in the admissions process, testing was the most commonly cited challenge, with 47% of parents identifying testing as the greatest challenge in the application process. Furthermore, parents cited a variety of reasons for believing that the testing was unfair. Some said that the test is culturally biased or that prior preparation could affect the results. A BPS teacher commented, "Some of our students who do not test well and therefore could not get into a criteria-based school would excel in specific programs." Parents also stated that, especially in the case of Olmsted 64, testing children at 4 years old to determine the future of their academic path is inappropriate. As one parent said, "I found the process for applying to Olmsted with my four-year-old to be incredibly awful. . . . These kids are babies, so I found that really daunting."

In addition to general disapproval of the testing requirements, participants noted a variety of ways in which the testing creates barriers for students. These factors included timing, awareness, frequency, location, accommodations for ELs and special education students, and lack of residency requirements for testing.

In terms of timing, as mentioned above, some parents believe that the testing occurs too early in the school year (October). Some parents expressed that they did not know when the testing was going to occur and might have missed the test date, in part because it was so early in the school year and they were not yet thinking about options for the following school year. District staff and some parents acknowledged that this early testing timeline is unfair to ELs, whose knowledge of English grows over the course of a school year and who might achieve higher test scores at the end of the year than in the fall. Other parents reported that they did not receive the test results far enough in advance of the deadline for applying to criteria-based schools. Since they were waiting to find out how their child performed on the test, they had to scramble at the last minute to complete the application form and submit it by the due date.

Parents also expressed disagreement regarding the limited number of options for testing—one regular testing date and one make-up date. Some parents suggested that the location of the testing (rotating annually between City Honors and Olmsted) was inadequate and might be inaccessible for some parents. Nearly two-thirds of BPS staff and teacher respondents (64%) indicated that transportation to testing sites was a barrier for some potential applicants. In several cases, the students' counselors drove them to the exam. Students were in agreement with this concern: As one student explained, "The most difficult part was getting to your exam if you had to take one."

District staff also raised concerns with the testing, and saw it as a barrier particularly for ELs and students in special education. Because the testing is language-heavy, it is very difficult for ELs to gain access to City Honors or Olmsted, as evidenced by the fact that there are no ELs at City Honors. One principal commented, "I do not have the test in another language. . . . I will be honest—I have never been posed with that issue." Staff suggested that criteria-based schools should consider the benefits of bilingualism as part of the criteria for admission rather than relying so heavily on the tests. District staff also believe that testing is a barrier for students in special education because these students do not receive appropriate testing accommodations. For example, as noted above, the tests are language-heavy, and many special education students have language disabilities.

Finally, parents suspect that numerous students who take the test to attend City Honors or Olmsted are suburban residents who are not currently attending BPS. They believe that it is unfair for these students to be taking seats, at City Honors in particular, and that students should be required to prove they are residents of the City of Buffalo prior to taking the test. A teacher commented, "A huge barrier is the number of suburban and private school students who apply and get in. There are students who live mainly in the suburbs but attend criterion schools because of special programs. These students often bump our city students who attend BPS schools for elementary school. These suburban and private school families do not even pay a testing fee!"

Participants suggested a variety of ways in which these barriers could be addressed. Principals and parents suggested that all students in BPS could be tested at their home schools. As one participant commented, "I really think that Buffalo might consider . . . offering families the opportunity to take this cognitive ability assessment right in the home buildings of the Buffalo public schools." Some principals recommended that every student in BPS be tested for schools that require it as a part of their admissions process. Alternatively, another principal questioned whether testing for admissions is necessary altogether. Some students suggested that admissions should not be based on a test but rather on an essay; one student specified that students should write an essay to describe their talents. It should be noted that essays were part of the application process at City Honors and Olmsted in the past, but the requirement was removed because of the high correlation between the essay and test scores. Several students suggested an interview as an alternative to testing so that schools can actually learn about the students and make the application process more personal.

Parent inventories and teacher recommendations. Some of the criteria-based schools require that parents complete an inventory as part of the application process. However, different schools require different inventories, creating a complicated process for parents to navigate. Some parents who participated in our study found the parent inventories to be straightforward and simple. However, many other parents, as well as district staff, expressed their belief that the parent inventories required by some schools are ambiguous, with language that is complex and culturally biased. Among all the parents who participated in our study, 10% of them viewed the parent inventory as the biggest challenge of all the criteria required for admission to criteria-based schools.

Teacher recommendations also present a challenge to students who want to apply to criteria-based schools and their parents. All eight of the criteria-based schools require that students submit teacher recommendations as part of their applications. Among the parents who participated in our study, 22% perceived the teacher recommendation to be the biggest hurdle in the application process. Thus, the challenge of providing a teacher recommendation appears to be even more pervasive than the parent inventory, since all the criteria-based schools require a teacher recommendation and an even higher percentage of parents find it to be the biggest challenge, compared with those who feel most challenged by the parent inventory.

Support Services

In general, all participants in the focus group sessions agreed that services rendered to ELs as well as to refugee students and families at criteria-based schools are insufficient. Only 6% of teachers surveyed believe that the current support provided to ELs is sufficient. A number of parents maintained that little effort is put forth by school and district personnel to provide support for ELs. Over two-thirds (67%) of teachers surveyed indicated that providing information in students' home languages is needed for ensuring appropriate support for applying to criteria-based schools. Further, a teacher commented, "BPS needs to provide translators so parents have the opportunity to ask questions." Generally, all principals agreed that outreach and testing materials should be provided in other languages. Administrators noted that some academic support services for students at criteria-based schools are currently provided in the form of after-school programs, tutoring, intervention classes, and part-time teachers of English as a second laguage (ESL). Criteria-based schools that are also Title I schools are provided additional accommodations such as supplemental teachers to assist students in core content classes, such as reading and mathematics.

The district staff expressed concern that there are insufficient resources for ELs at criteria-based schools. One teacher said that the biggest barrier for ELs at criteria-based schools is "not having services available to serve them in those schools, such as ESL and bilingual services." Additionally, staff recommended that all teachers at criteria-based schools, not just ESL teachers, receive training in working with EL students. Substantial percentages of BPS teacher and staff survey respondents expressed that the following might be helpful for supporting ELs: appropriate accommodations (77%), information provided in their language (67%), positive programs and welcoming school climate (62%), and more recruitment and information (51%). No non-White staff thought that support for ELs was sufficient as it currently exists. District representatives also acknowledged that the lack of ELs, specifically at City Honors, can be attributed to the difficulty that this particular student group faces in meeting the school's admissions requirements.

Another student population that the district staff recognized as in need of continued support services is the special education students. Over three-fourths (77%) of teachers and staff surveyed reported that appropriate accommodations are needed in order to support special education students in applying to criteria-based schools. Again, no non-White staff indicated that support for special education students is sufficient in its current state. There is a perception that the placement of special education students into schools (criteria-based or non-criteria-based) is dependent upon a student's disability. The staff reported that students with autism, for example, are more likely to be placed in criteria-based schools such as Olmsted and Hutch Tech, while emotionally disturbed students are enrolled at higher rates in non-criteria-based schools. In addition to special education student placement concerns, the district staff asserted that criteria-based schools are in need of differentiated learning, especially at the secondary level, as well as intervention programs addressing behavioral problems.

Availability of Choices

With only eight criteria-based schools and two that are in particularly high demand—City Honors and Olmsted—there is a limited number of desirable choices. The demand for access to these criteria-based schools exceeds the supply of seats, creating a shortage of high-quality educational opportunity that does not need to exist. As one parent stated, "There aren't enough desirable schools in the area." Additionally, a counselor remarked, "The fact that we have so many schools with small enrollment is the access problem."

Buffalo parents are generally very supportive of the criteria-based school system. In fact, only a small percentage of the total sample of parents we surveyed, about one-eighth, expressed negative attitudes toward criteria-based schools. We found that academic quality is the most important feature of the criteria-based schools for parents and students. Among parents, 59% of those whose children applied and 66% of those whose children did not apply to criteria-based schools ranked academic quality as the most important feature of criteria-based schools. Following academic quality, parents also identified other important aspects of the criteria-based schools, including teachers and school safety. Parents gave lower ratings to other factors, such as extracurricular activities, location, and athletics. Among students, two-thirds of respondents (67%) indicated that academic excellence influenced them to apply to or attend a certain criteria-based school; this aspect of criteria-based schools is by far the most influential for students as well. One-sixth of students also reported that the school's theme is an influential factor.

Almost half (44%) of teachers and staff members expressed that it would be very beneficial to create new criteria-based schools and another 24% indicated that it would be somewhat beneficial, suggesting that most staff believe the criteria-based schools offer important choices for students and that the system should be expanded. They also believe, by a large majority (87%), that criteria-based schools can be effective in competing for students with private and charter school options. Teachers and staff also prefer working in criteria-based schools—36% reported that they "much prefer" working in criteria-based schools, and another 45% indicated they had some preference for criteria-based schools. In combination, 82% of teachers prefer teaching in criteria-based schools. Only 1% said they prefer to teach in non-criteria-based schools.

When asked specifically about their interest in teaching in new criteria-based schools, most BPS teacher and staff respondents (90%) said that they would be interested in working in a new criteria-based school if such schools were created in BPS. They understand that viable educational options require appropriate faculty, and only 26% believe that those faculty should be assigned on the basis of seniority. Not surprisingly, those with the least seniority were the most unlikely to say that seniority should determine assignment to criteria-based schools. Instead, most teachers and staff (45%) believe that the selection of teachers for criteria-based schools should be done by the principals, with teacher and committee representatives, and without regard for seniority. The remaining 30% of respondents believe that teachers should be chosen by the district on the basis of expertise in the field, again without regard for seniority. This interest in creating and staffing new criteria-based schools suggests that expansion of criteria-based school options would be feasible in BPS.

If the criteria-based system were to be expanded by creating new schools, students would be most interested in five themes: science, technology, and mathematics (38%); medical/health sciences (38%); visual arts such as graphic/design arts, film, and fine arts (34%); honors/International Baccalaureate (30%); and performing arts such as instrumental and vocal music, theater, and dance (29%). The interest in science and art themes was widely shared among both White and non-White students as well as among students in both criteria-based and non-criteria-based schools.

In the course of our work, it became clear that the current limited availability of desirable choices affects the district's overall enrollment. In some cases, families whose children are denied admission to criteria-based schools subsequently choose to enroll their children in charter schools, private schools, or neighboring suburban districts. As one study participant noted, "People say, 'If I don't get into City Honors, I'm moving out of the city.'" These families reapply each year but do not reenter BPS unless they gain access to one of the desirable criteria-based schools. This phenomenon indicates a clear need for better educational options in BPS and the need for expanding the district's high-quality criteria-based schools, either by creating more seats within existing schools or by creating new schools with similarly high academic standards.

IDENTIFICATION OF ROADBLOCKS: A CRUCIAL STEP

Our findings highlighted five key areas of barriers described by stakeholders within the BPS district that deter access to criteria-based schools: information, preparation, admissions criteria, support services, and availability of choices. This knowledge was helpful in providing us and district administrators with some insights regarding the types of barriers that need to be addressed in order to create a more equitable and accessible system. While choice plans are designed to offer a variety of options, every student should have an equal opportunity to apply and have access to every school within a specified district. Barriers that impede or eliminate opportunity must first be identified and ultimately be removed, so that the pathway is cleared and all students have an equal chance at a quality education of their choosing.

NOTES

1. In this instance and some subsequent instances, the percentages add to more than 100 because of rounding.

2. This section is based on the findings reported on pp. 37–78 of Orfield et al. (2015).

REFERENCES

Frankenberg, E., & Siegel-Hawley, G. (2008). *The forgotten choice: Rethinking magnet schools in a changing landscape.* Los Angeles, CA: The Civil Rights Project/Proyecto Derechos Civiles.

Holme, J. J. (2002). Buying homes, buying schools: School choice and the social construction of school quality. *Harvard Educational Review, 72*(2), 177–206.

Kleitz, B., Weiher, G. R., Tedin, K., & Matland, R. (2000). Choice, charter schools, and household preferences. *Social Science Quarterly,* 846–854.

Orfield, G., Ayscue, J., Ee, J., Frankenberg, E., Siegel-Hawley, G., Woodward, B., & Amlani, N. (2015, May). *Better choices for Buffalo's students: Expanding and reforming the criteria schools system.* Los Angeles, CA: The Civil Rights Project/Proyecto Derechos Civiles.

Wells, A. S. (1996). African-American students' views of choice. In B. Fuller, R. Elmore, & G. Orfield (Eds.), *Who chooses? Who loses? Culture, institutions, and the unequal effects of school choice* (pp. 25–49). New York: Teachers College Press.

CHAPTER 6

How to Make Competitive Schools of Choice More Accessible and Equitable

Jennifer B. Ayscue and Genevieve Siegel-Hawley

Occupying a prominent place in the top tier of public education in America is a group of selective schools, often called exam schools, that admit students based on academic criteria such as test scores. These "public Ivies" (Moll, 1985) of the K–12 world include schools like Boston Latin, New York City's Stuyvesant, and San Francisco's Lowell High, all of which are regularly acknowledged as among the best in the country (Morse, 2012). Exam schools have been established over the past several centuries with different goals and foci.[1] Some were created as part of a commitment to preparing students for postsecondary education through rigorous curricula. In the 1970s, magnet schools emerged as part of desegregation orders (Finn & Hockett, 2012). As districts were released from court-ordered desegregation, some magnet schools became exam schools.

Despite their varied roots, many of these schools face a similar challenge today: They fail to reflect the racial and ethnic makeup of the largely urban systems in which they reside.[2] Consequently, within the last several years, federal officials have opened civil rights investigations against about a dozen exam schools, all relating to racial disproportionality in admissions.[3]

Layered beneath contemporary civil rights investigations is a string of 1990s-era court cases involving exam schools in Boston, San Francisco, and Buffalo (Hendrie, 1998; *Ho v. San Francisco Unified School District*, 1997; *Wessman v. Gittens*, 1998). These "reverse discrimination" lawsuits, among others that rolled back desegregation standards more generally, had a chilling effect on the use of race-conscious policies in K–12 education (Orfield & Eaton, 1996). They also prompted numerous exam schools to abandon racial diversity goals altogether (Finn & Hockett, 2012).

The most recent retrenchment on race-conscious policies in K–12 education came with the *Parents Involved* decision of 2007, when the U.S. Supreme Court curtailed the use of race in voluntary integration efforts. Chief Justice Roberts's now famous quote in the case, "the way to stop discriminating on the basis of race is to stop discriminating on the basis of race," validated earlier claims of reverse discrimination in exam schools. Yet, as Justice Sotomayor pointedly noted in a recent case dealing with affirmative action in higher education, the ongoing realities of race-based discrimination require direct acknowledgment and action. She wrote, "The way to stop discrimination on the basis of race is to speak openly and candidly on the subject of race, and to apply the Constitution with eyes open to the unfortunate effects of centuries of racial discrimination" (*Schuette*, 2014). Competitive-admissions schools, in many instances, have become a ground zero for K–12 debates over what advocates see as meritocratic systems of education versus the stubborn persistence of structural discrimination.

Given the unique opportunities that competitive-admissions schools provide—wide recognition as places of excellence, rigorous preparation for elite postsecondary experiences, and tight linkages with advantaged social networks that exchange information about college and career opportunities, to name a few—along with clear and mounting evidence that certain student groups disproportionately benefit from such opportunities, we seek to review and expand upon what we know about ensuring equitable access to and preparation for these selective-admissions programs. Since literature on selective-admissions schools is relatively scarce, we draw also on a wider body of research dealing with gifted and talented identification, magnet schools, school choice, higher education admissions, and testing. We first review the Buffalo context, followed by a review of relevant literature. Here we focus on understanding what is known about reducing barriers to equitable entry into competitive-admissions schools. We explore the same five categories of barriers that emerged from our interviews, focus groups, and surveys of Buffalo educators, parents, and students (see Chapter 5): admissions criteria, preparation, information, support services, and availability of choices. We review existing research related to these barriers and the practices and policies that have been designed to remove these barriers in competitive-admissions schools of choice. We close by explaining how these examples from practice and policy informed our recommendations for Buffalo.

TERMINOLOGY

As described in Chapter 2, we use the terms *competitive-admissions school of choice*, *selective-admissions magnet school*, and *criteria-based school* interchangeably throughout this chapter. When referring specifically to City Honors and/or Olmsted, we also use the term *exam school*, as both require testing for admission. In addition, in this chapter, we use the term *gifted and talented* to refer to a continuum of services provided to "students, children, or youth who give evidence of high achievement capability in areas such as intellectual, creative, artistic, or leadership capacity, or in specific academic fields, and who need services and activities not ordinarily provided by the school in order to fully develop those capabilities" (Elementary and Secondary Education Act, 2004). Typically, students are identified as gifted and talented through a process in which the student's performance and potential are assessed by a combination of objective and subjective instruments. Students who have been identified as gifted and talented access a variety of services, which might include accommodations in the regular classroom, part-time grouping with other gifted and talented students in a separate setting, or a full-time self-contained setting that is only for students identified as gifted and talented. These services and programs are offered in elementary, middle, and high schools. In essence, competitive-admissions schools of choice, such as Buffalo's criteria-based schools, are one approach to schooling for gifted and talented students.

BUFFALO CONTEXT

In 2014, a group of parents filed a civil rights complaint with the U.S. Office for Civil Rights (OCR) of the U.S. Department of Education, claiming that Black students were underrepresented in Buffalo Public Schools' (BPS's) competitive-admissions schools. OCR's subsequent investigation substantiated this claim. As a result of the agreement reached between BPS and OCR, our team of researchers from the Civil Rights Project was hired to independently identify barriers to equitable access in the recruitment, application, and enrollment processes in BPS's competitive-admissions schools, in addition to proposing changes that the school board would be required to consider. The Civil Rights Project team conducted this study as part of thinking through solutions to common problems of equity in choice systems, a topic that was earlier discussed in *Educational Delusions: How Choice Can Deepen Inequality and How to Make Schools Fair* (Orfield & Frankenberg, 2013). In this chapter, we provide recommendations for all of the district's criteria-based schools but pay particular attention to the two most highly-sought-after BPS high schools, City Honors and Olmsted. These two schools are also the only two BPS high schools that use a cognitive skills test as part of their admissions process. Moreover, they are the two schools where OCR found the most severe violations and disparities in enrollment by race. Although OCR did not require us to examine all of the criteria-based schools because they were not as severely disproportionate as City Honors and Olmsted, we chose to do so in an effort to create more comprehensive and systematic change that would impact students across the district. Individual schools are part of a system.

As described in Chapters 2 and 3, Buffalo has a decades-long history of civil rights issues related to segregation. In 1972, a coalition of parents, the NAACP, and the Citizens Council on Human Relations filed a lawsuit claiming both *de facto* and *de jure* segregation in Buffalo. In 1976, in *Arthur v. Nyquist*, Federal Judge John T. Curtin issued the first desegregation order in Buffalo, which led to the development of an innovative magnet school system rather than extensive busing. Two magnet schools opened in 1976, with eight additional magnets opening in 1977 and one more magnet in 1979. Roughly one out of three BPS schools was a magnet, and at that time, admission was determined through a lottery, not academic criteria. This was one of the most prominent magnet efforts in the United States at the time.

In 1995, the desegregation plan ended, and just 2 years later, in 1997, an individual civil suit was filed against BPS (Hendrie, 1998). In the case, Frank and Patricia Zagare alleged that their high-scoring daughter was denied admission to the 6th grade at City Honors while three minority students with lower scores were admitted. The Zagares contended that the district policies, specifically the racial quota at City Honors, discriminated against White students. This case, which occurred shortly before a similar case against Boston Latin (*Wessman v. Gittens*, 1998), prompted BPS to change its admissions procedures.

In the aftermath of unitary status and the reverse discrimination case, the district abandoned desegregation efforts. As of 2000, echoing conditions in many exam schools around the country, any consideration of race and poverty in determining access was dropped. Instead, BPS now has an extensive choice system and no diversity requirements. The students who attend these competitive-admissions schools of choice, especially City Honors and Olmsted, are disproportionately White and overwhelmingly middle-class in a city school system that is neither.

INCLUSION AND EXCLUSION CRITERIA FOR REVIEW OF RESEARCH

Research about selective-admissions magnet schools, and exam schools in particular, is quite limited. Thus, our review of research is not focused solely on competitive-admissions schools of choice and exam schools. We include research that examines schools of choice, whether the schools and researcher identify the work as being about magnet schools or not, and those that use academic criteria, including a test, to determine whether or not a student is admitted to the school. By adhering to these inclusion criteria, we include research about gifted and talented education, as competitive-admissions schools of choice are essentially whole-school programs that separate entire groups of gifted and talented students from those who are not identified with such a label. We also draw on literature from higher education because although there are differences, the use of admissions criteria and the process for admitting students to colleges and universities can be viewed as at least somewhat parallel to that of academically selective secondary schools of choice. Finally, we draw on broader school choice literature that is instructive for making choice systems more equitable in general.

This review includes research in peer-reviewed journal articles, books, and reports, as well as federal guidance and the news media. We include these varied sources because of the limited nature of peer-reviewed research about competitive-admissions schools of choice and the rapidly shifting legal and political terrain for such schools. For instance, federal guidance on "approaches to achieving diversity or avoiding racial isolation" for "admission to competitive schools and programs" was issued in 2011 (U.S. Department of Justice & U.S. Department of Education, 2011). The relatively recent date of this guidance means that there has been a short amount of time in which researchers could have conducted and published research through the more traditional channels of journal articles, thus prompting us to gather research from multiple types of sources. Reports from news media are used primarily for describing the context and developing a deeper understanding of policies being attempted, which is especially important given the limited quantity of peer-reviewed research.

There are no parameters around time, in part because of the scant research that exists about competitive schools of choice and also because these types of schools have been part of the national educational landscape since the start of public education.

PRIOR RESEARCH ON HOW TO MAKE CHOICE SYSTEMS MORE EQUITABLE

Prior research indicates that critical examination of the following issues can be helpful for making choice systems more equitable: admissions criteria, prior preparation, information and outreach, and school structure.

Admissions Criteria That Prevent Access to Competitive-Admissions Schools

Testing. Using test results to determine whether a student is granted admission to a school of choice creates multiple barriers for students of color and low-income students. A key barrier for students of color is stereotype threat. Stereotype threat occurs when individuals experience anxiety about confirming negative stereotypes about their social group; it often results in a lowered academic performance of individuals who belong to the negatively stereotyped group (Steele, 1997; Steele & Aronson, 1995). Numerous confirming studies have demonstrated that stereotype threat undermines the performance of stereotyped individuals through a variety of mechanisms (Spencer, Logel, & Davies, 2016). In the case of testing for competitive high school admissions, stereotype threat could be operating with students of color, low-income students, and English learners (ELs), and could hinder these students' performance on these high-stakes exams.

Further, the assertion that a test can validly measure a student's ability has been very strongly challenged. Cognitive ability tests, like the ones used in Buffalo, are intended to measure a student's reasoning and problem-solving abilities by combining a battery of verbal, quantitative, and nonverbal test items. However, using experimental methods, Fagan and Holland (2007) concluded that tests are often a reflection of students' knowledge, not their abilities. They found that knowledge is influenced by environmental factors and that not all students have access to the knowledge that is assessed on standard IQ tests. For example, the differences in scores on vocabulary knowledge across people of different races and native languages—regularly included on aptitude tests, including cognitive tests—reflect prior learning opportunities and not the ability to learn the vocabulary itself. Similarly, different scores on solving analogies can be explained by differences in prior education. Professional testing standards advise that in order to use test results fairly, students' opportunities to learn (i.e., the extent to which a student has been exposed to instruction or experiences that are assumed by the test developer) must be considered because the presence or absence of such opportunities might influence the fair and valid interpretation of test scores (AERA, APA, & NCME, 2014). Therefore, it follows that low-income students and students of color, who tend to be segregated (Orfield & Frankenberg, 2014) in lower-performing schools (Mickelson, Bottia, & Lambert, 2013; Mickelson & Heath, 1999) with more limited curricular options (Yun & Moreno, 2006), less experienced teachers (Clotfelter, Ladd, & Vigdor, 2005; Jackson, 2009), and more limited home access to traditionally valued educational experiences (Duncan & Murnane, 2011; Lareau, 2011), are at a disadvantage when cognitive skills tests are used as admissions criteria.

In addition to the use of a cognitive skills test itself, the manner in which the test is administered can also create secondary barriers. In BPS, for example, rather than offering universal testing, the test was offered at one location on a Saturday. This scheduling of the exam poses additional barriers in that students must first have knowledge that the test is occurring and then must secure transportation to the testing site. While referrals are not required for testing in BPS, students must either take the initiative and self-select to take the test or receive some encouragement from a teacher, counselor, or parent. In the field of gifted and talented education, when a teacher or parent recommendation is used to decide who is tested for gifted and talented programs, Hispanic, low-income, EL, and female students are systematically underreferred for testing; however, with universal screening, the test-taking patterns are much more equitable (Card & Giuliano, 2015). Thus, it is likely that when a cognitive skills test is required for admission to a competitive school of choice, a more diverse and equitable pool of applicants would be produced if the test were administered to all students.

Alongside concern with the cognitive abilities test, in the Buffalo context, the use of students' scores on the New York State English language arts and mathematics assessments is also a questionable criterion upon which to make admissions decisions. Beginning in April 2013, schools in New York administered tests that were aligned to the Common Core standards. Although this change is relatively recent, it was in effect during the year that we studied BPS. State-administered tests change with some regularity, which makes it difficult to rely upon them for multiple reasons. The use of the Common Core–aligned tests merits discussion because it raises an important consideration about the use of tests for admissions criteria to competitive schools of choice in BPS and more broadly. In 2015, the *New York Common Core Task Force Final Report* recommended that "until the new system is fully phased in, the results from assessments aligned to the current Common Core Standards, as well as the updated standards, shall only be advisory and not be used to evaluate the performance of individual teachers or students"

(Common Core Task Force, 2015, p. 35). The Task Force discouraged the use of the assessment results for evaluating teachers and students until the 2019–2020 school year, suggesting instead that the results should be used to guide further reform in the state. In BPS, the reliability and validity of the New York State test is uncertain, a concern that likely exists in other states in the early years following the adoption of new standards and assessments.

In short, both a report by the National Academy of Sciences, *High Stakes Testing for Tracking, Promotion, and Graduation,* and the Code of Ethics of the testing profession concluded that major decisions about students' life chances should not be based on a single test (AERA, APA, & NCME, 2014; Heubert & Hauser, 1999). The use of a cognitive ability test or an end-of-grade test and an absolute cut point below which students are eliminated from consideration is one such decision that could have a strong impact on students' life chances.

Teacher and parent recommendations. Along with testing, the use of teacher and parent recommendations as admissions criteria to competitive schools of choice could create barriers for students of color, low-income students, and ELs. In gifted and talented programs, Ford and Grantham (2003) assert, educators' deficit thinking about diverse students hinders their access to such programs. Along similar lines, Grissom and Redding (2016) found that Black students are referred to gifted programs at significantly lower rates when they are taught by non-Black teachers. This finding is particularly problematic as Black teachers account for only 7% of the public school teaching force (Goldring, Gray, & Bitterman, 2013). It could be inferred that a similar dynamic occurs for Hispanic students, who are disproportionately taught by non-Hispanic teachers; only 8% of public school teachers in the United States are Hispanic. In BPS, 5.0% of teachers in criteria-based schools and 9.4% of teachers in non-criteria-based schools are Black. Accounting for an even smaller proportion of teachers in BPS, 4.3% of criteria-based school teachers and 4.1% of non-criteria-based school teachers are Hispanic (Orfield et al., 2015). Mirroring national patterns, there is a significant gap between the share of students of color and teachers of color in BPS, which could contribute to the inequity in the representation of students of color in BPS's competitive schools of choice.

In addition to concerns about teacher recommendations, having a diverse teaching force is important for many other reasons. Racially diverse teaching staffs can be more effective in teaching students with a broad array of learning styles, serving as cultural links and communicating with families of different backgrounds, and serving as role models for students from diverse backgrounds (Nieto, 1994; Sleeter, 2007; Villegas & Irvine, 2010). Further, students of color who are taught by teachers of color often have higher academic achievement, fewer behavioral problems, lower dropout rates, and better attendance (Villegas & Lucas, 2005). Thus, the lack of teacher diversity in BPS criteria-based and non-criteria-based schools presents additional concerns, particularly for students of color.

Requiring parent recommendations can also create barriers, particularly for students of color, low-income students, and ELs. In the field of gifted education, researchers have found that the complicated and cumbersome nature of recommendation forms prevents some parents from completing them (Ford, 1998). Furthermore, parents who have difficulty understanding the forms are likely to either over- or underestimate their child's ability. In addition, parent recommendation forms and checklists lack reliability and validity, often lack cultural sensitivity, and tend to focus on intellectual or academic characteristics of giftedness without acknowledging characteristics that are relevant to minority students. With this multitude of problematic issues, it is likely that the use of parent recommendations or checklists in admissions criteria creates further barriers for students of color, low-income students, and ELs.

Inadequate Preparation Creates a Barrier to Accessing Competitive-Admissions Schools

In order to possess the academic credentials and ability to score above established thresholds on assessments, students must be prepared in earlier grades. In BPS (Orfield et al., 2015) and in other districts across the nation (Orfield & Frankenberg, 2014), schools have become increasingly segregated by race and poverty over the past 30 years. Segregation is related to both unequal opportunities and unequal outcomes, making it nearly impossible for students of color and low-income students to compete on a level playing field with White middle-class students. Segregated schools tend to have fewer experienced and less qualified teachers (Clotfelter et al., 2005; Jackson, 2009), high rates of teacher turnover (Clotfelter et al., 2010) and student mobility (Rumberger, 2003), and inadequate facilities and learning materials, including limited and less advanced curricular options (Yun & Moreno, 2006). In turn, students who attend segregated schools have lower academic performance (Mickelson et al., 2013; Mickelson & Heath, 1999), higher dropout rates (Balfanz & Legters, 2004), and lower graduation rates (Swanson, 2004). Segregation is systematically related to unequal educational opportunity and, in this case, preparation for attending competitive schools of choice.

Moreover, the gifted and talented pipeline is disproportionately White. In BPS, one elementary school, Olmsted 64, had a gifted and talented magnet program within the larger school. In 2013–2014, the share of White students attending Olmsted 64 was more than twice as large as that of the district—enrollment was 47% White at Olmsted 64 vs. 21% White in BPS; the share of low-income students enrolled at Olmsted 64 was half that of the district—enrollment was 38% low-income at Olmsted 64 vs. 76% low-income in BPS (Orfield et al., 2015). Nationwide, in 2011–2012, African American students accounted for only 9% of gifted and talented students even though they comprised 16% of the student population (U.S. Department of Education, 2012). Similarly, Hispanic students accounted for only 15% of gifted and talented students but 24% of the nation's student enrollment. Being excluded from access to gifted and talented programs in earlier grades would likely make it more difficult to access gifted and talented programs in high school and to gain admittance to an academically selective high school. For example, in New York City's schools, preparation to attend a specialized high school begins long before the time when students take the admissions test. Of the admitted students who had attended one of the top 30 feeder middle schools for the district's specialized high schools, 58% had been part of a gifted and talented program and 29% had attended a school that admitted students based on criteria such as exam scores (Wong, 2015). These patterns demonstrate how tracking students from the early years creates a pipeline from which some students, particularly students of color and low-income students, are excluded. Thus, students of color and low-income students face the barrier of unequal preparation in earlier grades, which makes it more difficult for them to access competitive schools of choice later in their educational trajectories.

Insufficient Information and Outreach Prevents Access to Competitive-Admissions Schools

Providing families with information about their options is essential for any choice system. When information is insufficient, confusing, or not provided directly to all families from the district or from schools—all of which we found to be the case in Buffalo—experience is often shared through informal channels of communication and social networks, which tend to be both racially and economically homogenous (Holme, 2002; McPherson, Smith-Lovin, & Cook, 2001). In the case of BPS's criteria-based schools, in which White students are overenrolled, a lack of formal communication likely results in White families who currently attend the criteria-based schools sharing information about the schools and navigating the application process with other White and/or middle-class families, thus perpetuating the existing segregation.

To break this cycle of segregation, it is necessary for schools and districts to provide information to diverse families. Further, it is important to use multiple modes of communication, such as the Internet, print, and telephone, as well as to provide information in multiple languages (Dougherty et al., 2013). The U.S. Department of Education (2017) also suggests numerous approaches to information dissemination, including an enrollment guide, school fairs, and expos. Outreach should be both broad and targeted, ensuring that as many families as possible have access to extensive information about educational options for their children.

School Structure Influences Access

Finally, choice programs are often structured in one of two ways—a whole-school model or a school-within-a-school program. With the whole-school model, the choice program is a school unto itself and occupies the entire school campus. With the school-within-a-school model, the choice program occupies part of the school campus; some students who attend the school are part of the choice program and others are not. A 2008 survey of more than 200 magnet schools found that school-within-a-school models are less likely to produce desegregation than the whole-school model (Frankenberg & Siegel-Hawley, 2009; Siegel-Hawley & Frankenberg, 2013).

REDUCING BARRIERS THROUGH PRACTICE AND POLICY

Practice

One of the most persistent gaps in the literature surrounding competitive entrance schools deals with alternatives for existing admissions criteria. Among the lonely voices in this field of study are Donna Y. Ford and John Harris. Ford and Harris (1991) examined existing research on strategies devoted to identifying and developing the talents of gifted minority students, and concluded that the lack of effort in this area is unconscionable. Between 1924 and 1990, in the 4,000 articles that have been written on gifted students, only 63 (2%) focused on minority students (Harris & Ford, 1991). In an effort to narrow this gap, Ford and Harris have created a rather extensive set of practical guidelines to help schools identify and strengthen the skills of gifted minority students. A summary of their findings is as follows (Ford & Webb, 1994; Ford & Whiting, 2008; Harris & Ford, 1991):

- Educators must move away from a reliance on traditional intelligence tests. Intelligence should be viewed as a trait that can be revealed in multiple ways and on multiple dimensions. Multimodal, multicultural, and multidimensional tests should be used to assess intelligence, *when given at all*.[4]
- Educators should adopt a culture-based definition of intelligence that recognizes a variety of talents as contributing to "giftedness." Instead of searching for universal attributes that describe intelligence, educators should examine aspects of giftedness that are valued by the culture of the student.
- Teachers should undergo multicultural preparation that will enable them to identify gifted students in the context of their unique cultures. Teachers should also receive gifted education preparation.
- Increased and substantive legislative commitment is necessary to ensure minority student representation in gifted education.

These recommendations should be examined more closely by educators and policymakers. The adoption of one or more of these proposals would help to alleviate increasing racial and socioeconomic stratification between competitive magnet schools and their urban school systems.

In practice, it can be difficult today to find examples of districts or schools that have committed to comprehensively addressing equity and access in gifted education. The rapidly shifting legal and policy context for race-conscious decisionmaking makes it difficult to evaluate recent interventions, since key parameters are subject to change. We focus here on a discussion of contemporary legal options for promoting voluntary integration in selective-admissions schools as outlined by recent joint guidance from the U.S. Departments of Justice and Education. We also include preliminary evidence from changes to selective-admissions schools in Chicago and proposed changes in New York. Although we do not delve into the desegregation standards applied to many exam schools prior to the judicial rollback of race-conscious policies that began in the 1990s, it is important to understand that some of the most prominent schools in Chicago, Boston, Buffalo, and San Francisco, among others, all employed racial guidelines for several decades (Shakarian, 2014), producing more equitable access to the schools and still maintaining a high standard of education.

Policy

In 2011, the Obama administration issued long-awaited guidance clarifying what school districts could and could not do in the aftermath of the Supreme Court's *Parents Involved* decision. The 2007 *Parents Involved* ruling limited the ways in which districts could consider the race of an individual student when making decisions about school assignment. Still, as outlined by the 2011 joint guidance, a number of strategies for promoting integration remain permissible—including several that deal specifically with schools that have competitive admissions processes. These strategies include the following:

- Establishing minimum criteria and then implementing lottery-based admissions for all students who meet the minimum;
- Giving greater weight to applicants who meet minimum requirements based on their socioeconomic background, prior attendance at an underperforming school, parent education level or background, or neighborhood income or poverty level;
- Admitting all applicants in the top quartile or tenth of their class at feeder schools;
- Granting special consideration or weight to applicants from particular types of neighborhoods (e.g., high-poverty or minority-segregated), provided that all students from the neighborhood are treated the same regardless of their race (U.S. Department of Justice & U.S. Department of Education, 2011).

Adhering closely to these recommendations, Chicago Public Schools crafted a new set of policies for admission to its many selective schools after being released from its longstanding desegregation order in 2009. One year later, the district implemented a plan that factored in consideration of a student's socioeconomic status via his or her neighborhood context. Although 30% of students gaining admission to the very selective high schools are admitted simply on the basis of grades and test scores, the remaining 70% of admissions are awarded to the top-performing students within four different socioeconomic strata (Quick, 2016). Those strata, or tiers, are defined by an analysis of the socioeconomic makeup (e.g., median family income, percentage of single-family homes, percentage of households where English is not the first language spoken) of census tracts, which are ranked from most to least advantaged. (It is worth noting that the 2011 guidance, issued after the Chicago policy was crafted, would also permit the consideration of the racial makeup of the neighborhood.)

Research on the impact of the new policy is relatively limited, but a quick analysis of the numbers shows that the percentage of Black students in Chicago's 10 selective schools is within 5 percentage points of the district breakdown, and the percentage of Latino students in selective schools is within about 15 percentage points (Shakarian, 2014). At the same time, enrollment of underrepresented minority students is uneven across the Chicago selective schools, with White students making up larger shares of the enrollment at the most high-ranking schools (Novak & Fusco, 2014). White student enrollment is higher in general under the race-neutral policy compared to the preceding era of race-conscious admissions under court-ordered desegregation (Wong, 2014). Chicago's highly touted selective schools received top rankings before and after the shift to an admissions policy that prioritized socioeconomic status rather than race (Quick, 2016).

In New York City, where the specialized high schools remain under civil rights investigation, a 2014 state legislative proposal sought to expand the admissions criteria for the top three high schools.[5] In addition to the single test that currently dictates admission, the legislation proposed that those three schools could also consider a student's GPA, scores on state tests, and attendance (Taylor, 2016). Although the shifts seemed promising, a detailed analysis conducted by the Research Alliance for New York City Schools simulated the impact of the proposed revisions, indicating that they would not produce appreciably more diversity in the specialized high schools, particularly in terms of Black or low-income students (Corcoran & Baker-Smith, 2015). This finding is due in part to the fact that using a broader array of measures did not create much change in the pool of applicants, who come from a very small segment of the region's middle schools. Many of the broader proposed criteria were already highly predictive of current admission, though the researchers found some unexplained differences between those factors and performance on the actual test itself (Corcoran & Baker-Smith, 2015). They suggested that differential test preparation was an area ripe for further research. Yet despite the inconclusiveness of the report's findings on the subject of test preparation, it became the centerpiece of recently proposed state legislation.

The 2016 legislation walked back on the idea of expanding admissions criteria, focusing on replicating an enrichment and test preparation program that had helped increase the numbers of Black and Latino students at one of the specialized high schools, growing gifted and talented programs in underserved areas, and adding outreach coordinators at the specialized schools (Taylor, 2016). The legislation seemed to have been crafted at least partly in response to the Research Alliance's finding that broadening the criteria in the manner suggested would do little to shift the demographics of the specialized schools, and aims attention at recruitment, another important aspect of underrepresentation.

However, the legislation ignores another key conclusion of the Research Alliance's analysis. The New York researchers found that a "top 10%" rule that would prioritize admission for the top 10% of all students from area middle schools would bring the specialized high schools much more in line with area demographics (Corcoran & Baker-Smith, 2015). Such a strategy also would be legally permissible under the 2011 guidance. The Research Alliance study did note that broadening the pool in such a way would produce lower average state test scores among the applicants; this observation is not necessarily surprising given the aforementioned close connections among socioeconomic status, concentrations of school poverty, racial segregation, and test scores (Kahlenberg, 2001). At the same time, as we turn next to higher education, it is important to note that the quality of our nation's flagship postsecondary institutions, many of which have valued diversity of background and perspective for centuries, is a reminder that more inclusive admissions policies do not diminish excellence.

Higher education policy. Although the higher education context is admittedly different from the K–12 one in important ways, research regarding admissions to selective colleges and universities contains some relevant lessons for exam schools. For instance, recent studies conducted to inform the often-shifting landscape of postsecondary admissions indicate that a 10% plan can be helpful in achieving a more diverse enrollment if feeder schools are racially segregated (Tienda & Niu, 2006). Yet basing the success of such a policy on a structure of discrimination is problematic in and of itself. Moreover, when universities use a policy that admits a specified percentage of the highest-achieving students (e.g., 10%), even with extensive outreach and recruitment, the enrollment patterns of students who qualify for admission are unequal across racial groups, with White students being disproportionately represented (Horn & Flores, 2012; Mexican American Legal Defense and Educational Fund et al., 2005). In colleges and universities that use a percentage plan, a holistic review process in admissions is a necessary complement.

Strong evidence indicates that a holistic review of students is connected to greater racial and ethnic diversity in postsecondary institutions. In a 2015 study of 338 nonprofit 4-year institutions of higher education, holistic application review including race as one of the factors considered was the most widely used strategy and was perceived to be the most widely effective strategy for supporting racial and ethnic diversity (Espinosa, Gaertner, & Orfield, 2015). In graduate and professional degree programs, the use of holistic admissions resulted in higher enrollment of African American and Latino students (Garces, 2012). Providing students of color with access to selective institutions of higher education is important for multiple reasons, including that African American and Latino students who attend selective flagship universities are more likely to graduate than comparable students who attend less selective institutions (Bowen, Chingos, & McPherson, 2011).

Relevant lessons from higher education also include research on the predictive power and validity of tests widely used in admissions. Although high school grades are sometimes viewed as unreliable predictors of college success because of differences in grading systems, research finds that they are a better predictor of college success than standardized tests. Not only are high school grades the best predictor of grades in the first year of college (Geiser & Studley, 2003), but they are also more predictive of 4-year college outcomes, including cumulative grade point averages and graduation (Geiser & Santelices, 2007). For students of color and other nonmajority students in particular, compared to SAT scores, high school grades are a better predictor of academic achievement in college (Hoffman & Lowitzki, 2005). While there are differences by gender and racial composition of the institution, overall SAT scores are a better predictor of academic success for White students than for Black students (Fleming & Garcia, 1998). Taken together, these findings demonstrate that grades are a better predictor of postsecondary success than are SAT scores, particularly for students of color. Based in part on these findings and also likely due to the way in which these tests reinforce disparities by race and gender, more than 850 colleges and universities across the United States are test-optional or test-flexible, meaning that they have deemphasized the use of standardized tests in the admissions process (Fair Test, 2016; Soares, 2012).

Given these findings in higher education, it is likely that similar mechanisms would be helpful in the admissions process for academically selective secondary schools, suggesting that a holistic form of admissions, rather than one that relies strictly on the academic performance of the highest-achieving students, would be far more effective at creating access for diverse groups of students.

RECOMMENDATIONS FOR BPS

Competitive-admissions schools of choice provide students with access to a rigorous and high-quality education in what are arguably the top public high schools in the nation. However, access to this opportunity is in high demand but short supply and is inequitably distributed among students by race and class. The basic strategy for our recommendations was to devise a system in which opportunity is allocated more equitably and standards are not changed or lowered. Rather than focusing on allocating scarce resources, our recommendations strive to expand those resources. Revising admissions criteria, providing adequate preparation, conducting outreach and disseminating information, supporting ELs and special education students, expanding the availability of choices, and working collaboratively with local and state agencies would facilitate more equitable access to selective magnet schools within a city that has been intensely segregated for generations (Table 6.1).

Each of the nation's competitive-admissions schools of choice operates in a unique context, and therefore, no one specific policy or set of criteria should be adopted by all these schools. Rather, the approach to expanding access to competitive-admissions schools of choice is context-dependent. To illustrate how policymakers might weave together context and evidence on what works, we outline our approach to the civil rights complaint against Buffalo's criteria-based schools in Table 6.1.

In Buffalo, we recommended an approach that differed from that of other cities, such as Chicago, because the contexts differ in important ways. A neighborhood model that focuses on race or socioeconomic status would likely provide Buffalo's Black students with greater access to academically selective magnet schools, but because there are not well-defined neighborhoods of Latino or Asian residents in Buffalo, this approach would likely not expand access for the city's Latino or Asian students. Using poverty as a criterion likely would be ineffective at creating more equitable access by race because there is widespread poverty in Buffalo, including among White families. Thus, this approach might have actually been counterproductive, privileging poor White applicants who were more likely to understand the admissions system. Instead, we recommended setting flexible goals for diversity, adopting expanded recruitment strategies, providing additional preparation for students who have been inadequately prepared for the competitive-admissions schools of choice, changing several aspects of the admissions criteria, and increasing the number of criteria-based schools. Non-English home language is another criterion that could be considered.

Information

We recommended that BPS develop a diversity plan and adopt recruitment strategies that would provide more accessible information to families. The plan would not contain quotas. Instead, the diversity goals would be flexible and would strive to increase diversity by race, ethnicity, poverty, and language at each school. These diversity goals would provide a benchmark for which the district could collect data and measure success.

To provide more accessible information, we recommended creating a Parent Information Center that would have at least one bilingual staff member. The Parent Information Center should organize visits to parent organizations in schools and explain that ELs and special education students do have access to criteria-based schools. We suggested redesigning the BPS website to make it more user-friendly and up to date. Information about using the district website should be posted in public libraries and in every school. We also recommended offering materials in the five most commonly utilized languages other than English. Brochures from all criteria-based schools in multiple languages should be available at public libraries and in an easily accessible section of the district's website. Community groups should be encouraged to link to the website and to organize visits to the criteria-based schools. Data about the achievement levels and graduation rates of each school by race and ethnicity should be posted as well as data about the average gain that students achieve in a year of attendance at each school, which would be a

How to Make Competitive Schools of Choice More Accessible and Equitable

Table 6.1. Recommendations for Addressing Barriers to Access in BPS Criteria-Based Schools

BARRIER	RECOMMENDATION
Information	
• Limited outreach and recruitment • Inadequate information at Central Registration • Unclear and complex application process • Lack of materials and support in languages other than English	• Develop a diversity plan and recruitment strategies • Create Parent Information Center with bilingual staff • Provide materials in top five languages utilized in district • Conduct in-person recruitment through road shows and school visits
Preparation	
• Disparate preparation in elementary school • Gifted and talented pipeline disproportionately White and middle-class • Higher acceptance rates for students who had attended criteria and charter schools	• Implement a summer preparatory program • Provide counseling and peer tutoring to support retention
Admissions Criteria	
• Cognitive skills test • New York English language arts and mathematics assessments • Parent and teacher recommendations	• Conduct holistic admissions with flexible thresholds • Discontinue use of NY assessment scores • Weight grades more than tests • Allocate 10% of seats for students deserving special consideration • End neighborhood preference for Olmsted Elementary
Support Services	
• Lack of services for ELs • Insufficient support for special education students	• Hire bilingual staff • Provide information about services for ELs and special education students
Availability of Choices	
• Limited number of schools and seats • High interest	• Create two additional criteria high schools • Create at least one additional criteria elementary school • Revise hiring process for new criteria-based schools
Regional and State Partnerships	
• City criteria-based schools operate in context of highly fragmented and residentially segregated region	• Launch a regional magnet school • Ask city government to prosecute residential discrimination • Clarify the state of the law

Source: Adapted from Ayscue et al. (2016).

better indicator of the school's effectiveness than the raw scores. In-person recruitment and "road shows" to showcase the options at school sites should be resumed.

Preparation

With regard to preparation, we recommended the creation of a summer preparatory program as well as counseling and a peer tutoring program during the school year. The summer preparatory program would provide students from less competitive elementary schools an opportunity to prepare for admissions prior to the admissions period. During these students' first year of attendance at a competitive school of choice, the counseling program would provide them with social support, while the peer tutoring program would provide academic support to aid in their retention.

Admissions Criteria

In terms of admissions criteria, we recommended eliminating absolute cut points for test score stanines below which students were automatically denied admission to the school. Based on guidance offered by the New York Common Core Task Force, we recommended eliminating the use of the Common Core–aligned tests as admissions criteria. We suggested that students' grades be weighted twice as heavily as students' test scores, since grades are a better predictor for academic success than are test scores. We also recommended that these various criteria be considered holistically rather than in isolation, with flexible thresholds for each.

In line with the 2011 guidance from OCR, we recommended that 10% of seats in each competitive-admissions school be set aside for the holistic consideration of students who are deserving of special consideration, based on factors such as obstacles overcome, exceptional dedication, unusual success in a school isolated by race and poverty, or coming from a section of the city that is rarely represented in the competitive schools of choice. This process could be accomplished by either relying on one factor, such as a remarkable recommendation that would trigger reconsideration, or having the district assign points for the factors described above.

Further, we found that the neighborhood preference for Olmsted Elementary, which is by far the most important point of access to City Honors, is unfair and should be eliminated. Since this opportunity is so scarce and so important, it should be fairly available to students from all parts of the city.

Although not part of our original report to the district, we would also recommend changes to the use of teacher and parent recommendations. Due to the subjective nature of a parent recommendation, we would recommend eliminating this requirement altogether. Given newly released research on how teacher biases influence gifted and talented recommendations from teachers, we also would suggest that districts deemphasize the weight given to recommendations provided by teachers.

Availability of Choices

To expand the number of choices, we recommended the creation of three new criteria-based schools, which could be phased in over a period of 2 years. Two of the new schools would be high schools, one of which would be similar to City Honors and another that would have a theme of interest to a diverse group of students in BPS, which at the time of our study seemed to be health sciences. We also recommended the creation of an additional criteria-based elementary school, which would be developed in collaboration with a local university. We also suggested that in the future the district consider creating a dual immersion criteria-based school that would provide instruction in Spanish and English. All of the new criteria-based schools should be whole-school programs, not program-within-a-school programs. We suggested that new criteria-based schools, except for City Honors II, should have enrollment criteria that focus primarily on student interest rather than academic criteria and that when demand for a school exceeds its capacity, a lottery should be used to determine admission. When excessive demand occurs repeatedly, BPS should consider expanding or duplicating the school on a different site.

To fill the faculty teaching positions at the new criteria-based schools, we suggested that rather than assigning teachers and administrators based on seniority, they should participate in interviews with a committee that includes a diverse group of experienced criteria-based school teachers, the deputy superintendent, and a university faculty member. Further, all criteria-based schools should have an affirmative action plan to support greater faculty diversity. A deputy superintendent should oversee the criteria-based system, aid in principal selection, supervise outreach, and monitor the effectiveness of the criteria-based schools. This comprehensive set of recommendations offers one blueprint for moving forward.

Working With Regional and State Partners

Finally, we recommended collaborative efforts that would require the district to work with other local and state agencies. We suggested that BPS seek funding for a regional magnet school in collaboration with the University of Buffalo. This regional magnet school could aid in overcoming the extreme segregation that exists across the broader metropolitan area and could offer opportunities that no individual district could provide on its own. We suggested that BPS seek funding for such a school from the state, the U.S. Department of Education, the Board of Cooperative Education Services, and private foundations.

As described in Chapter 3, BPS operated under court-ordered desegregation for two decades in large part due to the intense residential segregation across the city that also impacted the schools. Buffalo is one of the most intensely segregated cities, and very little has changed for generations. Given the reality of residential segregation that continues to plague the city of Buffalo, we recommended that the school board ask the city government to actively prosecute residential discrimination, including the steering of homebuyers or renters on the basis of race or school districts. We also suggested that BPS request that state and federal housing agencies support stable residential integration, avoid new construction of subsidized housing in areas with weak segregated schools, and provide counseling about better residential and schooling opportunities for families with rent subsidies or Section 8 housing vouchers, since the low cost of Buffalo-area housing could support considerable mobility to strong neighborhoods and schools.

Throughout our time in Buffalo, we encountered numerous statements in discussions as well as in documents that claim that the federal court forbade consideration of diversity and integration in making school assignment decisions in Buffalo. However, this is not the case. Therefore, we urged BPS to clarify the state of the law for its educators and the public.

EXPANDING ACCESS DOES NOT MEAN LOWERING STANDARDS

Ultimately, a strong base of evidence indicates clearly that the current approach to most competitive-admissions schools of choice is far off the mark. Overreliance on and misuse of testing instruments, along with the lack of diversity goals and holistic review processes, exacerbate stark inequities present throughout the K–12 experience. Arguments against change are backed by a firm belief in the existence of a meritocratic society but ignore the clear persistence of racial discrimination in a society that has both tolerated and perpetuated such discrimination since its founding. The contemporary example of Chicago and the stellar performance of exam schools across the country during the decades in which they relied on desegregation standards, not to mention our world-renowned universities, show us that well-designed policy can strive to take into account the complex relationships among socioeconomic status, race, and opportunity while offering more equitable access to high-quality schools—and still maintain elite status.

NOTES

1. Boston Latin, for instance, was established in 1635 and is considered the nation's first public school.

2. It is worth noting that Finn and Hockett's study of exam schools made a somewhat different argument, depending on their comparison groups. They found that exam schools enroll a disproportionately large share of Black and Asian students and disproportionately small share of White and Hispanic students in comparison to the *national* population of public school students. Most of these exam schools are located in urban areas that tend to have higher shares of students of color, thus making a comparison to the national high school population an inappropriate indicator of how representative exam schools are of the students who could possibly attend them. Acknowledging this issue, Finn and Hockett also compared exam schools in seven large cities to the public high schools in those cities, presenting a very different picture of the representativeness of exam schools—and one more in line with current civil rights complaints. In New York, Chicago, Boston, and Philadelphia,

Black and Hispanic students were underrepresented in exam schools compared to public high schools, while Asian and White students were overrepresented. In fact, between one-quarter and one-half of all Asian and White students who attended public high schools in these four cities were enrolled in selective schools. In Milwaukee and Washington, DC, selective high schools were more similar to the district. In Jefferson County (Louisville, KY), the demographic enrollment of selective high schools as a group was similar to that of the district, but upon examination of individual schools, significant differences emerged: one of Jefferson County's five selective high schools was 80% Black, and the other four were predominantly White. Finn and Hockett's more localized comparisons of the racial composition of exam schools indicate that their broad generalization that exam schools overenroll Black and Asian students and underenroll White and Hispanic students is misleading when trying to understand access to exam schools by students of different races.

3. All of Buffalo's selective-admissions schools have been under civil rights investigation, although only two would be considered exam schools under Finn and Hockett's definition. Two exam schools in Virginia, Thomas Jefferson High School for Science and Technology in Fairfax County and the Maggie Walker Governor's School in Richmond, are also under investigation. In addition, all eight of New York City's specialized high schools are still facing civil rights complaints. This year, for instance, among New York City's eight specialized high schools, 4% of offered seats went to Black students and 6% to Latino students (Taylor, 2016). Together the two racial/ethnic groups account for nearly 70% of the city's public school enrollment. Admission to New York's specialized high schools is governed by a student's rank-ordered performance on a single test, one of the central issues raised by a coalition of civil rights and community-based advocacy groups in a 2012 complaint filed with the U.S. Department of Education's Office for Civil Rights (NAACP LDF, 2012).

4. Ford and Harris provide a list of possible instruments to use. Some of these include the System of Multicultural Pluralistic Assessment, the Cattell Culture-Fair Intelligence Series, the Cartoon Conservation Scales, and the Ravens Progressive Matrices. None of these instruments was utilized by the Buffalo exam schools.

5. Changes to the admissions policy for specialized high schools require an act of the state legislature.

REFERENCES

American Educational Research Association (AERA), American Psychological Association (APA), & National Council on Measurement in Education (NCME). (2014). *Standards for educational and psychological testing*. Washington, DC: AERA.

Arthur v. Nyquist, 415 F. Supp. 904 (1976).

Ayscue, J. B., Siegel-Hawley, G., Woodward, B., & Orfield, G. (2016). When choice fosters inequality: Can research help? *Phi Delta Kappan, 98*(4), 49–54.

Balfanz, R., & Legters, N. E. (2004). Locating the dropout crisis: Which high schools produce the nation's dropouts? In G. Orfield (Ed.), *Dropouts in America: Confronting the graduation crisis* (pp. 57–84). Cambridge, MA: Harvard Education Press.

Bowen, W. G., Chingos, M. M., & McPherson, M. S. (2011). *Crossing the finish line: Completing college at America's public universities*. Princeton, NJ: Princeton University Press.

Card, D., & Giuliano, L. (2015). *Can universal screening increase the representation of low income and minority students in gifted education?* NBER Working Paper Series. Cambridge, MA: National Bureau of Economic Research.

Clotfelter, C. T., Ladd, H. F., & Vigdor, J. L. (2005). Who teaches whom? Race and the distribution of novice teachers. *Economics of Education Review, 24*(4), 377–392.

Clotfelter, C. T., Ladd, H. F., & Vigdor, J. L. (2010). Teacher mobility, school segregation, and pay-based policies to level the playing field. *Education, Finance, and Policy, 6*(3), 399–438.

Common Core Task Force. (2015). *New York Common Core Task Force final report.* New York, NY: Author.

Corcoran, S., & Baker-Smith, C. (2015). *Pathways to an elite education: Application, admission and matriculation to New York City's Specialized High Schools* (Working Paper). New York, NY: The Research Alliance for New York City Schools.

Dougherty, J., Zannoni, D., Chowhan, M., Coyne, C., Dawson, B., Guruge, T., & Nukic, B. (2013). School information, parental decisions, and the digital divide. In G. Orfield, E. Frankenberg & Associates, *Educational delusions? Why choice can deepen inequality and how to make schools fair* (pp. 221–239). Berkeley, CA: University of California Press.

Duncan, G., & Murnane, R. (Eds.). (2011). *Whither opportunity? Rising inequality, schools, and children's life chances.* New York: Russell Sage Foundation.

Elementary and Secondary Education Act, 20 USC 7801(22) (2004).

Espinosa, L. L., Gaertner, M. N., & Orfield, G. (2015). *Race, class, and college access: Achieving diversity in a shifting legal landscape.* Washington, DC: American Council on Education.

Fagan, J. F., & Holland, C. R. (2007). Racial equality in intelligence: Predictions from a theory of intelligence as processing. *Intelligence, 35*(4), 319–344.

Fair Test. (2016). *850+ colleges and universities that do not use SAT/ACT scores to admit substantial numbers of students into bachelor degree programs.* Jamaica Plain, MA: The National Center for Fair and Open Testing. Retrieved from www.fairtest.org/university/optional

Finn, C. E., & Hockett, J. A. (2012). *Exam schools: Inside America's most selective public high schools.* Princeton, NJ: Princeton University Press.

Fleming, J., & Garcia, N. (1998). Are standardized tests fair to African Americans? Predictive validity of the SAT in Black and White institutions. *The Journal of Higher Education, 69*(5), 471–495.

Ford, D. Y. (1998). The underrepresentation of minority students in gifted education: Problems and promises in recruitment and retention. *The Journal of Special Education, 32*(1), 4–14.

Ford, D. Y., & Grantham, T. C. (2003). Providing access for culturally diverse gifted students: From deficit to dynamic thinking. *Theory Into Practice, 42*(3), 217–225.

Ford, D., & Webb, K. (1994). Desegregation of gifted educational programs: The impact of Brown on underachieving children of color. *Journal of Negro Education, 63*(3), 358–375.

Ford, D., & Whiting, G. (2008). Culturally and linguistically diverse students in gifted education: Recruitment and retention issues. *Exceptional Children, 74*(3), 289–306.

Frankenberg, E., & Siegel-Hawley, G. (2009). *The forgotten choice? Rethinking magnet schools in a changing landscape.* Los Angeles, CA: The Civil Rights Project/Proyecto Derechos Civiles.

Garces, L. M. (2012). Necessary but not sufficient: The impact of Grutter v. Bollinger on student of color enrollment in graduate and professional schools in Texas. *The Journal of Higher Education, 83*(4), 497–534.

Geiser, S., & Santelices, M. V. (2007). *Validity of high-school grades in predicting student success beyond the freshman year: High-school record vs. standardized tests as indicators of four-year college outcomes.* Berkeley, CA: Center for Studies in Higher Education.

Geiser, S., & Studley, R. (2003). UC and the SAT: Predictive validity and differential impact of the SAT I and the SAT II at the University of California. *Educational Assessment, 8*(1), 1–26.

Goldring, R., Gray, L., & Bitterman, A. (2013). *Characteristics of public and private elementary and secondary school teachers in the United States: Results from the 2011–12 Schools and Staffing Survey* (NCES 2013-314). Washington, DC: U.S. Department of Education, National Center for Education Statistics.

Grissom, J. A., & Redding, C. (2016). Discretion and disproportionality: Explaining the under-representation of high-achieving students of color in gifted programs. *AERA Open, 2*(1), 1–25.

Harris, J., & Ford, D. (1991). Identifying and nurturing the promise of gifted black students. *Journal of Negro Education, 60*(1), 3–18.

Hendrie, C. (1998, May 13). Buffalo settles case challenging racial preferences. *Education Week.* Retrieved from www.edweek.org/ew/articles/1998/05/13/35buff.h17.html

Heubert, P., & Hauser, R. M. (Eds.). (1999). *High stakes: Testing for tracking, promotion, and graduation.* Washington, DC: National Academy of Sciences.

Ho v. San Francisco Unified School District, 965 F. Supp. 1316 (N.D. Cal. 1997).

Hoffman, J. L., & Lowitzki, K. E. (2005). Predicting college success with high school grades and test scores: Limitations for minority students. *The Review of Higher Education, 28*(4), 455–474.

Holme, J. J. (2002). Buying homes, buying schools: School choice and the social construction of school quality. *Harvard Educational Review, 72*(2), 177–206.

Horn, C. L., & Flores, S. M. (2012). When policy opportunity is not enough: College access and enrollment patterns among Texas percent plan eligible students. *Journal of Applied Research on Children: Informing Policy for Children at Risk, 3*(2), Article 9.

Jackson, K. (2009). Student demographics, teacher sorting, and teacher quality: Evidence from the end of school desegregation. *Journal of Labor Economics, 27*(2), 213–256.

Kahlenberg, K. (2001). *All together now: Creating middle class schools through public school choice.* Washington, DC: Brookings.

Lareau, A. (2011). *Unequal childhoods: Class, race, and family life.* Berkeley, CA: University of California Press.

McPherson, M., Smith-Lovin, L., & Cook, J. M. (2001). Birds of a feather: Homophily in social networks. *Annual Review of Sociology, 27*, 415–444.

Mexican American Legal Defense and Educational Fund, Americans for a Fair Chance, a project of the Leadership Conference on Civil Rights Education Fund, Equal Justice Society, & Society of American Law Teachers. (2005). Blend it, don't end it: Affirmative action and the Texas Ten Percent Plan after Grutter and Gratz. *Harvard Latino Law Review, 8*, 33–92.

Mickelson, R. A., Bottia, M. C., & Lambert, R. (2013). Effects of school racial composition on K–12 mathematics outcomes: A metaregression analysis. *Review of Educational Research, 83*(1), 121–158.

Mickelson, R. A., & Heath, D. (1999). The effects of segregation on African American high school seniors' academic achievement. *The Journal of Negro Education, 68*(4), 566–586.

Moll, R. (1985). *The public Ivy's: A guide to America's best public undergraduate colleges and universities*. New York, NY: Penguin Books.

Morse, R. (2012, October 8). How "exam schools" fared in the Best High Schools Rankings. *US News and World Report*. Retrieved from www.usnews.com/education/blogs/college-rankings-blog/2012/10/18/how-exam-schools-fared-in-the-best-high-schools-rankings.

NAACP Legal Defense and Educational Fund et al. (2012). "Admissions process for New York City's elite public high schools violates Title VI" Retrieved from www.naacpldf.org/files/case_issue/Specialized%20High%20Schools%20Complaint.pdf

Nieto, S. (1994). Lessons from students on creating the chance to dream. *Harvard Educational Review, 64*(5), 392–426.

Novak, T., & Fusco, C. (2014, April 28). Whites getting more spots at top Chicago public high schools. *Chicago Sun Times*. Retrieved from chicago.suntimes.com/article/chicago/whites-getting-more-spots-top-chicago-public-high-schools/sun-04272014-434pm/

Orfield, G., Ayscue, J., Ee, J., Frankenberg, E., Siegel-Hawley, G., Woodward, B., & Amlani, N. (2015). *Better choices for Buffalo's students: Expanding and reforming the criteria schools system* [A Report to Buffalo Public Schools]. Los Angeles, CA: The Civil Rights Project/Proyecto Derechos Civiles.

Orfield, G., & Eaton, S. E. (Eds.). (1996). *Dismantling desegregation: The quiet reversal of Brown v. Board of Education*. New York, NY: The New Press.

Orfield, G., & Frankenberg, E. (Eds.). (2013). *Educational delusions: How choice can deepen inequality and how to make schools fair*. Berkeley, CA: University of California Press.

Orfield, G., & Frankenberg, E. (2014). *Brown at 60: Great progress, a long retreat, and an uncertain future*. Los Angeles, CA: The Civil Rights Project/Proyecto Derechos Civiles.

Parents Involved in Community Schools v. Seattle School District No. 1, 551 U.S. 701 (2007).

Quick, K. (2016). *Chicago public schools: Ensuring diversity in selective enrollment and magnet schools*. Washington, DC: The Century Foundation.

Rumberger, R. (2003). The causes and consequences of student mobility. *The Journal of Negro Education, 72*(1), 6–21.

Schuette v. Coalition to Defend Affirmative Action, 572 U.S. ____ (2014).

Shakarian, K. (2014, November 11). Remaining elite, ensuring diversity: Boston, Chicago & New York wrestle with admissions to special high schools. *Gotham Gazette*. Retrieved from gothamgazette.com/index.php/government/5430-remaining-elite-ensuring-diversity-boston-chicago-a-new-york-wrestle-with-admissions-to-special-high-schools

Siegel-Hawley, G., & Frankenberg, E. (2013). Designing choice: Magnet school structures and racial diversity. In G. Orfield & E. Frankenberg (Eds.), *Educational delusions? Why choice can deepen inequality and how to make schools fair* (pp. 107–128). Berkeley, CA: University of California Press.

Sleeter, C. E. (2007). Preparing teachers for multiracial and historically underserved schools. In E. Frankenberg & G. Orfield (Eds.), *Lessons in integration: Realizing the promise of racial diversity in American schools* (pp. 171–189). Charlottesville, VA: University of Virginia Press.

Soares, J. A. (Ed.). (2012). *SAT wars: The case for test-optional admissions.* New York, NY: Teachers College Press.

Spencer, S. J., Logel, C., & Davies, P. G. (2016). Stereotype threat. *Annual Review of Psychology, 67*, 415–437.

Steele, C. M. (1997). A threat in the air: How stereotypes shape intellectual identity and performance. *American Psychologist, 52*(6), 613–629.

Steele, C. M., & Aronson, J. (1995). Stereotype threat and the intellectual test performance of African Americans. *Journal of Personality and Social Psychology, 69*(5), 797–811.

Swanson, C. B. (2004). Sketching a portrait of public high school graduation: Who graduates? Who doesn't? In G. Orfield (Ed.), *Dropouts in America: Confronting the graduation rate crisis* (pp. 13–40). Cambridge, MA: Harvard Education Press.

Taylor, K. (2016, 9 March). Legislators seek to promote diversity at elite public high schools. *The New York Times.* Retrieved from www.nytimes.com/2016/03/10/nyregion/legislators-seek-to-promote-diversity-at-specialized-schools.html

Tienda, M., & Niu, S. X. (2006). Capitalizing on segregation, pretending neutrality: College admissions and the Texas Top 10% Law. *American Law and Economics Review, 8*(2), 312–346.

U.S. Department of Education. (2012). *Civil rights data collection, 2011–2012: National and state estimations.* Retrieved from ocrdata.ed.gov/StateNationalEstimations/Estimations_2011_12

U.S. Department of Education. (2017). *Improving outcomes for all students: Strategies and considerations to increase student diversity.* Washington, DC: Author.

U.S. Department of Justice & U.S. Department of Education. (2011). *Guidance on the voluntary use of race to achieve diversity and avoid racial isolation in elementary and secondary schools.* Washington, DC: Author. Retrieved from www2.ed.gov/about/offices/list/ocr/docs/guidance-ese-201111.pdf

Villegas, A., & Irvine, J. (2010). Diversifying the teaching force: An examination of major arguments. *Urban Review, 42*, 175–192.

Villegas, A. M., & Lucas, T. F. (2005). Diversifying the teacher workforce: A retrospective and prospective analysis. *Yearbook of the National Society for the Study of Education, 103*(1), 70–104.

Wessman v. Gittens, 160 F.3d 790 (1st Cir. 1998).

Wong, A. (2014, December 4). The cutthroat world of elite public schools. *The Atlantic.* Retrieved from www.theatlantic.com/education/archive/2014/12/the-cutthroat-world-of-elite-public-schools/383382/

Wong, A. (2015, March 5). How to solve the diversity problem at NYC's elite public schools. *The Atlantic.* Retrieved from www.theatlantic.com/education/archive/2015/03/how-to-solve-the-diversity-problem-at-nycs-elite-public-schools/386944/

Yun, J. T., & Moreno, J. F. (2006). College access, K–12 concentrated disadvantage, and the next 25 years of education research. *Educational Researcher, 35*(1), 12–19.

CHAPTER 7

Research, Politics, and Civil Rights
What Happened to Our Recommendations

Gary Orfield and Jennifer B. Ayscue

Successful schools in big cities where there are few good options in the public school system generate serious conflict about these scarce and precious opportunities. In a city with a history of discrimination as well as present conditions of serious segregation by race and class, it is very likely that students are stratified by both and that opportunities are offered largely to the most successful students who come from families and schools with resources. When such schools were originally created as part of the solution to a history of racial discrimination, as Buffalo's were, they typically were set up with explicit goals for student and faculty desegregation alongside corresponding policies to assure that desegregation would occur. Once a federal district court's mandatory desegregation plan ends and the requirements are lifted, the tendency is for schools to become more and more selective. When they become exam schools requiring high test scores for admission, increasing selectivity is very likely to occur and to be defended as being based on merit, implemented by decisionmakers who assume that issues of racial discrimination are a thing of the past. Schools, like colleges, tend to want the most highly skilled students, and exclusiveness often strengthens their prestige.

The fact that there had been an official finding of a statistically significant lack of Black students in Buffalo's elite schools by the U.S. Department of Education's Office for Civil Rights (OCR) created the conditions for our involvement in Buffalo Public Schools (BPS). Producing change in the racially discriminatory practices that are part of the status quo and strongly defended locally is very hard. Accomplishing change in the allocation of very scarce spaces in highly valued schools is, of course, especially difficult.

One of the basic reasons the Civil Rights Project bid for this assignment was that we wanted to understand the dynamics of choice in big cities more clearly and to have the kind of access to the inner workings of a system and its data that researchers do not normally get. We wanted to think through remedies that could change the outcomes. Our goal was to find successful remedies for Buffalo students. We were also thinking about systems of choice schools across the country and looking for lessons to be learned and communicated.

We believe that we have designed methods and proposed remedies that can be applied in many different settings. Those remedies include voluntary plans that can be adopted by school districts that have a local majority of board members and administrators who want to make their choice systems both effective and fair, and to make schools of choice genuine community assets and strategic assets in the battle to preserve public schools. We wanted to generate solutions that would actually work and create real gains for the community and the school system, since a plan that does not work gives the victims of discrimination no gains and diminishes their right to make new claims.

THE SOCIAL AND POLITICAL CONTEXT FOR OUR RESEARCH

In taking this assignment, we knew that there would be many challenges, some of which were evident from a quick look at the basic racial statistics. Buffalo was hypersegregated and had been for a long time—stratified by neighborhoods, metro suburbs, and schools. We also knew, of course, that communities and school systems do not like being investigated for civil rights violations and that local educators sincerely believe that they are doing good things for communities of color.

We soon learned that the school board was deeply divided by both race and basic goals. Just months before our study began, the school board election in 2014 had produced a majority supported by business groups committed to both charter expansion and high-stakes testing, and in active conflict with the teachers union. As we did our work, all the members of the board majority were White. On the other side were four Black women members with considerable experience in the school district and the support of the teachers union, which had been working without a contract for years. There had been a succession of interim superintendents. The African American community and the growing immigrant communities had big problems but limited power, and the four African American board members were powerless to block the new majority. The city schools were short of money (the city government rather than the district controlled the budget), and most of the schools had been classified as failing by the state's new testing system—a system that had sharply raised the standards and that had mechanisms to put schools or even the district in receivership, thereby granting an independent receiver the authority to manage and operate the school or district. The state was pursuing a pro-charter policy, so "failing" schools were often given to charter operators. The pro-charter majority, who called themselves the "reform" group, was strongly committed to fight for a teacher contract that increased demands on teachers. When this group took over in 2014, they announced a six-point plan that included increasing seats in high-performing schools by 3,400 through a major expansion of charter schools (which they considered high-performing by definition though their actual performance varied widely) and a significant increase in the size of the public school system's most successful schools. The plan called for offering incentives to local and national charter groups to expand, allowing some students to transfer to suburban districts, providing private school vouchers, and increasing spaces in the two most successful public schools.

In the state of New York at the time, the state Regents testing system had placed increasing demands on the schools—demands which many urban schools and districts had been unable to meet. As a result, many high-poverty schools without high test scores had been placed in receivership or were threatened with that process, which could include measures such as closing the school and, under the charter law, transferring the school to a charter that would not face the same sanctions. These policies were strongly supported by the BPS board's majority.

The most politically and economically powerful member of the new majority was Carl Paladino. Buffalo was in the midst of a strong push for charter schools, actively supported by businesses in the city, including schools that Paladino was invested in or that were renting space from him while he was a board member. He was one of the wealthiest citizens of western New York and an archconservative who had run as a GOP candidate for governor and would later co-chair the New York presidential campaign of Donald Trump. His style was harsh and confrontational and involved personal and racial attacks on the school board's minority members. He was contemptuous of external pressure regarding civil rights and generated a bitter division within the board. He also had a strong personal involvement in the business side of charter expansion. A 2015 study analyzed Paladino's $25.6 million financial involvement with local charter schools:

> He is the sole investor in Tapestry Charter School, West Buffalo Charter School and will be finalizing the deal for the former Community Charter School Building which will become home to Charter School of Inquiry in 2015. He holds half a stake in Health Sciences Charter School, Charter School for Applied Technologies and Aloma D Johnson Charter School. (German, 2015, p. 35)

> Paladino also received $685,000 of tax incentives from the Erie County Development Agency. (German, 2015, p. 34)

Alongside the strong support for charter schools by the board's majority, another central factor in Buffalo was the state's very-high-stakes evaluation system. Governor Andrew Cuomo, in league with charter supporters, defined more than 170 New York schools in the lowest-scoring 5% of schools as failures or "priority" schools because of low test scores (Woodruff, 2015, p. 1). When priority schools did not make substantial progress, they were defined as "out of time" schools and were opened to charter conversion, which was treated as an educational remedy. In 2013, the state commissioner of education, John King (who became U.S. Secretary of Education at the end of the Obama Administration), had released the scores from a more demanding set of standards and reported drastic declines in the percentage of students attaining the state's prescribed scores to be defined as proficient. The state had raised the cut point to be considered proficient, and therefore a far larger share of students were thus defined as failing. But this outcome was often inaccurately reported as a dramatic decline in performance. A headline in *The New York Times* read, "Test Scores Sink as NY Adopts Higher Benchmarks" (Hernández & Gebeloff, 2013). This perception of an academic crisis, which was a direct misreading of changes produced by raising the standards and not by any decline in performance, was one of the factors that drove the accountability system (Cronin & Jensen, 2014) and supported the argument that more charters were needed (even though the charters were not subject to the same accountability system). When a public school was sold to a private charter company and public funds were used to pay off the mortgage, the public was actually transferring ownership to a private group or individual subject to very little public control. Charters were a highly organized lobbying force in the state.

The challenging circumstances we encountered in Buffalo reflected its history. As a city with classic problems of urban decay, Buffalo has a long history of racially polarized, poorly financed, and deeply divided educational policy. A study published a half-century ago described Buffalo as having "a political system that borders on chaos" and called it an "undeveloped democracy" (Crain, 1968, p. 59). The city was rife with scandals, and at that time, school politics and funding were caught in a battle between supporters of public and Catholic schools, as they are now divided between supporters of public and charter schools. The city was intensely segregated, and there were many largely unsuccessful battles over segregation (Crain, 1968, pp. 60–68) until the case finally went to a federal court, which changed things until the court order was dropped. The researcher of that earlier era noted the way in which individual board members could paralyze the district: "The presence of a single person who chooses to harass the superintendent and the other board members by taking campaigns to the public can almost immobilize the board" (Crain, 1968, p. 69). Our study, a half-century later, encountered a board that was profoundly divided between charter and public school supporters and a single person determined to disrupt the process, who mobilized such extreme racial hostility that his ideas triggered a huge local conflict. There was much about Buffalo that had deep historic roots.

Moreover, the divisions within the school board reflected the demographics of Buffalo and the greater metropolitan area. The 2000 Census showed that Buffalo was the seventh most segregated metropolitan area in the United States. The city had an unusually wide racial gap in earnings for both Blacks and Latinos, there were almost no Black-owned businesses, and Blacks were only one-sixth as likely as Whites to attend private schools. There has been a history of intense White opposition to school and housing integration efforts (Thomas, 2004). The history of discrimination by school and housing officials made Buffalo very vulnerable to the school desegregation lawsuit, *Arthur v. Nyquist*, which as noted above was decided in 1976, finding both the school board and city officials guilty of intentionally segregating the city's schools (Thomas, 2004). For the next 19 years, the board and city government were under court-ordered desegregation until the case was closed in 1995 and the schools rapidly resegregated. It was in this environment that we conducted our research.

CONFRONTING POLITICS

Being out-of-towners who had a temporary role and a responsibility to create the most credible possible independent data and findings, we tried to obtain all relevant data from as many sources as possible. Those sources included the district's data system; surveys of parents, teachers, and students; interviews of principals and district officials; focus groups; community meetings; a hotline; and others as described in Chapter 2. We successfully kept our work completely secret until it was done. During the course of our data-gathering, there was only one incident that became public.

An alumni group from one of the city's high schools wrote to Orfield, objecting to the proposed transfer of the facility for use by charter schools while our study was going on. Since there was already discussion within the study team about the need for new schools, Orfield responded to the group that it would not be a good idea to make potentially irreversible decisions about facilities in the midst of an investigation that would be finished soon and whose goal was to produce research-based solutions that could impact schools and facilities. When the alumni group sent the letter and the response to the school board, they became public documents and generated a debate and a fierce attack on our study by Carl Paladino. Paladino sent Orfield the following email:

> Thank you for your response Dr. Orfield. I'm sorry if I wasn't clear. You were retained to advise on one issue. Now in your own smug way you seek to control the future action of the BOE, obviously after being brainwashed by members of the BOE minority.
>
> Other majority members of the BOE and I have spent a great deal of time and resources planning changes to the dynamic of the dysfunctional BPS. The opposition wants to preserve the status quo and to do so they seek to co-opt your effort and delay our action. That will not happen. You say you don't want to get involved in the local dispute but you side with the opposition with your demand for a standstill.
>
> Your civil rights issue has nothing to do with our intended changes and we will not be intimidated nor will we slow our speed in implementing policy or other changes directed at educating our children while you and OCR deliberate. Our mandate from the citizens of Buffalo is to face down and destroy the obstacles to providing an education for 34,000 kids.
>
> Your effort to control our mission is exactly the type of impediment that has historically frustrated any effort to change the status quo. The nonsense of allowing you or the Justice Department to interfere and slow our process of change is the reason good people with common sense refuse to get involved and the reason that our urban systems are operated by idiot less than competent leadership intent on self empowerment with no regard for breaking down the cycle of poverty in our urban centers.
>
> **Stay out of our way Dr.** [emphasis added]

Paladino obviously believed that the district's majority group should decide the limits of the federal civil rights study, and his contemptuous attitude toward the OCR effort and the African American board members was unambiguous. Orfield sent his letter to OCR, and we made no changes to our study design. The incident was a strong warning of conflict to come.

UNEXPECTED CHANGES TO THE CONTEXT FOR OUR STUDY

We did not, however, know what was happening at the same time we were doing our work. In the fall of 2014, as our civil rights study was under way, the New York commissioner of education, John King (a former charter school principal and, as noted above, future Obama administration Secretary of Education), designated two Buffalo high schools as "out of time" and cited two other schools for poor state test performance. His letter to the district asked for a response to the commissioner in less than two weeks.

In response, the very next day, the board majority requested that the commissioner approve an extra round of charter applications for the four schools. After less than an hour's discussion, the five-member "reform" group made this request. Subsequently, the four African American members of the board protested that the commissioner's rapid decision to authorize more charters might undermine the ongoing civil rights study. Their letter pointed out that Buffalo was the only city in New York that faced this additional charter school round and said that the process "raises serious questions about whether or not a concerted effort exists to intentionally frustrate remedial options necessary to bring the Buffalo Public School District into compliance with federal anti-racial discrimination laws" (Belton-Cottman, Harris-Tigg, Kapsiak, & Seals-Nevergold, 2014). The district was being changed right in the middle of our study.

PRESENTING OUR REPORT

When the report was completed in May 2015 (Orfield et al., 2015), Orfield returned to Buffalo to brief the school district staff, meet with each school board member, meet with the reporters and editorial board at the *Buffalo News*, and make a public presentation to the board. He outlined and discussed the report with each board member except Paladino, who refused to attend a meeting. The report presented strong data on the obstacles that students faced; their relationships to educational opportunity; the desires of the parents, teachers, and community; and the ideas of principals and administrators regarding what was feasible. The report identified many problems and suggested solutions for them.

The briefing of administrators went well. The interim superintendent was in broad agreement with the report and saw it as an important opportunity for the district. We asked district staff for any factual corrections and received very few.

The state-appointed monitor for the district praised the report as an important opportunity for the system.

Then the report was posted on the Internet for all to see. The local media covered the report seriously. The team did not have funds for more trips to Buffalo but said repeatedly that we would be happy to answer questions or discuss the issues with anyone who wanted information or to exchange ideas.

It became clear that advocates of the most successful schools were especially worried about two things—that we would make recommendations that would lower the standards of those schools and that we would suggest changes in the admissions process that would decrease the opportunities for their children or their community. We took a strong position that high academic standards were important and proposed no changes in curriculum, but broader admissions standards were essential to expand access to the benefits of those standards to low-income students of color who were so strongly underrepresented. The schools were seen locally as very important assets, and admissions were viewed as a zero-sum game.

Our basic answer was that BPS should not reallocate the existing pie but that the district should expand the pie or create more equally good pies. We proposed a second City Honors High School, which was the central focus of the battle, with no lowering of academic demands on the students but with much more effort to diversify admissions, much like the affirmative action policies at leading colleges. A conscious change in recruitment strategies and policy would be needed in order to increase the diversity of admissions. Once our report was complete, the district was then obliged to respond to our recommendations.

THE CHALLENGES OF CIVIL RIGHTS ENFORCEMENT

The first part of a civil rights enforcement process is documenting the violations. The second part is determining what kinds of remedies could address the problem. The third part is having an appropriate authority adopt and order the changes, if they cannot be agreed to voluntarily. Then comes the most critical and difficult part of the process—getting the institution that created the violations to administer a remedy it usually does not want. A fundamental reality is that the places where the violation is most obvious and where big changes are needed are also the most difficult places to institute remedies. Although federal officials and courts have a great deal of potential power, those who implement changes are hired and their careers unfold under local administrators and boards of education.

The problems in Buffalo were the result of social pressures and practices in a city that had been extremely segregated and polarized for generations, with actions by officials that fostered inequality, divisions within the school district, and a school administration with limited expertise and no clear vision. All of these problems persisted throughout our investigation and continued after we made our recommendations. Particularly difficult were the divisions within the school board and the instability of the district's leadership. The report came in the midst of a very strong division on the school board between a White conservative majority and a Black minority, which was allied with the teachers union and strongly supported civil rights but was unable to act. The four African American members were repeatedly voted down and sometimes insulted. The divisions were raw.

NEGOTIATIONS BETWEEN OCR AND BPS

Once the report was out, however, our formal job was done, and except for some media inquiries, we had very little involvement in what happened next. Our recommendations formed the basis for negotiation between the district and OCR. Fortunately, we had filed an extensive written report explaining the basis for our conclusions and recommendations, and that document remained on record and accessible (Orfield et al., 2015). The Civil Rights Project always demands the right to publish its findings when undertaking a study.

After receiving our recommendations in May 2015 (Table 7.1), BPS deliberated about how to move forward and negotiated with OCR through October 2015. While BPS accepted many of our recommendations about information and convenience, they ultimately did not comply with some of the most essential remedies regarding actually changing the basic criteria or increasing capacity—recommendations that were central to our approach. Specifically, BPS did not accept our

Table 7.1. Recommendations for Expanding Equity and Access in BPS Criteria Schools

Information	• Develop a diversity plan and recruitment strategies • Create Parent Information Center with bilingual staff • Provide materials in top five languages utilized in district • Conduct in-person recruitment through road shows and school visits
Preparation	• Implement a summer preparatory program • Provide counseling and peer tutoring to support retention
Admissions Criteria	• Conduct holistic admissions with flexible thresholds • Discontinue use of NY state assessment scores • Weight grades more than tests • Allocate 10% of seats for students deserving special consideration • End neighborhood preference for Olmsted Elementary
Support Services	• Hire bilingual staff • Provide information about services for ELs and special education students
Availability of Choices	• Create two additional criteria high schools • Create at least one additional criteria elementary school • Revise hiring process for new criteria schools
Regional and State Partnerships	• Launch a regional magnet school • Ask city government to prosecute residential discrimination • Clarify the state of the law

Source: Adapted from Ayscue et al. (2016).

recommendations to discontinue the use of New York state assessment scores (although the state officials themselves expressed serious reservations), deemphasize the cognitive admissions test, set aside 10% of seats for students demonstrating potential in other ways, end the neighborhood preference for Olmsted Elementary School, and create a second City Honors High School.

On August 14, 2015, BPS submitted an initial response to OCR. In the response, BPS outlined the ways in which the district would or would not comply with our recommendations. However, on September 1, 2015, OCR rejected BPS's response because it failed to address each and every one of our recommendations. OCR requested that BPS revise its response to indicate its intentions regarding each recommendation that had not been addressed in the initial response (Cash, 2015). In this letter, OCR reminded the district that "OCR may initiate administrative enforcement or judicial proceedings to enforce the specific terms and obligations of the agreement, which could result in the suspension of federal financial assistance from the Department" (Cash, 2015, p. 7).

In turn, on September 24, 2015, BPS submitted a more detailed reply to OCR that addressed all recommendations (Buffalo City School District [sic], 2015). In this response, BPS accepted many, but certainly not all, of the recommendations that we had proposed. To guide the overall process, BPS agreed to develop mission and vision statements as well as a diversity plan with a recruitment strategy that would include specific outreach activities such as holding a district-wide high school showcase, reestablishing road shows, and providing materials in the district's top five languages. The district agreed that the BPS superintendent would appoint a cabinet-level administrator to oversee the criteria-based schools. To address outreach and information dissemination, BPS agreed to create a Parent Information Office at the Central Registration building, redesign the district website, and provide easily accessible information about applications, admissions, and enrollment. To expand the available choices, the district agreed to transform a current school into a high-standards, arts-focused elementary school, seek funding for a regional magnet, focus on whole-school magnets instead of school-within-a-school magnets, and consider a dual-language-immersion, criteria-based school. At the existing and new criteria-based schools, BPS agreed to change staffing procedures, create a summer bridge program, and provide after-school programs. Finally, BPS agreed to clarify the state of the law (since the incorrect belief that the law forbade positive integration steps was common in the district) and to request that the city government actively prosecute residential discrimination. While these agreements addressed many of our recommendations, BPS "modified" some of our largest and potentially most influential recommendations for structural change that would have expanded opportunity and access.

Regarding our recommendations on admissions criteria, BPS proposed to accept some of them and reject others. Importantly, BPS agreed to end the use of absolute cut points for any single criterion and instead proposed to use cumulative scoring to examine admissions criteria in a more holistic manner. It planned to hire an outside agency to develop an algorithm based on the prior four years of student success at the criteria-based schools in order to determine how to weight different criteria. The district also agreed to administer the entrance exam for City Honors and Olmsted at students' home schools rather than on Saturdays at single locations. However, it rejected our recommendations to discontinue the use of the state assessments. The district also chose not to include personal assets as part of its algorithm, instead choosing to explore this recommendation after an initial period of using the algorithm and determining how effective it was at improving equity in admissions.

Rather than agreeing to set aside 10% of seats for students demonstrating potential or those coming from neighborhoods that are not normally represented in criteria-based schools, the district stated it would explore the idea further, solicit feedback, and conduct legal review of the recommendation. Essentially, the district agreed to consider the idea but did not agree to implement any change.

Similarly, the district rejected our recommendation to end the neighborhood preference for Olmsted Elementary, arguably the most important point of access for criteria-based schools. Instead, BPS agreed to task the school staff with making recommendations about how to expand citywide access to the school and to seek public input. Again, BPS essentially agreed to consider the idea but did not commit to any course of action after the exploratory work.

Likewise, the district did not accept our recommendation regarding faculty diversity. BPS agreed to a legal review of our recommendation to adopt an affirmative action plan for faculty diversity. However, it stated that it would consider moving forward with such a plan only after legal review. Affirmative action employment plans for faculty are widespread across the country.

In terms of expanding access by creating new criteria-based schools, the district laid out a plan that essentially appeared to take its preexisting plans for school redesigns and plug them in as solutions for our recommendations, without truly considering the intent behind our recommendations or the desired outcome. One of our most important recommendations was to create a second high school in the model of City Honors, the most academically successful school in the district. However, BPS rejected this recommendation altogether. Instead, the district explained that it would comply with our recommendation to create two new criteria-based schools each year for the second and third years of this reform by creating four new schools in upcoming years, as follows. In 2015–2016, the district proposed to expand Emerson School of Hospitality. In 2016–2017, BPS would create a Montessori High School that would be aligned with the existing Montessori Elementary School and would also create Research Laboratory High School for Life Sciences and Bio-Informatics. In 2017–2018, BPS planned to integrate a gifted and talented strand at Marva J. Daniels Futures Prep Academy. While these proposed schools would be important additions to the options for the district, none of them would provide the expanded opportunity that was intended through the creation of a second City Honors. A number of them had already been part of the district's preexisting plans.

OCR did not accept the second version of the district's plan. On October 15, 2015, OCR responded to BPS and asked for further clarification about numerous issues (Blanchard, 2015). OCR sought clarification about the district's decision to delay or reject our recommendations to set aside 10% of seats, end the neighborhood preference at Olmsted Elementary, and create a City Honors II. In addition, OCR asked for clarification regarding the proposed admissions algorithm, especially the choice to include state assessment scores and not consider personal assets. The OCR staff never communicated with our team.

BPS replied to OCR's questions on October 23, 2015, in a document that contained 53 responses (Buffalo Public Schools, 2015). While BPS provided additional clarification, the district did not change its stance on any of the responses. OCR accepted BPS's reply, and negotiations concluded. Barbara Nevergold, who would become president of the BPS school board after the 2016 election switched control of the board, sees the failure of OCR to continue applying pressure on key issues as a fundamental weakness of the process (B. Nevergold, personal communication, August 28, 2017). OCR never discussed these issues with our research group.

CHANGE IN DISTRICT LEADERSHIP

In August 2015, the board unanimously appointed Superintendent Kriner Cash, an African American educator who had led the Memphis public school system. The program he brought to BPS, the New Education Bargain, included community schools, smaller class sizes, early literacy programs, and more career programs. His commitment to accountability and testing policies won him support from the conservative board members and from state officials. As he took over, "nearly half of the Buffalo schools [were] in receivership, and many more could follow," and the entire district was threatened with receivership (Lankes, 2015). Cash was also seen favorably by a number of African American educators for his other initiatives.

Cash named Kevin Eberle to the position of chief operating officer. Eberle was a former principal who had managed the campaign of one of the "reform" group members and had been Carl Paladino's choice for superintendent.

Cash did not name Rashondra Martin to continue as the district's general counsel. She had been personally insulted at a board meeting when, in February 2015, Paladino had attacked her, saying, "How can you be so ignorant?" She had filed a civil rights complaint but was subsequently fired by the board. She was replaced by a new lawyer, Edward Betz, who had been a campaign manager for one of the "reform" board members (Williams, 2016). Although he had no school law experience when he took the position, Betz received a 26% salary increase over what Martin had earned.

THE TWO SUBSEQUENT SCHOOL YEARS

After the negotiations concluded early in the 2015–2016 school year, BPS implemented several changes that had the potential to lead to improved access and equity in the criteria-based schools. The cognitive abilities assessment was administered at students' home schools rather than at one location on Saturdays, resulting in 1,900 students taking the test, a substantial increase of 700 students (Lankes, 2016). BPS also changed the admissions formula, thereby ending absolute cut points on the test. In addition, the district hired an outside agency, rather than using school committees, to rank students for admission, but the same basic process was used.

During the 2016–2017 school year, after the previous minority took 6–3 control of the board, BPS took additional steps to remove more barriers to accessing the criteria-based schools. The district eliminated the requirement for teacher recommendations in order to address any potential for implicit bias. In a separate decision, unrelated to our recommendations, the board suspended the use of New York state assessments, and it plans to reconsider the use of such assessments after the New York State Education Department completes its revisions to the assessments. BPS also eliminated the application process for City Honors and Olmsted; rather than adding a student to the applicant pool only after the parents submitted an application, the new approach specified that by completing the cognitive abilities assessment, students would automatically be entered into the applicant pool. These changes contributed to a more than doubling of applicants for City Honors and Olmsted, from 750 applicants in 2015 to 1,658 in 2016 (Keresztes, 2016).

However, without adopting several of our most important recommendations, the results were disappointing. Instead of expanding access and creating a more racially diverse student body, the opposite occurred. The share of African American students at City Honors and Olmsted decreased slightly between the 2015–2016 and 2016–2017 school years, from 18.0% to 17.6% and 41.9% to 40.8%, respectively (Keresztes, 2016). Acknowledging this setback, Associate Schools Superintendent and Chief of Intergovernmental Affairs Will Keresztes, who had been centrally involved throughout this process, stated, "With regard to the criteria-based schools, we still have more work to do." Sam Radford, president of the District Parent Coordinating Council and one of the original parties who brought this complaint to OCR, said, "I think that we need to look at the structural changes that will lead to more minority students in top-performing schools," and emphasized the need for a more diverse teaching force. He referred to the changes that had thus far been implemented, such as administering the admissions test at students' home schools, as "window dressing." Underscoring the need to address the opportunity gap in the district, Associate Superintendent Keresztes stated, "We think all of the barriers will be removed to access admissions into these schools, but that doesn't mean we have closed the achievement gap, so we need to ask the hard question, and that is, are schools across the district and parents adequately preparing students so that they can compete for a spot at these schools?" (Buckley, 2016, para. 5). In November 2016, the board discussed our recommendation to set aside seats for students demonstrating potential. They considered developing a policy to "apportion seats for qualified students underrepresented in student enrollment at any school." As of fall 2017, nothing had been done about creating the recommended new schools to expand the spaces for demanding academic training, but a report to the board showing a second year of failure to increase the Black enrollment at City Honors revived local discussion.

In September 2017, the district released a report finding that not only had their plan failed for the second year, but that there was actually a slight decline in the number and share of African American students at City Honors and Olmsted, despite an increase in the number of applicants (Keresztes, 2017). At City Honors, the proportion of African American students declined from 17.6% to 16.4% between 2016–2017 and 2017–2018. At Olmsted, the share of African American students dropped from 40.8% to 38.92% over the same time period. Sam Radford, president of the District Parent Coordinating Council, said that the district was just recycling the same old choice process without adequate changes.

In addition to the district's failure to expand access to criteria-based schools, another disappointment arose from the district's lack of interest in using the extensive information about parent and teacher preferences that our report provided. Having been involved with the release of many sensitive documents related to other reports, the study director and staff reached out as broadly as possible for information in this investigation. We took extraordinary steps to obtain information and make contact with BPS constituencies that are usually hard to reach and often ignored—low-income families of color from the poorest parts of the district. Local survey experts told us that a paper or online parent survey would get little response, especially from these groups, and that a telephone survey was impossible because most parents communicated on cell phones and many of their cell phone numbers changed during the school year. Heeding these warnings, we adopted extensive procedures to reach out to parents. As described in Chapter 2, we asked all the homeroom teachers to update and submit a new list of cell phone numbers just before the survey. We then had the numbers called up to 15 times to obtain the best possible response. This approach was critical to generating some of the important findings of the report, such as the fact that only 5% of the parents were accessing information about the schools on the Internet, which was the key information source according to the district's plan. We had the only valid information on parent preferences from our challenging and expensive survey, but their responses were largely ignored by BPS. In the process of our work, we learned that the school district had little real communication with the district's parents. It was disappointing to see how this kind of information, which is rarely available to school policymakers, was ignored on some of the most important issues in our report, issues on which the three sectors—parents, students, and staff—had very similar views. Likewise, our recommendations for making changes in the union contract, particularly for staffing the choice schools more effectively rather than through seniority preference, were favored by most teachers who responded to the survey but went nowhere.

THE RACIAL AND POLITICAL CONTEXT
IN WHICH CIVIL RIGHTS NEGOTIATIONS OCCURRED

As an indication of the racial and political polarization in which these negotiations and plans for the future of BPS were unfolding, a major racial scandal on the board exploded in late 2016. When asked by a local reporter about his hopes for the New Year, board member Paladino expressed his wishes in the most classic, extreme racist imagery, suggesting that Black people belong in the jungle with primitive animals. Escalating the impact of the statement even further was the focus of the comment—President Barack Obama and First Lady Michelle Obama. Responding to questions from the local publication *Artvoice*—"What would you most like to happen in 2017?" and "What would you like to see go away in 2017?"—Paladino expressed his hopes as follows:

1. Obama catches mad cow disease after being caught having relations with a Hereford. He dies before his trial and is buried in a cow pasture next to Valerie Jarret {a senior advisor to President Obama], who died weeks prior, after being convicted of sedition and treason, when a Jihady cell mate mistook her for being a nice person and decapitated her.
2. Michelle Obama. I'd like her to return to being a male and let loose in the outback of Zimbabwe where she lives comfortably in a cave with Maxie, the gorilla. (Moses, 2016, Carl Paladino section)

The racial attack on President and Mrs. Obama in the last days of the administration triggered a tidal wave of protest, as thousands of local citizens signed petitions calling for Paladino's removal from the school board. The statement was widely denounced, including by the Trump transition team and New York Governor Cuomo, and the board passed a resolution asking for his immediate resignation a week later, calling on state officials to remove him if he refused. Paladino refused, and the process dragged on, with protesters at every meeting until he was finally removed (on other grounds) in August 2017.

Before his removal, he fought the reelection of Barbara Nevergold as the board president in July 2017. Paladino himself was nominated and, though defeated, he received three votes in spite of the Obama racial incident scandal and the pending state investigaton, thus illustrating the continuing polarization of the board (Rey, 2017). At one of the last meetings he attended, Paladino objected to a ruling by the chair permitting protesters to participate in the meeting. He called 911 and City Hall to urge the arrest of the protesters during that meeting. Even after his dismissal for improperly disclosing confidential information in August 2015, Paladino attacked the school budget in hearings by the city government and sued the state board of education. His removal led to a new appointment giving the more progressive part of the board a 7–2 majority and, ironically, opening up the possibility of more action on the issues that Paladino had fought against. These incidents underscore the reality that doing policy work on civil rights issues can be unique in its intensity.

THE ABSENCE OF STRONG LEADERSHIP FROM BPS AND OCR

As noted above, the OCR report came to a bitterly divided school board in which the civil rights supporters had a minority, the vocal majority was hostile toward civil rights, and no superintendent was in place. Two months after the report was released, Kriner Cash was appointed superintendent. Barbara Nevergold, who later became board chair, says (and a memo from Paladino confirms) that Cash was selected because he favored high-stakes testing and charter school expansion. None of the interim or regular superintendents provided any strong leadership on the OCR issues. Although the charter supporters were finally defeated in the 2015 election, the three new board members were, Nevergold said, overwhelmed by learning the job and were unable to focus on these issues (B. Nevergold, personal communication, August 28, 2017).

Board President Nevergold further noted, in retrospect, that OCR did not provide strong feedback or follow-through and therefore, the board felt "no push from OCR," which could have moved the process forward. In addition, time was of the essence, she added, because the entire board would be up for reelection again in 2019 (B. Nevergold, personal communication, August 28, 2017).

In September 2017, two years after BPS had rejected key elements of the plan we designed, the district reported that the changes in the way the cognitive abilities assessment tests were administered (doing them at the students' home schools rather than at a central location) had indeed greatly increased participation in the test. However, it had produced no progress in terms of representation at City Honors, and the Black share of the enrollment had actually declined more (Keresztes, 2017). The *Buffalo News* responded with a recognition of the failure and a strong editorial endorsement of the creation of a second City Honors high school, as we had recommended two years earlier (News Editorial Board, 2017). "It makes no sense for the district to limit access to its top-flight education to the number of slots available and relegate other qualified students to decidedly weaker schools" (News Editorial Board, 2017, para. 13). The District Parent Coordinating Council concluded that the plan outlined in the report would work only if all major elements were implemented and called on the board to take action. What had seemed to be a dead end was turning in a new direction, reflecting both leadership changes and the evidence that piecemeal procedural changes were simply not working. Superintendent Cash expressed his view that a new approach was necessary to achieve the needed progress. It is important for researchers to remember that policymaking is not an event but a process, and that ideas defeated at one stage may become viable again following political changes or changes in professional beliefs. Good research can have a second life under the right circumstances.

REFERENCES

Arthur v. Nyquist, 415 F. Supp. 904 (1976).

Belton-Cottman, S., Harris-Tigg, T., Kapsiak, M. R., & Seals-Nevergold, B. (2014, November 15). [Letter to Merryl H. Tisch, Robert M. Bennett, & John B. King]. Copy in possession of Barbara Seals-Nevergold.

Blanchard, T. C. J. (2015, October 15). [Letter to Kriner Cash]. Buffalo Public Schools. Retreived from www.buffaloschools.org/files/news/ocr%20letter%20dated%2010%20 15%2015-2.pdf

Buckley, E. (2016, June 23). Looking toward changes to admissions for criteria-based schools. *WBFO*. Retrieved from news.wbfo.org/post/looking-toward-changes-admissions-criteria-based-schools

Buffalo City School District [sic]. (2015, September 25). Table of response(s) to consultant's recommendations and implementation plan (Case No. 02-14-1077). Buffalo Public Schools, Buffalo, NY.

Buffalo Public Schools. (2015, October 23). Working draft of letter to the U.S. Department of Education, Office for Civil Rights (Case No. 02-14-1077). Buffalo Public Schools, Buffalo, NY.

Cash, K. (2015, September 2). Letter to board members, Buffalo Public Schools.

Crain, R. L. (1968). *The politics of school desegregation*. Chicago, IL: Aldine Press.

Cronin, J., & Jensen, N. (2014). The phantom collapse of student achievement in New York. *Phi Delta Kappan*, 96(2), 60–67.

German, K. R. (2015). *A financial analysis of Buffalo charter schools: Are charter schools getting their fair share of public funds* (Master's thesis). Retrieved from digitalcommons.buffalostate.edu/mpa_projects/13/

Hernández, J. C., & Gebeloff, R. (2013, August 7). Test scores sink as New York adopts tougher benchmarks. *The New York Times*. Retrieved from www.nytimes.com/2013/08/08/nyregion/under-new-standards-students-see-sharp-decline-in-test-scores.html

Keresztes, W. (2016, November 16). OCR update criteria-based schools (#02-14-1077). Retrieved from www.buffaloschools.org/files/122064/ocr%20ppt.%20update.pdf

Keresztes, W. (2017, September). OCR update, criteria-based schools [PowerPoint Presentation] (Case No. 02-14-1077). Buffalo Public Schools, Buffalo, NY.

Lankes, T. (2015, August 19). New superintendent has support for agenda from board, Albany. *Buffalo News*. Retrieved from buffalonews.com/2015/08/19/new-superintendent-has-support-for-agenda-from-board-albany/

Lankes, T. (2016, February 20). Civil rights expert calls Buffalo's efforts over criteria schools admissions "disappointing." *Buffalo News*. Retrieved from buffalonews.com/2016/02/20/civil-rights-expert-calls-buffalos-efforts-over-criteria-school-admissions-disappointing/

Moses, J. (2016, December 23). What do we want for 2017? We have a lot of different opinions. *Artvoice*. Retrieved from artvoice.com/2016/12/23/want-2017-lot-different-opinions/#.WdkBmGiPI2y

News Editorial Board. (2017, September 28). Editorial: District should create a City Honors II. *Buffalo News*. Retrieved from buffalonews.com/2017/09/28/editorial-district-create-city-honors-ii/

Orfield, G., Ayscue, J., Ee, J., Frankenberg, E., Siegel-Hawley, G., Woodward, B., & Amlani, N. (2015, May). *Better choices for Buffalo's students: Expanding and reforming the criteria schools system*. [A Report to Buffalo Public Schools]. Los Angeles, CA: The Civil Rights Project/Proyecto Derechos Civiles.

Rey, J. (2017, July 6). Nevergold re-elected School Board president despite Paladino opposition. *Buffalo News*. Retrieved from buffalonews.com/2017/07/05/nevergold-re-elected-board-president-despite-paladino-opposition/

Thomas, G. S. (2004, October 29). Turning points #5: Black and white. *Buffalo Business First*. Retrieved from www.bizjournals.com/buffalo/news/2014/06/20/turning-points-5-black-and-white.html

Williams, D. (2016, January 6). Buffalo School Board fires Martin, hires Betz as general counsel. *Buffalo News*. Retrieved from buffalonews.com/2016/01/06/buffalo-school-board-fires-martin-hires-betz-as-general-counsel/

Woodruff, C. (2015 March 16). Cuomo uses "failing" schools label to push receivership takeover model. *On Board Online*. Retrieved from www.nyssba.org/news/2015/03/12/on-board-online-march-16-2015/cuomo-uses-failing-schools-label-to-push-receivership-takeover-model/

Postscript: What We Learned

Gary Orfield

A major challenge is an opportunity to learn, and the Buffalo investigation challenged us to learn fast. We learned a great deal about the barriers to collecting data even under good conditions; we now know more about researching the context needed for understanding mechanisms of inequality and necessary elements of solutions; we witnessed the strength of the political forces and the willingness to attack what we struggled to make a nonpartisan professional study; and we were stimulated to think more deeply about how to communicate priorities effectively in a complex study. Because we were outsiders commissioned to provide expert evidence and advice to both sides, we kept our work confidential until it was published and strictly avoided local politics—but local politics didn't avoid us. We learned how becoming part of a civil rights investigation backed with governmental power offers unique opportunities to researchers but imposes harsh demands and sometimes frustrating conditions.

THINKING ABOUT THE SCOPE

Our work was generated by a conflict over the very limited access of the city's Black students to its best schools. The situation was generated by a choice process and admissions requirements (criteria) that produced a lopsided enrollment of Whites in a heavily non-White system. The system was defended as a merit system by the district and by those who were benefitting from it, but it was seen as discriminatory in the African American community. Because we knew about the deep roots of educational inequality, we had to look very carefully into the nature of the community and the structure of preparation in very unequal schools. Solving severe problems of racial inequality is not about programs, though programs matter; it is about context and structures. It is about strategies to change outcomes in the face of powerful obstacles, often in a politicized environment. In research terms, it means a broader focus and not only thinking through the evidence on likely benefits but also consideration of the fact that changes must be implemented against ongoing opposition. The history of the city's race relations and its great success in creating well-integrated magnet schools a generation ago were important in understanding what needed to change if the problems were to be solved.

We learned a great deal over the course of this intense project. The reality of doing work that really matters, in a tense environment, with a concrete deadline differs in so many ways from classroom exercises or writing for a journal. Good civil rights research differs from traditional academic research because it is interdisciplinary, must take into account legal parameters, has high-stakes deadlines, and unfolds in politically charged contexts that are critical for the outcomes. It is typically not just looking at how one factor impacts one outcome but instead investigating how multiple causes and various structures lead to certain consequences. Civil rights problems tend to have long histories, and making systems fair in a lasting way requires that deep barriers be overcome. These and similar factors no doubt need to be considered further in many studies of reform efforts.

WHAT SEEMS SIMPLE BUT ISN'T

A seemingly simple response to the severe underrepresentation of African American students in the best schools might have been proposing a mechanism that could have transferred some seats at the schools from White to Black students. That could not be done by simply setting aside a certain number of seats because, without a specific official finding of intentional discrimination, that would be illegal under the Supreme Court decision in the 2007 *Parents Involved* case. However, there are other methods for achieving greater representation; for example, we could have recommended a set-aside of seats for students in segregated African American parts of town. But if such a plan was adopted, it would have provoked immediate political and possibly legal attacks, and many students might not have been prepared to succeed in the much more demanding school. That solution would have left the definition of merit unchanged and would have implied that the added students of color did not have merit. Making a very explicit exception to the criteria which many in the city thought were central to the high quality of those schools would have created a destructive zero-sum game where one side lost and the other won. We did not think that this was a good or lasting solution. It would likely have been challenged, and it might not have lasted since civil rights agencies and courts rarely maintain active supervision over a long period of time. Anyone familiar with civil rights remedies knows that they must be defensible over time if they are to last. We knew that there are very few opportunities for communities of color to use the power of civil rights law to precipitate change, so it was very important to our team that the remedies work and continue to work.

A SOLUTION OF EXPANDING OPTIONS

Thinking about alternatives requires understanding of the research and the practical possibilities of creating new structures. One thing about schools of choice that those of us who had worked on magnet school research knew is that creating new magnet schools is not rocket science. A good magnet school needs a leader and faculty dedicated to and able to deliver the curriculum, a focus that is or becomes sufficiently compelling to create a market of people wanting to come to the school, a basic commitment to diversity and outreach, the provision of good information to all, and fair methods of selection. No one is coerced to come to a new magnet school. If it is well done, it expands the opportunities for all groups in a community.

We already knew that City Honors High School had a record of solid academic success and a very positive image, turning away many students who wanted to enroll. So we asked the leaders of the school for their advice about whether it could be duplicated, and we asked the parents and students whether they wanted more choice. We already knew that the demand was far greater than could be handled by the existing school, which the leadership held could not be significantly expanded on site. So duplicating City Honors by creating City Honors II while changing the criteria and admissions processes for both were key recommendations. We were convinced that this solution was feasible and would work. The great advantage would be that this approach would double capacity rather than reallocate scarcity, creating a win-win for both Whites and non-Whites in the city and giving the city another outstanding school. Reaching this decision rested on practical experience, knowledge of research on magnets, and careful checking of conditions on the ground.

We knew from a great deal of research on school and college inequalities that students admitted from weak schools and underresourced families might well have the brains and determination to succeed in a much more difficult school but that they would have a much better start if they were drilled on key academic skills before school opened, which we recommended.

OPERATIONALIZING THE MANDATE

We were firmly committed to carry out the assignment given to us by the agreement between the federal and local authorities, but it was a very vague mandate, as legal and policy statements often are. We were faced with the challenge of translating the stated goal into operational analyses and systematically gathering evidence to support what would become the eventual recommendations for resolving the problem. The Office for Civil Rights (OCR) investigation that triggered this study had only reached conclusions about statistically significant underrepresentation of students of color in two key schools. Our task was to propose solutions for a problem that was the product of a much broader set of issues. The solutions needed not only to propose the creation of a better method for selecting students but also to address the reasons why so few Buffalo students of color were ready to take advantage of what could be a life-changing opportunity.

GAINING ACCESS TO DATA

The great advantage of this assignment compared to normal research was that we had power to not only get data from the school district's files and from data sets but to also create data through original questionnaires and interviews of school leaders and visits to the schools at will. Compared to the normal process of gaining access to a school district and waiting for appointments that have very little priority, we had easy and guaranteed access. Instead of looking at a single aspect, we could look at many components.

The school district complied with our data requests to the extent that they had data and means to retrieve it. Because the district was required to respond to our recommendations, we had real influence, and people wanted to explain their perspectives and give us useful information and ideas. That meant that with a relatively small staff and very limited time in the city, we could learn a great deal and gather good advice and insights from many people. These conditions were remarkably positive. On the other side, the deadline and our limited time in the city meant that we had to focus on findings and recommendations in a short period of time, which was a great challenge.

Researchers should realize that there are some very important opportunities that come together with many challenges of conducting high-stakes policy research. Researchers have to be ready to respond quickly when a policy window creates an opportunity and identify the issues on which it may be possible to reach a firm conclusion in the allotted time. We are glad we took the challenge.

LISTENING TO PARENTS

We cannot assume that a school district or anyone else knows what parents actually want, especially low-income families of color. We dealt with the realities of communications with poor families of color in a big city, which has great implications for research. Most of these families, we learned, did not have high-speed Internet connections at home, and few used them in a way that the schools could count on. Yet middle-class professionals in the district had developed basic information systems that assumed that people were connected. There is an enormous class bias in any system that relies on such communications. We also learned that not only is the phone the most important way to communicate with parents but also that phone numbers in these communities change so often that lists quickly become obsolete, making the schools' robocall system severely inadequate. Even after updating numbers and having professional surveyors call 15 more times after the original call, we were not able to reach many families. Researchers have to be aware that they may not be getting representative information, particularly from low-income families of color, whose children make up the largest group in many urban schools and districts. It quickly became obvious to us that the district had no effective ways of communicating with parents. The best information we could obtain showed that many of these parents were interested in choice and options and that they were getting poor or no information from the system. These facts underscored the importance of our qualitative research. More research is needed since policy often assumes that silence indicates consent or disinterest, but we found that it may be a product of barriers.

Our demographic work in Buffalo and many other areas pointed to an often ignored reality that the growing population of students is related to immigration, and many of these families do not speak or read English. School districts and schools of choice often ignore the family languages of a changing population, even as the district is creating choice systems that require the parents to understand the choices. The underrepresentation of these students in the choice system was severe. Research that speaks to the future of these communities must pay attention to those groups, even though longstanding severe racial issues affecting African American students remain unresolved and the often powerless new groups are not organized. Researchers committed to racial justice must take existing and predictable changes into account in remedies. Communities are constantly changing, and a lasting remedy cannot ignore major changes that are already taking place.

CHALLENGES OF UNSTABLE LEADERSHIP

One of the general problems of school reform in the United States is the lack of consistent policy over time, often correlated with unstable school leadership. The frequent turnover of leadership and its impact were evident in our work. There is nothing, of course, that researchers can do about this, and there was instability at a very high level during the process of our research. We experienced several interim leaders and a new superintendent who came in after the process began, as well as changes on the school board both shortly before we came into the case and not long after we were done. This instability means that researchers are working on very sensitive issues affecting a divided community in an inherently unpredictable environment. We tried to be open to all and wrote a report that documented the evidence and reasoning for our conclusions. The lengthy report we wrote had limited impact on some key issues at first but later turned out to have a greater impact than seemed possible at the time. We did not, however, have any contact with the man who became the superintendent after our work was finished until much later.

FORMULATING REMEDIES

One thing that we learned from our experience is that too complex a remedy makes it too easy for the district to agree on secondary issues, giving the impression of compliance while ignoring some fundamental recommendations. On substantive issues, it is normal for researchers to think about multiple dimensions. It is important, however, to think about clarity and to carefully emphasize the most essential priorities while considering the capacity of the institution to manage complexity. We thought we had done that, but we did not have contact after the report was filed, so we could not interact with those making decisions in the administration and on the board. What happened after the report was presented showed us that if you make too long a list of recommendations and do not sufficiently highlight those that are absolutely central, the organization can say that it is complying with a number of details while it actually rejects the most important recommendations and those that may be the most difficult to implement amid local politics.

THE ROLE OF RESEARCHERS

Researchers play a special role because of their expertise. We had no previous contacts with the key actors in Buffalo. It was vital to us that the research be carried out professionally and reported honestly. Too often government agencies and school districts select researchers or firms whose work can be controlled and directed and with whom they have a continuing relationship. These conditions do not lead to good research. The researchers here were not selected because of political skills, and the team had the right to publish their data and conclusions without approval or review by either side. We had no preexisting conclusions or ongoing roles in Buffalo and knew we would not be making the policy decisions. We built no alliances with any faction, though, of course, there were many rumors about such things and it would probably have been easy to exchange information with those most supportive of civil rights changes. Such research, we thought, must be presented as clearly as possible to a nonacademic readership, and the basis for our recommendations was spelled out. Being strictly professional and nonpolitical does not, of course, mean that you will be treated that way by those who disagree with the recommendations.

In a context of high stakes and high conflict, the research and/or the researchers are likely to be regarded with suspicion and attacked by those who disagree with their findings. This reality makes it very important to use language carefully and to resist being drawn into inherently political discussions, even while being attacked. Those inclined to see everything as political or through a racial lens often ignored our serious efforts.

DECONSTRUCTING TESTING—HARD BUT ESSENTIAL

Part of what must be done in any effort to produce major change in exam schools is to educate people about testing, something which is very widely misunderstood and overestimated. Exam- or test-based admissions policies are based on the assumption that tests fairly represent students' capacity for challenging work and are neutral measures of merit that can be fairly used to make high-stakes decisions about life-changing educational opportunities. Taking on the testing issue was even more difficult than we had expected.

In the research world and among educational testing organizations, there is a broad understanding that test results are strongly linked to earlier home and school advantages and that both are unequal for non-White children. Making high-stakes decisions on the basis of tests alone will, on average, reward those who are most privileged and identify Whites and higher-income students disproportionately. Tests do, of course, measure important dimensions of readiness for the next stage of education, but they do not measure how less-prepared students would do in an educationally richer environment.

Any serious effort to change the outcome of test-based choice for students cannot simply equate tests with educational capacity. As we pointed out in the report, the code of ethics of the testing profession concludes that single tests should not be used for high-stakes life decisions, and access to a great high school in a poor community is such a decision. Many educators and officials, as well as many White parents, have typically viewed tests as valid and adequate measures of merit—as scientific tools that would spare the schools from sensitive decisions that might be subjected to political and social pressures. We devoted considerable space in our report to those issues but did not reach some key decisionmakers. Shifting understanding of this issue is fundamental to making people understand the need to change admissions processes. We had little time to do it, and we fell short. It is important, we think, to make the point that highly selective colleges almost never base their admissions decisions solely on test scores and to explain why, in order to open up the conversation about the needed changes. Changing people's understanding of testing requires much more community education than we were able to do.

Since requiring the highest test scores is seen as the key to quality by many people, changes will often be seen as threats to quality. However, the belief in quality is essential to recruitment to selective-admissions magnet schools, such as Buffalo's City Honors. Researchers and policymakers need to explain that quality can be preserved as it has been in our great universities and that there are tangible academic and social benefits from integration for all groups of students. Research by colleges has shown that admitting some students with significantly lower test scores does not threaten academically strong colleges, and those students very often rise to the challenge and graduate at higher rates than similar students enrolling in weaker colleges. Admissions practices should open opportunity and maintain quality—not passively preserve inequality.

CONSIDERING CHARTER SCHOOLS

In retrospect, one lesson we learned in Buffalo is that charter schools must be included in civil rights investigations and in remedies where they constitute a significant and growing part of local educational opportunities. We looked statistically at the charters but had no charge to consider them since they were not part of the case. However, they are, obviously, a large part of the system of choice among publicly funded schools. When their share is large and growing and the same school can quickly change from public to charter, they cannot be ignored in thinking about opportunity and rights. It makes no sense that a school can be held accountable for participating in a civil rights remedy, but that if it is closed and quickly reopened as a charter school, it has none of the responsibility. One thing that should be done in a case like this is to freeze the status quo of the division of schools between publics and charters while the consideration of the remedy is proceeding. This kind of provision would be very normal in an enforcement process within a public school system. Information, choice, integration, and transportation policies should be similar for all schools of choice in an area funded with public resources.

All of these schools should be included in a strong and lasting remedy. This is one of the important issues that this experience revealed for future urban research. The public and charter schools are highly interactive components of a differentiated publicly funded system. Proposing changes to public schools but ignoring charters is like trying to pump up a tire while a large hole is being made in the other side.

UNSETTLED QUESTIONS

Research often yields new questions. After this experience, there are a number of questions that we think deserve attention from researchers, civil rights officials, and educators. Would it have been better if we had maintained active communication with the supporters of civil rights on the board, especially after it became clear that our effort would be blasted by the other side that ignored our careful separation from local politics? Would it have been important to communicate continuously with the OCR staff as the negotiations proceeded, or at least to have clarified the most critical aspects of our plan and the fact that implementing selected recommendations would have little impact if the most powerful parts were ignored? Should there be some way to facilitate peer review of a draft report by experts from local universities and engage those experts in ongoing oversight?

On all of these issues, we maintained professional distance, did our work, filed our report that fulfilled our contract, and did not take any initiatives. We took a passive stance, defining that as our professional role. Nevertheless, the opponents of the plan saw us as conspiring with the other side. So in terms of having our plan adopted, we were blamed unfairly, and we also lost the advantages that more proactive communication might have created. Once researchers get involved in local politics, of course, they are on a path that they cannot control, which was one of the reasons for our approach. These kinds of questions linger, prompting thought about what to do after the basic research has been done and the policy decisions are under way. There are no simple answers.

All in all, this experience taught us a great deal and made us think more deeply about causes and possible ways to change the results of school choice policies. We did our best to untangle and explain those issues, and while many of our recommendations were adopted, some of the most crucial ones were not. Researchers, consultants, and educational leaders can learn from our experience. We are convinced that test-driven choice plans are likely to replicate and perpetuate inequality, and many approaches are available that have the potential to limit or reverse the outcomes. The rapid spread of test-driven access to elite public schools is very likely to further perpetuate inequality. Excellent schools of choice need to face these issues and so must the civil rights and educational authorities regulating them, as almost all of our colleges have, if we want the outcome to be better and the civil rights problems to be resolved. Researchers can contribute to that effort and learn a great deal in the process.

We had a rare opportunity and have no regret for undertaking this task. We think that we proposed a moderate and effective remedy that would have expanded opportunity for high-quality education for non-White students in Buffalo while also expanding opportunities for White students and for the school district. After negotiations with OCR, the school district agreed to implement many specific and useful changes that we proposed as part of an overall plan. So far, however, those changes have not substantially changed access to the best schools for African American students. But the ideas are not dead; in fact, they are being strongly advocated by parent groups. In the meantime, however, the federal government has changed hands and the OCR has been greatly altered by a far more conservative administration, which will reinject itself into active enforcement of the rights of student of color, at least until there is a major political change. To our great surprise, as this book was nearing publication, a major community group in Buffalo demanded that our full report be implemented, and the superintendent contacted us to earnestly discuss the possibilities. A final lesson, then, is that policy is an ongoing stream and that ideas rejected at one point may have another life.

About the Contributors

Gary Orfield is distinguished research professor of education, law, political science and urban planning at the University of California, Los Angeles. Dr. Orfield's research interests are in the study of civil rights, education policy, urban policy, and minority opportunity. He was co-founder and director of the Harvard Civil Rights Project, and now serves as co-director of the Civil Rights Project/Proyecto Derechos Civiles at UCLA. Recent works include eight co-authored or co-edited books since 2004 and numerous articles and reports. Recent co-edited or co-authored books include *Educational Delusions? Why Choice Can Deepen Inequality and How to Make Schools Fair* (2013), *The Resegregation of Suburban Schools: A Hidden Crisis in American Education* (2013), and *Twenty-First Century Color Lines* (2008). In addition to his scholarly work, Dr. Orfield has been involved in the development of governmental policy and has served as an expert witness or special master in dozens of court cases related to his research, including *Grutter v. Bollinger*, the University of Michigan Supreme Court case that upheld the policy of affirmative action in 2003. He has been called to give testimony in civil rights suits by the U.S. Department of Justice and many civil rights, legal services, and educational organizations. He was awarded the American Political Science Association's Charles Merriam Award for his "contribution to the art of government through the application of social science research." Among many other awards, he received the 2007 Social Justice in Education Award from the American Educational Research Association for his work, "which has had a profound impact on demonstrating the critical role of education research in supporting social justice." He is also a member of the National Academy of Education.

Jennifer B. Ayscue is an American Educational Research Association Congressional Fellow in the United States Senate. Previously, Dr. Ayscue was research director of the Initiative for School Integration at the Civil Rights Project/Proyecto Derechos Civiles at the University of California, Los Angeles. Her research interests focus on desegregation in K–12 schools and the role of policy in shaping students' access to diverse and equitable educational opportunities. Dr. Ayscue's work has explored expanding access, equity, and diversity in magnet schools; suburban school responses to increasing racial diversity; school segregation trends in the Eastern states; and segregation in charter schools. Her research has been published in *Educational Policy, Peabody Journal of Education,* and *Phi Delta Kappan*. Prior to earning a PhD in education from the University of California, Los Angeles, she taught elementary school in East Palo Alto, California, and in Charlotte, North Carolina.

Natasha Amlani is a student at the UCLA School of Law who is interested in pursuing a career in public interest litigation. As a coordinator and research assistant for the Civil Rights Project/Proyecto Derechos Civiles, she coordinated CRP's amicus briefs for several Supreme Court affirmative action cases and planned a webinar that provided guidance for university counsel and admissions officials in response to the Supreme Court's decision in *Fisher v. University of Texas-Austin* (2013). Amlani earned her BA in philosophy with a minor in public affairs from the University of California, Los Angeles.

Jongyeon Ee is a postdoctoral researcher at the Civil Rights Project/Proyecto Derechos Civiles at the University of California, Los Angeles, with experience and expertise in quantitative research design and analysis. Dr. Ee has been responsible for data analysis for multiple reports released by the CRP. Her recent work has focused on school segregation, racial inequality, and school discipline in K–12 schools. She also is deeply interested in education for language-minority students and immigrant students. Dr. Ee has conducted several studies exploring bilingual education and bilingualism, including the economic advantages of bilingual abilities and parents' thoughts and attitudes toward dual language programs. In 2016, she received the Outstanding Dissertation Award from the National Association for Bilingual Education. Dr. Ee completed a PhD in Education at the University of California, Los Angeles, and earned an MA degree in the teaching of English as a second language from the University of Illinois at Urbana-Champaign.

Genevieve Siegel-Hawley is an associate professor in the School of Education at Virginia Commonwealth University. She has been involved in numerous studies examining the relationship between school choice and student body diversity. Together with colleagues, she has written several reports and articles on the state of segregation in charter and magnet schools, and has specifically examined how policies dealing with transportation, admissions requirements, programmatic offerings, diversity goals, and outreach relate to access to schools of choice. Dr. Siegel-Hawley is the author of *When the Fences Come Down: Twenty-First-Century Lessons from Metropolitan School Desegregation* (2016). She has served as a consultant to a major Southwestern school district interested in redesigning its magnet schools to promote more desegregation, in addition to her involvement in the Buffalo study. In addition, Dr. Siegel-Hawley recently oversaw a major study of federally funded magnet schools. She graduated from a criteria-based regional magnet high school in Richmond, Virginia, that served students from the city and 11 participating districts. Her experiences there led to an ongoing interest in issues of race and educational equity. Prior to earning her doctorate at the University of California, Los Angeles, Dr. Siegel-Hawley taught high school history in the Baltimore City Schools and Richmond Public Schools.

Jenna Tomasello is a Buffalo-area native and a policy associate at the American Youth Policy Forum, a nonpartisan intermediary organization located in Washington, DC. Her work involves the development of learning events and the dissemination of policy and practice guidance to frame issues, inform policy, and convene conversations that improve education and the lives of traditionally underserved youth. Ms. Tomasello is also the co-founder of Learn Together, Live Together, a diverse, bipartisan coalition of education stakeholders striving to promote diversity, equity, and inclusion in schools. Ms. Tomasello has a background in philosophy and legal studies, and holds a master's degree in educational policy from the University of Rochester Warner Graduate School of Education and Human Development.

Brian Woodward is a doctoral candidate in the Graduate School of Education and Information Studies at the University of California, Los Angeles. A former high school history teacher, Mr. Woodward is a research associate with the UCLA Civil Rights Project/Proyecto Derechos Civiles and presently studies school resegregation trends across the country as well as policies that promote educational equity for all students. His research has been published in *Educational Policy* and *Spectrum: A Journal on Black Men*.

Index

The letter *f*, *t*, or *p* after a page number refers to a figure, table, or photo, respectively.

Abrams, C., 43
Abrams, D., 62
Absence of leadership, 130
Academically selective magnet schools. *See* Criteria-based schools
Academically selective schools of choice. *See* Criteria-based schools
Academic curriculum, 16, 75, 99, 122
Academic excellence, 21, 89, 103, 105, 134, 139
Academic performance. *See* Buffalo Public Schools (BPS): student achievement
Accountability in education, 118–119
Administrators, 78, 88
Admissions criteria
  and access, 75–76
  algorithm, 124–125, 126
  alternatives, 102–105, 107t, 108, 110, 124, 139
  and BPS, 29–30, 31t, 32
  parent inventories and teacher recommendations, 87–88, 98–99
  and race discrimination, 27–28
  recommendations, 108, 123–127, 123t, 135, 139
  testing, 79t, 82, 84–87, 96–98, 141
Admissions processes. *See* Admissions criteria
Admissions rates, 85
Admissions-testing procedures, 86–87, 97, 110, 124, 127, 130, 139
Affirmative Action programs, 6, 13, 93, 109

Alexander, M., 13
Algorithm for admissions, 124–125, 126
Allensworth, E. M., 5
American Educational Research Association, 6, 97, 98
American Psychological Association, 6, 97, 98
Amlani, N., 46, 48–49, 50, 98, 99, 121, 123
A Nation at Risk, 19
Applicant pool, 104, 127, 128
Aronson, J., 96
Arthur v. Nyquist, 27, 32, 48, 50, 94, 119
Asian students, 27, 71, 77, 92n2, 111. *See also* Buffalo Public Schools (BPS): segregation data; Buffalo Public Schools (BPS): total enrollment demographics
Attendance zones, 48
Availability of choices
  background, 2, 20–21, 31
  findings, 75, 76, 79t, 87, 89–90
  recommendations and negotiations, 105, 107t, 116, 123t, 125, 135
Ayscue, J. B., 13, 46, 48–49, 50, 98, 99, 107t, 121, 123

Baker-Smith, C., 103, 104
Balfanz, R., 99
Belton-Cottman, S., 121
Betz, E., 126
Bischoff, K., 13
Bitterman, A., 98

147

Black students, 47, 50. *See also* Buffalo Public Schools (BPS): segregation data; Buffalo Public Schools (BPS): total enrollment demographics
Blanchard, T. C. J., 28, 126
Board of Education of BPS, 78, 120, 121
Board of Education of Oklahoma City v. Dowell, 15, 17, 27, 49
Bok, D., 6
Bonilla-Silva, E., 6
Boston Latin School, 4
Bottia, M. C., 97, 99
Bowen, W. G., 6, 104–105
BPS (Buffalo Public Schools). *See* Buffalo Public Schools (BPS)
Brown v. Board of Education, 2, 11, 19
Buckley, E., 127
Buffalo, city and metro area of
　background, 11, 12–13, 42–44, 44f, 45f, 94–95, 137
　Civil Rights Project, 21–23, 94
　residential segregation, 2, 22, 44–47, 52, 108–109, 124
Buffalo Academy for Visual and Performing Arts 192, 30t, 59, 59f, 67, 67f, 68, 69f
Buffalo City School District, 65f, 124
Buffalo News, 39, 121, 130
Buffalo Public Schools (BPS)
　background, 2–5, 21, 27–29, 47–50, 52, 123, 124
　Central Registration, 35, 78–79, 82–84, 124
　civil rights history, 47–48, 50
　comparison of criteria-based and non-criteria-based schools, 58–59, 58f, 62–65, 63t, 65f, 70–71
　description of criteria-based schools, 29–31, 30t
　desegregation order and plan, 2–3, 4, 32, 48–49, 50, 92, 116, 119
　individual school data, 58–61, 58f, 59f, 60t, 61f, 67f, 68–70, 68f, 69f, 70f

　leadership, 19, 117–123, 120, 126, 130
　post-negotiations period, 126–129, 130
　recommendations, 105–110, 107t
　segregation data, 55, 62–65, 63t, 71–72
　student achievement, 65–70, 67f, 68f, 69f, 70f
　teaching force, 65, 65f
　total enrollment demographics, 50–52, 52f, 55–56, 57t
Buffalo Vocational Technical Center, 49
Bush (George H. W.) administration, 17
Bush (George W.) administration, 17, 18, 19, 20, 22
Business interests, 117, 118
Business regulations, 8
Busing, 48
Byrnes, M., 50

California, 18
Card, D., 97
Carter, P. L., 13
Cash, K., 124, 126, 130
Central Registration. *See* Buffalo Public Schools (BPS): Central Registration
Charter schools, 3, 8, 18–20, 121, 140
Chavez, L., 18
Chicago Public Schools, 102–103
Chingos, M. M., 104–105
Choice programs, 3, 14–20, 28–29, 94, 135
Chowhan, M., 100
Chubb, J. E., 19
Citizens Council on Human Relations, 48
City Data (Buffalo), 43
City Honors 195
　and access, 85, 87, 94
　background and description, 2, 28, 29, 30t, 32, 33p, 49–50
　demographic and segregation data, 59, 59f, 60t, 61, 67, 67f, 68f, 69, 70, 70f, 72
　recommendations and negotiation, 108, 124, 127, 128, 130, 135
City Honors high school. *See* City Honors 195

Index

City Honors II, 109, 125, 126, 130, 135
Civil rights
  and Buffalo history, 1, 2, 15–18, 20, 47
  enforcement process, 122–123
  federal legislation, 16, 20, 22, 47, 61
  investigations, 4, 55, 72, 92
Civil Rights Project (UCLA), 18, 28, 55, 75, 76, 94, 116, 140. *See also* Current research
Class. *See* Socioeconomic class
Class bias, 136–137
Class-ranking criteria, 102
Climate of education, 8–9, 39–40
Clinton administration, 19
Clotfelter, C. T., 13, 97, 99
Cobb, C. D., 14
Code of Ethics of the testing profession, 98, 139
Cognitive-ability testing. *See* Cognitive-skills testing
Cognitive-skills testing, 85–87, 96–97, 124, 127
Collaborations, 107t, 108, 123t
College admissions, 3–4, 5, 6, 21, 22, 104–105, 139, 141
Colorblind racism, 5, 6–8, 10–11, 22, 95, 102
Common Core standards, 67, 68, 71, 97
Common Core Task Force, 97–98
Competition for enrollment. *See* Availability of choices
Competitive-admissions magnet schools. *See* Criteria-based schools
Competitive-admissions school of choice. *See* Criteria-based schools
Complexity of remediation plan, 138
Compliance, 138
Conservative view of education, 8–10, 19, 141
Controlled choice, 15, 16
Cook, J. M., 100
Corcoran, S., 103, 104
Counseling, 108

Court cases. *See by name*
Coyne, C., 100
Crain, R. L., 119
Crandall, R. W., 43
Creswell, J. W., 33
Criteria-based schools
  background, 27–29
  benefits to attending, 4–5, 93
  BPS enrollment data, 56, 57t, 58–64, 58f, 59f, 60t, 61f, 63t, 71
  BPS system, 29–33, 30t, 33p
  terminology, 27, 29
Cronin, J., 119
Crystal, D., 62
Cultural bias in testing, 139
Cultural inferiority/superiority notion, 6–7, 10
Cuomo, A., 118
Current research
  admissions criteria, 85–88
  availability of choices, 89–90
  background, 1, 3, 21, 133
  context, 39–40, 117–119, 121
  data analysis, 38
  data collection methods, 36–38, 76
  implementation, 122–123
  information access, 78–84, 79t
  lessons, 116–117, 133–141
  participants, 34–36, 77–78
  presentation, 121–122
  recommendations and negotiations, 94, 105–110, 107t, 123–126, 123t, 129–130, 138
  researcher role, 22–23, 33–34, 36, 120–121, 138–139, 141
  review of prior research inclusion criteria, 95–96
  support, 88–89
Curtin, J. T., 32, 94

Davies, P. G., 96
Dawson, B., 100
De facto segregation ruling, 48

De jure segregation ruling, 11, 48, 94
De la Torre, M., 5
Denton, N. A., 13
Desegregation, 14–18, 19–20, 21–22, 86, 106
Desktop Explorer, 47
Dickerson, C., 11
Disabilities. *See* Special education
Discrimination and the courts, 20–21, 134. *See also court cases by name*
Dissimilarity index, 12
District Parent Coordinating Council, 130
Divergence measure, 11–12
Diversity, 74, 95, 104, 110, 122, 124, 139–140
Divisive climate, 8–9, 39–40, 117, 130, 133–134, 138–139
Double segregation, 9–10, 13, 55, 64–65, 72
Dougherty, J., 100
Dual-language immersion school, 108, 124
Duncan, G., 13, 97

Early education, 49, 84–85, 99–100
Eaton, S. E., 13, 15, 92
Eberle, K., 126
Economically disadvantaged students, 51, 52t, 56, 98–99. *See also* Socioeconomic class
Economic mobility, 13
Educational Delusions (Orfield & Frankenberg), 94
Education policy. *See* Office for Civil Rights (OCR); U.S. education policy
Ee, J., 46, 48–49, 50, 55–56, 98, 99, 121, 123
Elementary and Secondary Education Act, 93
Elmore, R. F., 14
Emerson School of Hospitality 302, 30n1, 30t, 58, 58f, 59, 59f, 67, 67f, 125
Energy, 43
Enforcement. *See* Implementing recommendations
English learners (ELs). *See* Limited English proficiency (LEP)
Erie Canal, 42
Espinosa, L. L., 104
Essay option, 87
Essential recommendations, 138, 140, 141
Every Student Succeeds Act, 19
Exam schools, 3–6, 29, 92, 93, 94, 139, 141
Excellence. *See* Academic excellence
Exclusivity, 3, 116. *See also* Availability of choices
Expanding access, 1, 10, 105, 122, 124, 128. *See also* Availability of choices
Exposure index, 11–12. *See also* Intergroup contact

Facilities and materials, 99
Faculty. *See* Teacher and staff perspectives; Teachers
Fagan, J. F., 96
Failing schools. *See* Low-performing schools
Fairness of tests, 139
Fair Test, 105
Federal funding, 17, 20, 21, 49
Finn, C. E., 4, 29, 92
Fleming, J., 105
Flores, S. M., 104
Ford, D. Y., 98, 99, 101
Formulating remedies, 138
Frankenberg, E., 9, 13, 14, 15, 18, 46, 48–49, 50, 55–56, 75, 76, 94, 97, 98, 99, 101, 121, 123
Frederick, C. B., 66
Free and reduced-price lunch. *See* Economically disadvantaged students
Freedom-of-choice plans, 19
Freeman v. Pitts, 16
Frey, W. H., 13
Fuller, B., 14
Fusco, C., 103

Gaertner, M. N., 104
Gallup Editors, 7
Garces, L. M., 104
Garcia, N., 105

Index

Gebeloff, R., 119
Geiser, S., 105
German, K. R., 118
Gifted and talented programs, 31, 93–94, 98–102, 125
Giuliano, L., 97
Glaeser, E. L., 42, 43–44
Glass, G. V., 14
Goldring, E., 15
Goldring, R., 98
Grades as predictors, 105, 108
Graduation rates, 106
Grain production, 42–43
Grantham, T. C., 98
Gray, L., 98
Greenberg, E., 13, 16
Green v. Board of Education of New Kent County, 19
Grewal, E. T., 13, 16
Grissom, J. A., 98
Guruge, T., 100

Harris, J., 101
Harris-Tigg, T., 121
Hauser, R. M., 6, 98
Heath, D., 97, 99
Hendrie, C., 92, 95
Hernández, J. C., 119
Heubert, P., 6, 98
Hiaasen, S., 8
High academic standards. *See* Academic excellence
Higher-education policy, 104–105
High-stakes life decisions, 139
High Stakes Testing for Tracking, Promotion, and Graduation (National Academy of Sciences), 98
High-stakes tests, 5–6, 98
Hockett, J. A., 4, 29, 92
Hoffman, J. L., 105
Holistic review, 104, 105, 108, 110, 124, 139
Holland, C. R., 96
Holme, J. J., 75, 100

Horn, C. L., 104
Hours of operation, 82
Housing discrimination, 119
Housing patterns. *See* Residential segregation
Ho v. San Francisco Unified School District, 92
Hutchinson Central Technical High School 304, 30t, 59, 59f

IB World School, 32
Implementing recommendations, 126, 127–128, 130, 135–136, 138, 140. *See also* Negotiations
Incarcerations, 13
Independence. *See* Passive stance
Inferior schooling, 47–48, 50
Influx of Southern Blacks. *See* Migration of Southern Blacks
Information dissemination
 background, 14–15, 16
 findings, 74–75, 78–82, 100, 103–104
 recommendations, 106, 107t, 108, 122, 124, 136–137
Instructions for completing application, 83
Integration, 2, 75–76, 102. *See also* Desegregation
Intelligence testing, 47, 101
Intention to discriminate, 20–21, 134
Interest-based admissions, 108
Intergroup contact, 11–12, 55, 62–64, 63t, 71–72
Internet, 83, 122, 136–137
Interviews and focus groups, 34–36, 78
"Invisible hand," 8
Irvine, J., 98
Isolation measure, 11–12
Isolation of Black schoolchildren, 47

Jackson, K., 13, 97, 99
Jacobs, H., 45
Jefferson County (KY), 18
Jensen, N., 119
Johnson administration, 19

Kahlenberg, K., 104
Kalogrides, D., 13, 16
Kapsiak, M. R., 121
Kennedy, A., 17
Keresztes, W., 127, 128, 130
Keyes v. School Dist. No. 1, Denver, 48
Kiersz, A., 45
Killen, M., 62
King, J., 118, 121
King, M. L., Jr., 7
Kleitz, B., 75
Kucsera, J., 13, 27, 45, 46, 48, 49, 50
Kurlaender, M., 18

Ladd, H. F., 13, 97, 99
Lambert, R., 97, 99
Language barrier, 82, 83, 88, 106, 124, 137
Language support, 88
Lankes, T., 126, 127
Lareau, A., 97
Latino students, 80, 82, 83, 86, 88, 92n2, 98–99, 106, 124, 137. *See also* Buffalo Public Schools (BPS): segregation data; Buffalo Public Schools (BPS): total enrollment demographics
Lee, C., 66
Legal investigations of discrimination. *See court cases by name;* Discrimination and the courts
Legal segregation, 11
Legters, N. E., 99
Leonardo da Vinci 212, 30t, 59, 59f
LEP (limited English proficiency). *See* Limited English proficiency (LEP)
Liberal view, 10, 19
Limited English proficiency (LEP)
 and access, 14, 80, 86, 88, 98–99
 BPS enrollment, 56, 57t, 60t, 61, 61f, 62, 63t, 64–65, 72
Local power, 122–123
Logel, C., 96
Lottery admissions, 94–95, 102, 108
Lowell High School (San Francisco), 4
Lowitsky, K. E., 105

Low-performing schools, 118, 121
Lubin, G., 45
Lucas, T. F., 98

Magnet schools, 2, 3, 14–15, 20, 29, 48–49, 94, 135
Magnet Schools Assistance Program, 16, 49
Mandatory desegregation programs, 15–16
Market theory, 8–10
Martin, R., 126
Marva J. Daniels Future Prep Academy, 125
Massey, D. S., 13
Math assessment. *See* Buffalo Public Schools (BPS): student achievement
Matland, R., 75
McConney, A., 66
Mcgrory, K., 8
McPherson, M., 100
McPherson, M. S., 104–105
Measuring segregation, 11–12, 12n1
Merit, 39, 134, 139
Merriam, S. B., 33
Mexican American Defense and Educational Fund, 104
Mickelson, R. A., 62, 97, 99
Middle Early College 415, 30t, 58, 58f, 59, 59f, 67, 67f, 68, 69f
Migration of Southern Blacks, 43, 47
Milliken v. Bradley, 16
Minimum criteria, 102
Mission and vision statements, 124
Missouri v. Jenkins, 16
Moe, T. M., 19
Moll, R., 92
Montessori High School, 125
Moore, P. T., 5
Moreno, J. F., 97, 99
Morse, R., 92
Moses, J., 129
Mosey, G. J., 47–48, 49
Moxley, H., 47
Moynihan, D. P., 49
Multicultural preparation for teachers, 101

Multilingual staffing, 106
Municipal funding, 49
Murnane, R., 13, 97

NAACP, 48, 94, 111
NAACP Legal Defense and Educational Fund, 111
National Academy of Sciences, 98
National Council on Measurement in Education, 6, 97, 98
National Park Service, 42, 43
Negotiations, 123–126
Neighborhood preference, 124, 125, 126
Neighborhood segregation, 46–47, 106
Nevergold, B., 126, 130
New Education Bargain, 126
New questions, 140–141
New schools, 108, 125, 127–128, 130, 135
New structures, 135
Newsweek, 32
New York City schools, 4, 103
New York Common Core Task Force, 97–98, 108
New York Office for Civil Rights, 28
New York State Education Department, 50–51, 51f, 57t, 58f, 59f, 60t, 61f, 63t, 67f, 68f, 69f, 70f
New York State Regents assessment, 65–70, 67f, 68f, 69f, 70f, 72, 97–98, 118, 123, 126, 127
New York State school enrollments, 50–51, 51f, 52f
New York Times, 48
Niagara Falls (NY), 44, 47, 51
Nieto, S., 98
Niu, S. X., 104
Nkomo, M., 62
No Child Left Behind Act, 19
Non-criteria-based schools, 58–59, 58f, 62–64, 63t, 71
Non-public schools, 8
Non-residents, 87
Novak, T., 103
Nukic, B., 100

Obama, M., 129
Obama administration, 19, 20, 22, 102, 129
Office for Civil Rights (OCR)
  desegregation goal, 3, 21–23, 27–29, 42, 50, 94
  recommendations and negotiations, 108, 116, 123–126, 135
Olmsted Elementary 64, 30t, 31, 60t, 61, 72, 99, 108, 125
Olmsted Middle and High 156
  and access, 85, 87, 94
  background and description, 28, 29, 30t, 31
  demographic and segregation data, 59, 59f, 67, 68f, 70, 70f, 72
  recommendations and negotiation, 127, 128
Online application, 83
Operationalizing the mandate. *See* Implementing recommendations
Opportunity in education, 1, 2, 12–13, 22, 39, 122
Orfield, G., 9, 13, 14, 15, 18, 27, 45, 46, 48–49, 50, 55–56, 66, 92, 94, 97, 98, 99, 104, 107t, 121, 123
Out-of-district students, 87
"Out of time" status, 118, 121
Outreach and recruitment. *See* Information dissemination
Oversight lack, 8
Overview of the book, 23–24

Paladino, C., 118, 120, 121, 126, 129
Palardy, G. J., 66
Parent coalition, 48, 94
Parent Information Center, 106
Parent Information Office, 124
Parents as participants, 34–35, 76–77, 128, 136–137
Parents Involved in Community Schools v. Seattle School District No. 1, 17, 18, 92, 102, 134
Parents' perspectives
  admissions criteria, 85–88, 98–99

Parents' perspectives *(continued)*
  availability of choices, 94
  information, 78–84, 79, 80, 81, 82–83
  preparation, 84–85
  support services, 88–89
Partnerships. *See* Collaborations
Passive stance, 138–139, 141
Peer intergroup contact. *See* Exposure index; Intergroup contact
Peer networks, 81
Peer-tutoring program, 108
Percentage plans, 104, 108, 124, 125, 127–128, 134
Performance standards, 118–119, 122. *See also* Common Core standards
Perry, L. B., 66
Peters, J. W., 11
Pettigrew, T. F., 62
Phone communication, 136–137
Piecemeal changes, 130
Policies for admission. *See* Admissions criteria
Policy impact on access, 102–105
Political climate of district. *See* Divisive climate
Post-negotiations years, 127–128
Poverty, 9–10, 13, 42, 44, 51, 52t, 55, 56, 64–65, 72, 98–99
Practice and policy, 101–105
Predictive power, 105
Preparation, 79t, 84–86, 99–100, 103, 107t, 123t, 135
Presentation of report, 121–122
Prior learning opportunities, 96–97
Prior research
  choice systems, 74–76, 96–101
  gifted programs, 101–102
  inclusion in the current research, 95–96
  policy effects, 102–105
Private schooling, 78
Pro-charter policy, 117–119
Professional distance. *See* Passive stance
Property values, 43–44, 47
Protest over racial attack, 129

Proving discrimination. *See* Intention to discriminate
Public control, 119
Putnam, R. D., 66

Quick, K., 103

Race and schooling, 11–13, 47–50
Race-class-language connection. *See* Triple segregation
Race-conscious civil rights policies, 10, 92, 102
Race-poverty connection. *See* Double segregation
Racial attack, 129
Racial composition of research participants, 77
Racial quotas, 49–50
Racial separation, 11–12, 47–48
Racism, 5, 6–11, 95, 102, 129
Radford, S., 127, 128
Ready, D., 62
Reagan administration, 17, 19, 49
Reardon, S. F., 13, 16, 18, 66
Receivership schools, 117, 118
Recruitment. *See* Information dissemination
Redding, C., 98
Regional magnet school, 108, 124
Research. *See* Current research; Prior research
Research Alliance for New York City Schools, 103–104
Resegregation, 49–50, 119
Residential segregation, 2, 22, 42, 43, 44–47, 108–109, 124
Resistance to change, 39
Responsibility and charter schools, 140
Reverse discrimination lawsuit, 49–50, 92, 95
Reville, E., 49
Rey, J., 44, 129
Roberts, J., 92
Robocall, 136–137

Ruck, M., 62
Rumberger, R. W., 66, 99

San Francisco (CA), 4
Santelices, M. V., 105
Sartain, L., 5
Saul, S., 11
Scarcity of seats. *See* Availability of choices
Schedule of testing, 86, 97
School board. *See* Buffalo Public Schools (BPS): Board of Education
School closings, 48, 118
School demographics. *See* Buffalo Public School (BPS): total enrollment demographics
School effectiveness data, 106, 108
School-within-a-school program, 100–101
Schuette v. Coalition to Defend Affirmative Action, 92
Scott, J., 14
Seals-Neverhold, B., 121
Seattle (WA), 17
Segregation
 BPS, 55, 57t, 62–65, 63t, 71–72
 and civil rights legislation, 16, 20, 22, 47, 61
 court rulings, 11, 48, 94
 language, 55, 64–65
 by neighborhood, 46–47, 106
 race, 9–10, 13, 55, 64–65, 72
 residential, 2, 22, 42, 43, 44–47, 108–109, 124
 and social science research, 11–12
 socioeconomic class, 9–10, 13, 55, 64–65, 72, 116
Segregation index, 12
Selective-admissions schools. *See* Criteria-based schools
Selective magnet schools. *See* Criteria-based schools
Selectivity, 3, 116. *See also* Availability of choices
Seniority, 90, 109, 128
Set-aside seats. *See* Percentage plans

Shakarian, K., 102, 103
Siegel-Hawley, G., 13, 15, 46, 48–49, 50, 55–56, 75, 76, 98, 99, 101, 107t, 121, 123
Silander, M., 62
Sleeter, C. E., 98
Smith, A., 8
Smith-Lovin, L., 100
Smrekar, C., 15
Snellman, K., 66
Soares, J. A., 105
Social science research and segregation, 11–12
Social support, 108
Socioeconomic class
 academic performance, 6, 66–68, 67f, 68f
 and admissions, 102–103
 BPS enrollment, 56, 57t, 60t, 61, 61f, 63t, 72
 and information dissemination, 136–137
 and language, 64–65
 and race, 58–59, 58f, 64–65
 segregation, 9–10, 13, 55, 64–65, 72, 116
Sotomayor, S., 93
Special education, 14, 80, 86–89
"Special schools," 47
Spencer, S. J., 96
Staff, 78, 80, 82, 83, 84, 85, 86, 87, 89, 106
Standardized tests, 97–98, 105
Standards of excellence. *See* Academic excellence
Steele, C. M., 96
Stereotype threat, 96
St. Lawrence Seaway, 43
Students. *See also* Asian students; Black students; Latino students
 achievement data, 65–70, 67f, 68f, 69f, 70f
 BPS total enrollment, 50–52, 52f, 55–56, 57t
 disabilities, 14, 80
 from low income households, 51, 52t, 56, 98–99
 mobility, 99
 as participants in research, 35, 77–78

Students *(continued)*
 perspectives on access, 80, 81, 83, 84, 85–86, 87, 88–90
 race/ethnicity, 50–52, 52f, 55–56, 57t, 62–65, 63t, 71–72
 segregation data, 55, 62–65, 63t, 71–72
Studley, R., 105
Study sources, 95–96
Suburbs, 43, 46, 47
Summer preparatory programs, 108
Supervision of civil rights remediation, 134
Supply of choice schools. *See* Availability of choices
Support services, 79t, 88–89, 107t, 108
Sussman, D., 11
Swanson, C. B., 99
Systematic racism, 6–11

Taylor, H. L., Jr., 43–44, 46, 47
Taylor, K., 103, 111
Teacher and staff perspectives, 79–83, 85, 86–90, 109, 128
Teachers. *See also* Teacher and staff perspectives
 quality of, 5, 13, 99
 race/ethnicity, 65, 65f, 98, 125
 as research participants, 35, 37–38, 77–78
 teaching assignments, 88, 89–90, 109, 128
Teachers unions, 8, 19, 117, 128
Tedin, K., 75
Terminology, 11–12, 29, 93–94
Test administration. *See* Admissions-testing procedures
Test anxiety, 96
Test-based admissions. *See* Admissions criteria: testing; Exam schools
Test bias, 139
Testing locations, 86, 87
Test reliability, 97–98
Test scores. *See* Admissions criteria
Test validity, 96–97, 98

Thee-Brenan, M., 11
Thomas, G. S., 44, 119
Tienda, M., 104
Timeline for applications, 83–84
Timing of information distribution, 81–82
Tompkins-Stange, M. E., 8
Town-hall discussions, 78
Tracking, 47–48, 99–100
Trade, 42–43
Transportation, 14, 42–43, 75, 86
Triple segregation, 55, 64–65
Tropp, L. R., 62
Trump administration, 3, 19
Types of schools, 95

Unitary status, 49, 52, 95
Universal access to quality education, 2–3
Universal screening, 97
University of Buffalo, 108
University of Minnesota Law School, Institute on Metropolitan Opportunity, 44, 46
Unofficial pipeline, 85, 99, 108
Unstable leadership, 137–138
U.S. Census Bureau, 43, 45, 45f
U.S. Commission on Civil Rights, 43
U.S. Dept. of Education, 3, 8, 28, 94, 95–96, 99, 100, 102
U.S. Dept. of Justice, 22, 95–96, 102
U.S. education policy
 and Affirmative Action programs, 6, 13, 93, 109
 and civil rights legislation, 16, 20, 22, 47, 61
 and the Constitution, 11
 Dept. of Education, 3, 28, 94, 102
 higher education, 6, 13, 93, 104–105
 and presidential administrations, 3, 17, 18, 19, 20, 22, 49, 102, 129
 and the Supreme Court, 17, 19, 27, 48, 49, 92–93, 102, 134
U.S. schools, 13, 55–56

Index

U.S. Supreme Court, 17, 19, 27, 48, 49, 92–93, 102, 134

Validity of tests, 105
Vigdor, J. L., 13, 97, 99
Villegas, A., 98
Voluntary integration, 48–49, 92, 102, 117. *See also* Choice programs; Magnet schools
Voluntary transfers, 19–20

Ways and terms of testing, 86
Webb, K., 101
Website, 81, 124
Weiher, G. R., 75
Wells, A. S., 75
Welner, K. G., 13

Wessman v. Gittens, 95
White flight, 43–44, 47
Whiting, G., 101
Whole-school model, 100–101, 108, 124
Williams, D., 126
Winerip, M., 49
Wong, A., 100, 103
Woodruff, C., 118
Woodward, B., 46, 48–49, 50, 98, 99, 107t, 121, 123
World War II, 43

Yin, L., 43–44, 45, 46–47
Yun, J. T., 18, 97, 99

Zagare, P., 95
Zannoni, D., 100